PROOFREADING MANUAL AND REFERENCE GUIDE

by Peggy Smith

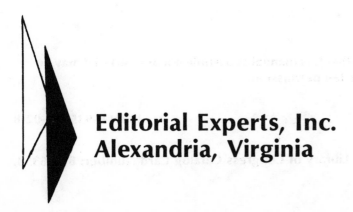

Editorial Experts, Inc.
Alexandria, Virginia

I'll bet you ten to one
that most people will not
not notice anything wrong
with this message.

ISBN 0-935012-02-8

Library of Congress Catalog Card Number: 81-66353.

EDITORIAL EXPERTS, INC.

5905 Pratt Street • Alexandria, Virginia 22310 • (703) 971-7350

Preface

These books were written to fill the need for an up-to-date reference and instructional manual on proofreading. Through the text and its accompanying workbook, both novices and experienced proofreaders can learn practical, modern techniques that can be applied to copy prepared by typing, word processing, computer typesetting, and photocomposition, as well as by older, traditional forms of composition. The information in this set of books is useful, furthermore, in dealing with all printing processes.

Several years ago, Editorial Experts published a manual for its freelance proofreaders, all of whom were professionally experienced but who had learned a variety of ways to approach their trade. The manual gave all EEI proofreaders a common set of techniques and symbols to use. It also set out speed and accuracy standards.

The usefulness of that book, along with our failure to find a current, comprehensive reference book on proofreading techniques, encouraged us to expand the in-house manual for a larger audience. Our efforts led to this two-volume set, which is addressed to anyone who must read proof professionally.

Experienced publications specialists can use this set as a refresher course and a reference work, and will find new tips, shortcuts, and useful background information here. For example, if you have worked alone (single-proofing), the books can help you adapt to working with a partner or a tape recording. If you have worked only as part of a two-person team, the books will help you learn to work alone.

If you have never proofread or have proofread only occasionally and informally, these books will teach you the marks and techniques professional proofreaders use. Quite frankly, if you master the textbook and do well in all the accompanying exercises, you should be a top candidate for any proofreading jobs available.

Part I of the manual is designed primarily as a textbook on proofreading techniques. It covers the standard marks, how and when to make them, and when to adapt them. Part I is accompanied by many workbook exercises to allow novices to try new skills and experienced proofreaders to check how good they really are.

Part II provides the general background proofreaders need to understand their role in the publications process.

WRITING • EDITING • RESEARCH • PROOFREADING • INDEXING • TYPING • CONSULTING
ARTICLES • BOOKS • BROCHURES • CONFERENCES • NEWSLETTERS • PUBLICITY • REPORTS • SPEECHES

Part III is a collection of reference materials and practical tools, including summaries of two major editorial styles and rules to use to measure copy.

Part I has been tested on several hundred students in the George Washington University Publication Specialist Program. We especially thank those students for helping us perfect this book by sharing their reactions to early drafts and finding our errors.

The major credit for conceiving, researching, and writing these books goes to Peggy Smith, one of Editorial Experts' first proofreading managers and current editor of our newsletter, <u>The Editorial Eye</u>. The instruction sheets and forms that she designed for her proofreaders eventually led to the publication of our first, much smaller, in-house proofreading manual, a work that is still used in our company.

Our company and the editorial profession owe Peggy Smith a great deal of gratitude for her willingness to tackle enthusiastically the difficult task of collecting information about a subject that at first glance would seem tedious and boring. In fact, as you will see as you work your way through the material Peggy has compiled, proofreading is a fascinating subject. I am sure you will be enlightened as well as inspired by this book and that it will help your editorial development, no matter what stage you have reached in your career.

Laura Horowitz

Laura Horowitz
Publisher

April 1981

Author's Preface

My preface has already been written by somebody else. I can express myself best by quoting from the preface to the first edition of <u>Pens and Types: Hints and Helps for Those Who Write, Print, Teach, Read or Learn</u>, written in the 1880's by Benjamin Drew after his retirement from nine years of proofreading for the "Government printing-office, at Washington":

> This volume gives the results of a proof-reader's experience, and such suggestions derived therefrom as may . . . be useful to all who prepare reading-matter for the press, to all who assist in printing and publishing it, and, finally, to the reading public.
>
> But as a vein of imperfection runs through all human achievement; and as the most carefully issued volume must contain errors,--so this work, if critically examined, may perhaps be found to violate, in some instances, its own rules; nay, the rules themselves may appear to be, in some points, erroneous. Still, the inexperienced, we feel assured, will find herein many things of immediate benefit; and those who need no instruction may have their opinions and their wisdom re-inforced by the examples used in illustration. So, believing that on the whole it will be serviceable; . . . we send this treatise to press. And if its perusal shall incite some more competent person to produce a more valuable work on the topics presented, we shall gladly withdraw, and leave him, so far as we are concerned, the undisputed possession of the field.

> --Peggy Smith
> Annandale, Virginia 1981

Acknowledgments

Thanks for help in preparing these books for publication are due to many talented people:

Laura Horowitz, the genius who founded Editorial Experts, Inc. (EEI), never lost patience when the book took four years to write instead of six months. She followed every step of production and did much of the editing herself.

Laura's students at George Washington University were responsible for a great many improvements in Part I.

Faye Hanson, Alison Heckler, and Adrienne Mills, expert proofreaders, shared their know-how, experience, and wisdom.

Technical reviewers included Faye Hanson; EEI proofreading manager Patricia Caudill and editing manager Priscilla Taylor; Charles Reid, Coordinator, Graphic Arts Department, Algonquin College of Applied Arts and Technology; Jeane Schultz, student proofreader, who also helped with the paste-up; and three publication managers with special expertise in production--Mara Adams, Chisholm Gentry, and Robert Solomon.

Many EEI typists, word processor operators, and proofreaders deserve to be congratulated because they finally learned to ignore their best instincts and leave intentional errors alone. Barbara Hughes, Margaret Morrison, Kathleen Richardson, Elaine Sullivan, and Floyd Anderson were especially good at typing or proofing revisions.

Lee Mickle, Barbara Anderson, and Nan Fritz, in turn, were project managers for the book. Nan also edited the book before seeing it through its final stages.

Andrea De La Garza did the final copyediting. Stephanie Orhan and Betsy Colgan did much of the graphics and paste-up.

And Rufus Smith never complained about his preoccupied wife; his moral support was the biggest help of all.

--PS

Acknowledgments

Contents

List of Figures

PART III. APPENDIXES. RESOURCES AND REFERENCES

Part I
Mechanics of Proofreading

Chapter 1

Introduction to Professional Proofreading

Read the following sentence slowly:

FROZEN FOODS ARE THE RESULT OF YEARS OF SCIENTIFIC STUDY AND THE
DEVELOPMENT OF REFRIGERATION

Now count aloud the <u>f</u>'s in that sentence. Count only once.

The average person finds four <u>f</u>'s. Identifying all seven is un-
usual--an indication of a mind already attuned to letter-by-letter
reading. Because the mind knows there is an <u>f</u> in the unimportant
word "of," it is difficult to recognize the letter when reading
for sense as well as for <u>f</u>'s.
> --<u>The Complete Guide to Editorial Freelancing</u>
> Carol L. O'Neill and Avima Ruder
> Dodd, Mead & Company, 1974.

CHAPTER OVERVIEW

This chapter defines professional proofreading and discusses some
of the job opportunities for proofreaders, the differences between
proofreading and editing, proofreading's place in the publication
process, the future of proofreading, optimum work conditions, standards for speed and accuracy, and proofreaders' qualifications and
general responsibilities.

PROOFREADING DEFINED

A <u>proof</u> is a test copy of type or artwork prepared for printing,
taken for examination to "prove" its quality. The person who
methodically examines a proof and marks it for correction is
a <u>proofreader</u>.

Proofreaders also read and mark copy other than printer's proofs--
typewritten copy, for example.

Professional proofreading involves (1) comparing new typeset or
typewritten copy letter-by-letter to an earlier version to be sure
the contents of the two versions match exactly; (2) scrutinizing
the old copy to be certain all specifications for typesetting or
typing have been followed correctly; (3) inspecting the technical
quality of the new copy to catch problems such as misalignment,
defective type, and bad spacing; (4) marking the new version for
correction of deviations from the earlier version, from specifications, and from good technical quality; and (5) <u>querying</u> (raising
questions about) errors overlooked by the author or editor, such
as misspelling, bad grammar, and inconsistent <u>editorial style</u>
(compounding, capitalization, abbreviation, and so on).

Traditionally, two people proofread together, one reading aloud from the earlier copy (<u>dead copy</u>), the other marking corrections on the new copy (<u>live copy</u>). Other methods, including one-person proofreading, are discussed in Chapter 6. By any method, a thorough job adds two stages after the basic proofreading: (1) <u>reviewing</u>, which is a quick scan of the finished work by the proofreaders themselves; and (2) <u>checking</u>, which is a more thorough scan, usually by a supervisor.

JOB OPPORTUNITIES

Many organizations hire professional proofreaders as employees or as freelancers, full time or part time. Employers include the following:

- Printing establishments

- Commercial typesetters

- Publishers, including those of newspapers, magazines, and books

- Advertising agencies

- Public relations firms

- Trade and professional associations

- Government agencies

- Organizations such as consulting firms that print, publish, or distribute reports, proposals, or other publications, often printed in-house

- Direct-mail marketing firms

- Companies that provide editorial services to offices and agencies.

Skillful proofreading can lead directly to a supervisory job, to copyediting, or to production editing; indirectly, it can lead to administrative work, to sales, or to other jobs.

SOME FAMOUS PROOFREADERS

Proofreaders are in distinguished company. The early printers hired eminent scholars as correctors of the press (proofreaders). In 1716, a book was published in Germany containing the biographies of 99 celebrated proofreaders.* The names in the book include John

---

*John Conrad Zeltner, <u>Correctorum in Typographiis Eruditorum Centuria, Speciminus Loco Collecta</u>, printed by Adam Jonathan Felsecker, Nuremberg, 1716.

Foxe, author of the <u>Book of Martyrs</u>; Rabelais; and Erasmus, who was ordained a priest in the year Columbus discovered America but who "was more at home reading proofs in a print shop than working in a monastery."*

Important scholar-printers read proof. Aldus Manutius, who introduced italic type, did; he also printed a Greek dictionary and a Greek grammar when he found that proofreaders needed such reference books. Bodoni read proof (he did it poorly; his books are full of errors), as did Caxton, Baskerville, Estienne, and Ben Franklin.

Louis Quatorze, with his press at The Louvre, and Madame de Pompadour, with her little print shop in the Tuileries, very likely read proof. People with private presses certainly did; they include Horace Walpole, William Morris, Robert Graves, and Virginia Woolf. Add to the list typesetters Mark Twain and Walt Whitman; professional proofreaders Edgar Allan Poe, Bret Harte, Horace Greeley, and William Dean Howells; and, of course, all authors who have read author's proofs of their own work.

PROOFREADING AND EDITING COMPARED

Proofreading is not editing. It is not normally part of a proofreader's job to correct nuances of editorial style, to improve or change wording, or to correct grammar. (Proofreaders are always expected to catch English misspellings.)

If a manuscript needs a systematic, thorough review for editorial style, including wording, consistency, spelling of foreign words, accuracy, tone, punctuation, and logic, an editor should do the work. Such a review is not a proofreader's responsibility.

Many proofreading jobs, however, contain editorial errors. To distinguish between editing and proofreading, a useful guideline is this: Proofreaders should not spend more than five minutes an hour on "editing" work unless specifically authorized to do so. If more time is authorized, workers are doing more than simply proofreading.

Traditional proofreading and <u>copyediting</u> (editing for consistency in editorial style) are akin but have three major differences:

1. <u>Different kinds of copy</u>. An editor works with only one kind of copy, usually a draft; but a proofreader generally works with two kinds, the dead copy and the live.

2. <u>Different markings</u>. An editor writes corrections once only, in the running text; but a proofreader writes in the text and in the margin, making two marks for every correction.

3. <u>Different functions</u>. An editor's functions are to clarify the author's intent by correcting and improving a manuscript

---

*John Lewis, <u>The Anatomy of Printing</u>, Watson-Guptill Publications, New York, 1970.

to conform to good usage and a specified editorial style, and to prepare the manuscript for the next step in the publication process. An editor <u>corrects</u> bad grammar and inconsistencies overlooked by the author.

A proofreader's functions are to check the live copy against the dead to detect typist's or typesetter's errors and to be sure all of the editor's and publisher's instructions have been followed. A proofreader has no authority to make any changes at all--not even to correct errors made in the draft and duplicated in the final copy. A proofreader <u>queries</u> (rather than corrects) bad grammar or inconsistencies in editorial style overlooked by the editor or the author. (Querying is discussed in Chapter 7.)

THE CONTINUING NEED FOR PROOFREADING

We have invented the linotype and other aids to speed accuracy. Yet the human finger is still fallible, the human eye far from perfect, and upon these agencies we must depend for the operation of our machines.
> --Ben Abramson
> "Reading and Collecting"
> September 1937

Proofreading is true quality control. Good proofreading can turn a bad job into an acceptable one, a good job into an excellent one. Bad proofreading can ruin a well written, well edited, well designed job.

Printed words confront us everywhere. Books, pamphlets, magazines, catalogues, newspapers, reports, and proposals are the most common publications. But we are also bombarded with job printing--handbills, calendars, greeting cards, tickets, checkbooks, office forms, business stationery; display printing--posters, billboards, road signs; printed packaging materials--boxes, labels, tin cans, decals, record sleeves; decorative and novelty printing on paper, cloth, and plastic--napkins, towels, playing cards, baseball cards, gameboards, yard goods, shower curtains, shopping bags, T-shirts; not to mention music, maps, stamps, and titles for films and television.

All this printed material is subject to error--to the gaucheries of misspelling, typographical errors (<u>typos</u>), and gross grammatical errors, and to the ugliness of careless printing or reproduction. As a scholar-proofreader wrote in 1889, "So long as authors the most accomplished are liable to err, so long as compositors the most careful make occasional mistakes, so long as dictionaries authorize various spellings, just so long must there be individuals trained and training to detect errors . . . proofreaders."*

---

*Benjamin Drew, <u>Pens and Types</u>, Lee and Shepard Publishers, Boston, 1889.

Whatever the method of printing or reproduction, most publications in the foreseeable future will begin with a draft that is to be converted to at least one other form of copy through the agencies of the human finger and the human eye--and that conversion will be subject to error and will need proofreading.

However, the technology is changing rapidly, and proofreading techniques and methods will have to adapt to new methods of typesetting and printing; for example:

● When computer typesetting produces a coded printout, proofreaders must be able to decipher the code.

● When typesetting can be done by anyone able to type, the conventional proofreader's marks and language of printing are not always understood. Proofreaders must write out instructions or explanations for those who don't know proofreading marks.*

● When dead copy is compared to live copy that must be "proved" on a video display terminal (VDT)--a machine that looks like a typewriter keyboard attached to a TV screen (a cathode ray tube--CRT)--instead of on paper, the electronic cursor replaces the pencil, and proofreaders combine proofreading with typesetting by finding the errors and making the corrections themselves.

● When copy is typed directly on a computer keyboard, the editors who check the copy combine editing, proofreading, and typesetting. Comparison proofreading is eliminated.

Comparison proofreading may disappear entirely as technology advances. But when all writers exchange their typewriters for computer stations, the output will still have to be proved for the inevitable misspelling, inconsistency, and loss of word sense that occurs even in the best writer's work. And when computers transcribe directly from voice input, the result will still have to be edited for coherence and then examined for the editor's oversights and computer malfunction. We suspect that the people who work behind writers, editors, and computers to control quality will be called proofreaders.

QUALIFICATIONS FOR PROOFREADING

To be a good proofreader, you must start with certain qualifications: a feeling for English, an alert and orderly mind, a good memory, and an "eye." Most of the rest can be learned.

---

*I firmly recommend the traditional marking system; anyone producing copy to be proofread should learn standard marks or the simplified version described in my book, Simplified Proofreading, National Composition Association and Editorial Experts, Inc., Alexandria, Va., 1980.

A feeling for English includes the ability to spell, or at least an awareness of which words you cannot spell and a willingness to look them up. It also includes the ability to recognize bad grammar. You do not need a college degree in English or journalism to be a proofreader (to some employers a degree is desirable, to others it is an overqualification). You do need a solid grounding in language skills. People with such a grounding are often book lovers, familiar with good literature and good writing.

You need an alert and orderly mind to recognize disorder or illogic in the copy, to follow instructions, and to meet deadlines.

Good memory is important because you must recognize such major defects as repeated matter (we have seen eight pages of copy mistakenly repeated) and such minor defects as inconsistencies in editorial style (for example, the abbreviation r.p.m. on one page and R.P.M. several pages later).

The "eye" is essential. It is a unique quality. (A good eye would readily have caught the repetition of the word "not" in the handwritten insert at the beginning of this manual.) The ability to spot a typo, to have it leap at you from the page, is only a part of it. You must also spot such evidence of poor workmanship as disparities in the amount of space between lines; defective letters, for example, a broken f̲ (f), a capital O̲ instead of a zero (0); and minute misalignments, for example, the two fives and the decimal points before them in the box below.

| 27.2 |
| 23.9 |
| .5 |
| 1.9 |
| 4.7 |
| 3.8 |
| .5 |
| 0.0 |

Some people seem to be born with a proofreader's eye; others seem unable to develop it, although it can be developed. Journeyman printers have developed it to a high degree. An Editorial Experts, Inc., proofreader developed her eye through lessons in photography and art appreciation that taught her to see the details and the entirety of what she looks at. Copyeditors may or may not have the eye; their job is to look at words. But proofreaders look at words, at individual characters (letters, numerals, punctuation marks, and symbols), and at whole pages, too. Highly educated people or those who read a great deal are not likely to have such an eye without training; they read for content rather than for individual words and characters.

To test your spelling ability and your aptitude for comparison reading, turn to the Proofreading Aptitude Test at the beginning of the Workbook. Return to this page after taking the test.

Because a proofreader should understand exactly what a typesetter must do to make corrections, good proofreading requires familiarity with type, with typesetting methods, and with the procedures used to produce artwork. Chapters 10 and 11 offer an introduction to these aspects of proofreading. Further theoretical knowledge can be gained from further reading, but nothing is so valuable as practical knowledge. Proofreaders should watch typesetters at work, ask questions, read typesetting equipment manuals, and try to set type themselves.

Flexibility is highly desirable--to adapt to different sets of specifications and to changes in marking techniques for different kinds of copy; to adjust to the pressures of deadlines and the piecemeal nature of much proofreading work. Neat work habits, a sense of proportion, pride in the profession, good vision, and good hearing are also desirable.

GENERAL RESPONSIBILITIES OF PROOFREADERS

As a professional proofreader, your responsibilities include the following:

1. Meeting deadlines

2. Having available all necessary tools, supplies, and reference books (see Part III for lists)

3. Following job specifications exactly; this means being competent to detect all problems but marking and querying selectively, ignoring problems irrelevant to the particular job

4. Using neatly the proofreader's marks specified (see Chapters 2, 3, and 9)

5. Distinguishing properly between marking for correction and querying (see Chapter 7)

6. Maintaining speed and accuracy of the highest standards

7. Keeping your supervisor informed of your progress and difficulties.

THE PLACE OF PROOFREADING IN THE PUBLICATION PROCESS

To understand where proofreading fits into the publication process, see Figure 1, which shows a typical sequence from the point of view of a publisher who provides all the proofreading for a book. A description of how proofreading fits into the picture in a typesetting shop is given in Chapter 11.

Proofreading for the same publication progresses in several stages. At each stage, as new live copy is produced, the previous stage's live copy becomes the dead copy. (This is the reason the terms "live" and "dead" are used throughout this manual. "Copy" and "proof," as the two sets compared by proofreaders are often called, are terms too imprecise.) Any earlier corrected proof (or dead copy) is a <u>foul proof</u>. The progression of proofreading as shown in Figure 1 is as follows:*

---

*Note that some numbers in Figure 1 have no labels.

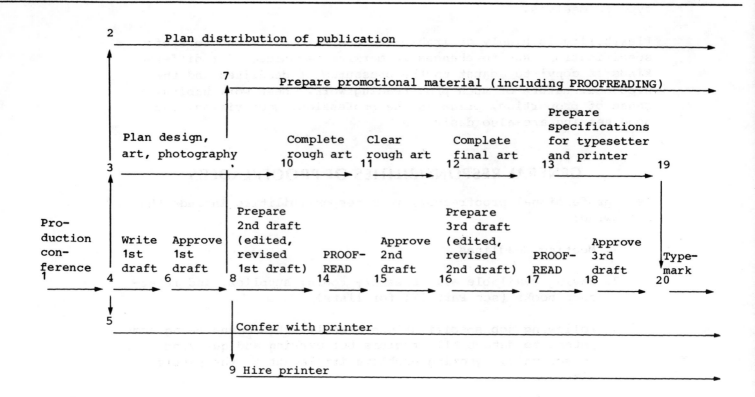

Figure 1.   Typical sequence

Step	Dead Copy	Live Copy
14	dead second draft (first draft with editor's marks added)	live second draft (typed as marked in dead copy)
17	dead third draft (second draft with proofreader's marks from step 14 and new editor's marks added)	live third draft (typed as marked in dead copy)
24	third draft from step 17 with typemarks (instructions to the typesetter) added	first galley proofs (typeset proofs)-- sometimes called green proofs
28	green proofs with proofer's marks from step 24	revises (revised galley proofs corrected as marked on green proofs)
30	revises with proofer's marks from step 28	page proofs (galleys made up into pages) with corrections made as marked on revises

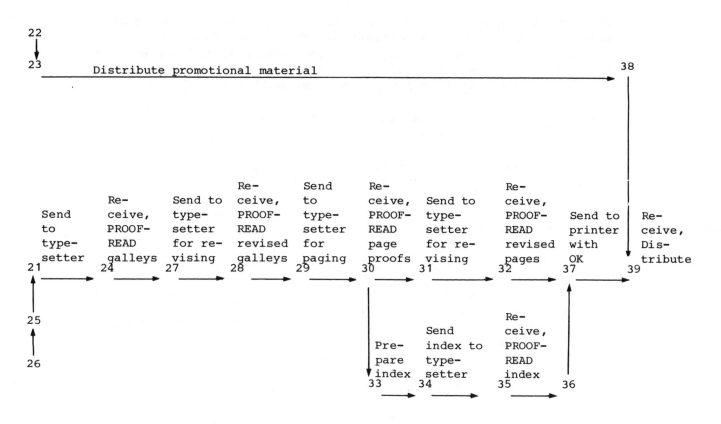

22
↓
23   Distribute promotional material   38

            Re-   Send   Send   Re-   Re-
            ceive,   Send to   ceive,   to   ceive,   Send to   ceive,
Send   PROOF-   type-   PROOF-   type-   PROOF-   type-   PROOF-   Send to   Re-
to   READ   setter   READ   setter   READ   setter   READ   printer   ceive,
type-   galleys   for re-   revised   for   page   for re-   revised   with   Dis-
setter   vising   galleys   paging   proofs   vising   pages   OK   tribute
21   24   27   28   29   30   31   32   37   39

25
26
                                                                     Re-
                                                          Send   ceive,
                                               Pre-   index to   PROOF-
                                               pare   type-   READ
                                               index   setter   index
                                               33   34   35   36

in book publishing

32   page proofs with proofer's   revised page proofs cor-
        marks from step 30   rected as marked on first
                                            pages

Promotional material follows the same sequence from typed draft to
galley proofs to page proofs.

An index follows a shortened sequence, perhaps from edited draft to
retyped draft to page proofs.

In proofreading material other than books, some of the steps shown
may be omitted, and new steps may be added. Even in the publication of books, significant variations may occur; for example,
the publisher may provide camera-ready copy--final pages ready to
be printed by photographic or other means--or may provide input
that can be read by computerized typesetting equipment. But after
any stage in which a new version of live copy is made, proofreading
needs to be done.

SETS OF PROOFS

Commercial typesetters and commercial print shops that do typesetting usually employ proofreaders. From such shops, proofs received by a publisher usually have been proofread and corrected at
least once (most shops require two readings, especially on critical
jobs). Proofs read in the type shop are called <u>office proofs</u>.

The type house usually furnishes the publisher with several sets
of proofs called (or stamped) as follows:

1. <u>Customer's proof</u>, or <u>proofreader's set</u>. The proofreaders
   mark corrections and queries directly on this set.

2. <u>Author's set</u>. The author may mark corrections and make
   changes on this set.

3. <u>Master proofs, marked proofs, or printer's set</u>. When corrections marked on the proofreader's set are checked and
   queries are resolved, marks are transferred from the proofreader's set (and the author's set) to this set, which is
   the one returned to the printer. The publisher's editorial
   unit keeps the proofreader's set and the author's set
   until the publication is printed.

4. <u>Dummy set</u>. This set is often used to make a page dummy.
   A dummy must have all corrections marked on it to show
   what corrections will eventually be incorporated; those
   that add or take away lines are especially important. The
   typesetter almost never makes corrections from a dummy.

Some publishers use only two sets, one for proofreading and one
for dummy paste-up.

TYPEWRITTEN AND TYPESET COPY

Typeset copy--galley proofs and page proofs--is not the only copy
professional proofreaders work with. Because whole books can be
printed from typewritten copy (as is this one), professional proofreaders must understand typewritten copy as well as typeset copy.
Throughout this manual, typed copy (<u>typescript</u>) and typeset copy
are distinguished from each other as follows:

Typescript comes from a standard typewriter or from a machine that
strikes letters onto paper and prints pages that look like they
came from a typewriter. Typescript is <u>monospaced</u>--every character
is the same width as every other. An <u>M</u> takes the same amount of
horizontal space as an <u>i</u>; a zero takes the same space as a period;
and the space bar, used between words, leaves blank the same amount
of space that one character takes.

Typeset copy can come from many kinds of machines (see Chapter 11).
There are far more variables in typeset copy than in typescript,
and thousands of typefaces in many sizes are available. Typeset

copy does not look like typescript because the characters are proportionally spaced--different characters have different widths. An
<u>M</u> is much wider than an <u>i</u>; a zero is wider than a period. In type-
setting, the space between words can be adjusted minutely, as can
the space between lines. (Although there are proportionally spaced
typewriters and monospaced typeset faces, the foregoing descriptions
hold true in general.)

Here are some examples of the two kinds of copy:

Typed:

ABCDEFGHIJKLMNO abcdefghijklmno

ABCDEFGHIJKLMNO abcdefghijklmno

ABCDEFGHIJKLMNO abcdefghijklmno

ABCDEFGHIJKLMNO abcdefghijklmno

Typeset:

ABCDEFGHIJKLMNO abcdefghijk

ABCDEFGHIJKLMN abcdefghijlmn

ABCDEFGHIJKLMN abcdefghijklmn

ABCDEFGHIJKL abcdefghijkl

RECOMMENDED STANDARDS

Work Conditions

Whether you work in a printing plant, a publisher's office, or at
home (as do many freelance proofreaders), you need quiet, minimum
distraction, good lighting, a comfortable temperature, and ade-
quate ventilation. You should have an adjustable-angle reading
board if you prefer one to a flat surface.

You need written instructions; they produce far greater accuracy
than oral ones. You must have a basic reference library and all
the appropriate tools.

Hours

Properly done, proofreading is hard, intensive work. To maintain
accuracy and avoid eyestrain, every hour of work should include
a five-minute break, and work should be limited to seven hours a
day (not including lunch hour or breaks longer than five minutes).

Speed

With relatively clean, easy-to-follow dead copy and good live copy,
a professional team should be able to proofread about as fast as a
fast talker can speak; a team should average 5,000 words an hour;
a single proofreader, 4,000. Many teams on certain jobs can reach
7,000 or more words an hour. Several factors will, of course,
reduce speed: small type, a hard-to-read typeface or format,

extensive editorial marking, handwritten copy, frequent errors in the live copy, many words or figures that need to be read character by character, many footnotes or bibliographic references, many tables, or the need for extensive querying.

To time the rate per hour, count the number of words on a typical page and multiply by the number of pages read in an hour. (A typical double-spaced typewritten page contains 250 words.) Remember that the first hour on a new job is usually the slowest.

Accuracy

A minimum acceptable standard of quality allows a proofreader to miss only one printer's or typist's error in an hour's work. The count of errors includes author's (or editor's) misspellings. It does not usually include other author's or editor's errors (although in many jobs such errors should be caught, particularly if they are blatant).

In freelance work, penalties may be imposed when a proofreader or team misses more than the acceptable number of errors, fails to follow job specifications exactly, uses improper marking, or damages camera-ready copy. Payment may be reduced to compensate for the extra time used in checking, repairing, and redoing the work if necessary. By Editorial Experts, Inc., standards, missing more than one error in 3,000 words may be grounds for dismissal or nonpayment.

A high rate of error on a job should alert the checker to review the work more carefully than usual.

QUESTIONS FOR STUDENTS

1. After the basic stage of reading proof, which two additional stages should follow in careful work?

2. What four main qualifications should a proofreader start with?

3. Why must a proofreader understand printing and typesetting processes?

4. Why do bibliographies or tables take longer to read than straight text?

5. How many words an hour should a team average with good dead and live copy?

6. For every 8,000 words proofread, how many missed typographical errors are acceptable?

7. Which of the following three-line paragraphs are typewritten and which typeset? Make a checkmark at the typewritten ones. List the reasons for your decision.

1. Proofers are expected to see the forest, the trees, and every little leaf.

2. Proofers are expected to see the forest, the trees, and every little leaf.

3. Proofers are expected to see the forest, the trees, and every little leaf.

4. Proofers are expected to see the forest, the trees, and every little leaf.

5. Proofers are expected to see the forest, the trees, and every little leaf.

6. Proofers are expected to see the forest, the trees, and every little leaf.

7. Proofers are expected to see the forest, the trees, and every little leaf.

8. Proofers are expected to see the forest, the trees, and every little leaf.

9. Proofers are expected to see the forest, the trees, and every little leaf.

10. Proofers are expected to see the forest, the trees, and every little leaf.

11. Proofers are expected to see the forest, the trees, and every little leaf.

12. Proofers are expected to see the forest, the trees, and every little leaf.

13. Proofers are expected to see the forest, the trees, and every little leaf.

14. Proofers are expected to see the forest, the trees, and every little leaf.

15. Proofers are expected to see the forest, the trees, and every little leaf.

16. Proofers are expected to see the forest, the trees, and every little leaf.

Chapter 2

Fundamentals of Marking

Blot out, correct, insert, refine,
Enlarge, diminish, interline.
                    --Jonathan Swift

CHAPTER OVERVIEW

Standard marks are the proofreader's language. They show what errors have been found in the copy and how they must be corrected. (For a beginner, to learn the marks is also to learn what kinds of errors to watch for.)

This chapter introduces standard proofreading marks for the basic operations of deletion, insertion, replacement, and transposition, and describes when and how to use these marks. The next chapter presents further details on marking.

WHY USE STANDARD MARKS?

The marking system used by professional proofreaders has proved its efficiency over the centuries. Without proofreading marks, specific instructions to correct the errors in the following sentence take more words than the sentence itself:

insert t in thirty   Thiry days hath SEptember   *lowercase first e in September*

With standard proofreading marks in the text and in the margin, the instructions are specific and brief:

t   Thiry days hath S/eptember

Standard proofreader's marks and marking techniques are practical, then, for several reasons:

* They are widely understood.

* They ensure that a job divided among proofreaders will be marked uniformly.

* In the evolution of printing, they are examples of the survival of the fittest--designs that achieve maximum accuracy, speed, and clarity for proofreaders and typesetters.

* They are basic to traditional forms of printing and typesetting. Slightly modified, they work with any form. A proofreader who knows them well can adapt them with ease as different jobs may require. (Chapter 9 deals with some of the modifications that may be needed.)

WHEN TO USE STANDARD MARKS

Use standard marks and marking techniques as described in this chapter and the next, when you know the typesetter or typist understands them, for the following:

- Galley proofs

- Page proofs

- Machine copies (those made by copying machines) of <u>reproduction proofs</u> (repros)--text or artwork

- Machine copies of <u>camera-ready copy</u> (artwork, type proofs, or typewritten material ready to be photographed or otherwise prepared for reproduction)

- Any preliminary printouts, such as from word processing machines, computerized typewriters, or computerized printing equipment.

If machine copies are not available, standard techniques, and sometimes the use of standard marks, must be modified, as described in Chapter 9, for the following:

- Repros

- Camera-ready copy

- Film or photographic paper

- Mimeograph stencils

- Original artwork, original photographs

- Direct-use typewritten copy (such as letters and address labels)

- Cases when the typesetter or typist does not understand standard marks.

NAMES OF CERTAIN MARKS

In this chapter, some marks will be referred to by name:

<u>caret</u> ∧ or λ

<u>caron</u> ⟩ or ———⟨

<u>cancel</u>
<u>slash</u> } /

<u>dele</u> (pronounced "deely") or <u>take-out sign</u> ∫

octothorp or space mark   #

close-up sign   ◯

Note that the cancel or slash is a symbol with many names. It is also called a shilling, virgule, slant bar, oblique, stroke, solidus, separatrix, and diagonal. Note also that there are many variations in the shape of the dele (some are shown at the end of Chapter 3 under Alternative Proofreader's Marks). This book uses a simple, quickly written dele that accords with the U.S. Government Printing Office (GPO) Style Manual.

HOW TO USE STANDARD MARKS

General Rule 1. Mark an Error Twice—Once in Text, Again in Margin

In proofreading, nearly all corrections must be marked twice, once in the text and again in the margin. The two marks are often different.

Most in-text marks show where to make a correction; most marginal marks show what correction to make (and also serve as signals to the typesetter or typist, who cannot be expected to search the text for corrections). The examples that follow in this chapter all illustrate this rule.

General Rule 2. Use Slashes in the Margin

In the margin, use a slash for three purposes:

    1. To call attention to an inconspicuous mark; for example:

r/   poofreading

    2. To separate marks for corrections to be made in the same line; for example:

r/i   poofreadng

    3. To indicate that the same correction must be made consecutively in the same line as many times as there are slashes; for example:

r‖   poofeading

Slashes to count consecutive corrections of the same kind and slashes to separate marks may appear in the same line, and the same set of slashes may serve both to count and to separate. In the following example, the first two slashes show that r must be inserted twice in succession; the same two slashes also separate the r from the next mark. Only one slash separates the a from the u.

r‖a/u   Poofeading Mnal

You may correctly use a slash after any mark, but it saves time
and effort (and makes a cleaner margin) to reserve slashes for
the three purposes described.

General Rule 3. Mark in Both Margins

Unless otherwise instructed, mark in both left and right margins.
Divide the type area in half with an imaginary vertical line
through the center. Mark in the left margin the errors you find
in the left half, and mark in the right margin the errors you
find in the right half; for example:

y︡/r   Commend me to ˄our proof˄eaders. They are ˄he soul ˄ad   t︡/w
  w   prosperity of a printi˄g office.

                                              --Crapelet

This system, recommended by the U.S. Government Printing Office,
prevents overcrowded margins.

General Rule 4. Mark from Left to Right

Unless otherwise instructed, mark from left to right when more
than one error occurs in one line. The example for rule 3
illustrates this principle.

General Rule 5. Ring Instructions

Draw a ring around explanatory words directed to the typesetter
or typist to indicate that these words are not to be set in type.
The following example shows a ringed instruction to clean up dirty
lowercase e's:

> Oh, that they who set the types and they who read the
> proofs would free their texts from errors.
>   --Peter Schoeffler

Cautions

Confusion and Repetition of Marks

Do not confuse in-text and marginal marks, and avoid repeating an
in-text mark in the margin or a marginal mark in text. Here are
examples of correct and incorrect techniques:

ɔt   wrong in-tex˄ and marginal marks   right in-tex˄ and marginal marks   ɔt
                  t
 k   (repetitious mar˄ing)   (nonrepetitious mar˄ing)   k
                  k

Guidelines

You are learning here the book system of proofreading marks. Another standard system is the guideline system. Guidelines (path-
lines, kitestrings) invite confusion, as they create the sort of
maze shown on the next page. Do not use them.

Human society, the world, the hole of man is in the alphabet. Masonry, astronomy, philosophy, and all the sciences find it an invible but real point of departure; and that is as it should be. The alphabet is a source all things.

—Victor Hugo

Spacing and Positioning Changes Resulting From Corrections

Ordinarily, when you mark for deletion or insertion of type, you should leave it to the corrector to adjust wordspacing, linespacing, and word division. For example, if you mark for a letter to be inserted between words, you do <u>not</u> mark for the space that must be added to separate the words:

Proofreader's Mark	Corrected Copy
lette added	letter added

Do not try to keep the live copy line for line the same as the dead copy; for example, if you delete extra words, do <u>not</u> mark for the adjustment that must be made in the lines of copy:

Proofreader's Mark	Corrected Copy
Proofreading proves whether the live copy copy matches the dead copy.	Proofreading proves whether the live copy matches the dead copy.

Handwriting

It is generally advisable to make marks and write characters about the same size or a little larger than the capital letters in the type you are marking.

The system fails if your marks are misinterpreted. Neatness is important. Good handwriting is essential.

To evaluate your handwriting, turn to Exercise 1 in the Workbook. Return to this page after doing the exercise.

Take a hard look at your handwriting:

- Do you make ascending and descending lines long enough to distinguish clearly between <u>a</u> and <u>d</u>, <u>e</u> and <u>l</u>, and <u>b</u> and <u>f</u>?
  a d e l b f

- Do you point and round to differentiate clearly among <u>m</u>, <u>n</u>, <u>r</u>, <u>u</u>, <u>v</u>, and <u>w</u>? *m, n, r, u, v, w*

- Do you dot <u>i</u>'s and cross <u>t</u>'s precisely? (A terminal un-
  crossed <u>t</u>--as in *ʃet* --is unacceptable; cross all lowercase <u>t</u>'s.)

- Do you make loops where they could be mistaken for another
  letter? Do you close all loops?
  Write carefully *g d k s*

  Avoid *g d h b*

- Could any of your capitals* be mistaken for each other or
  for a delete sign?
  Print G̲ I̲ J̲ Q̲ L̲ O̲

  Avoid *G I J L L O*

If you are writing a single character in the margin, any of the
following can be misinterpreted; do not use the letterforms in
the column headed "unacceptable."

Character	Unacceptable	Acceptable
<u>e</u>	*ℓ*	*e*
<u>n</u>	*𝓃*	*n*
<u>r</u>	*𝓇*	*r, 𝓇*
<u>l</u>	*|*	*ℓ*

If your handwriting is in any way ambiguous, change it or print.
The following alphabet is acceptable for hand printing:

- Block capitals:

  A̲B̲C̲D̲E̲F̲G̲H̲I̲J̲K̲L̲M̲N̲O̲P̲Q̲R̲S̲T̲U̲V̲W̲X̲Y̲Z̲

- Lowercase (the <u>l</u> in this alphabet may be used only in
  words; for a single letter, write a tall *ℓ*):

  abcdefghijklmnopqrstuvwxyz

---

*The triple underscore is the proofreader's symbol for a capital
 letter. Use it for every handwritten or hand-printed capital.

Be sure you write numbers clearly: 1234567890

BASIC PROOFREADING MARKS

Errors requiring basic marks fall into four categories: (1) surplus characters or words, to be marked for <u>deletion</u>; (2) omitted characters or words, to be marked for <u>insertion</u>; (3) wrong characters or words, to be marked for <u>replacement</u>; and (4) out-of-order characters or words, to be marked for <u>transposition</u>.

Deletion

"Delete" means "take out and leave white space (or set spacing material) here."

Deletion differs from replacement, which is discussed later.

<u>Doublets</u> (repeated characters, words, or lines, also called <u>dupes</u> for duplicates), <u>repeaters</u> (longer erroneous repetitions), and surplus characters or words are marked for deletion.

Simple Deletion

For simple deletion, use the dele (ꝭ) in the margin.

In text, it is important to mark deletions so that the typist or typesetter can read what is to be deleted. As a general rule, use a diagonal cancel (/) for a single character and a horizontal crossthrough (⌒) for more than one character, as shown in Figure 2-A.

Haven hotel (an overdose). Her ether-eal sister Bridget discovered she had

Your Little Ones will have a Great Time, and be carefully tended by our trained hostessess

identifying jurisdictional boundaries, and and in thinking about the kinds of evidence and informa-

The use of plant material is also important, Ives said. "You don't want an evergreen in front of a house with a southern exposure because it would block the house in winter when you want exposure because it would block the house in winter when you want the sun coming through. You'd put something like a honey locust there to diffuse sunlight in summer and allow it in the winter."

Figure 2-A.   Deletion of doublets and repeaters

For maximum clarity, do the following:

● Cancel

  - one character standing alone,

- one or two characters at the beginning of a word, or   ∫∥

∫∥

- one or two characters at the end of a word not immediately followed by punctuation.

● Cross through

- more than one character standing by alone, or   ∫

- entire surplus words, phrases, words, phrases, or   ∫
  passages. Be sure the mark clearly crosses through
  or, as shown, overscores punctuation marks.

It does not matter which doublet you mark when both appear in one
line or when each constitutes an entire line. However, when doublets appear on different lines, you must often decide which deletion will cause fewer resetting or retyping problems. In the example below, the second doublet is chosen because only one line
will need redoing; the first would involve two lines.

∫

A word . . . is the skin of a living thought and may
vary greatly in color and context according to the
the circumstances and the time in which it is used.
                                  --Oliver Wendell Holmes

Deletion With Closing Up

To a typesetter, a dele alone may mean, "take out the marked char-
acter(s) and insert (or leave) space instead." To avoid unwanted
space, combine the dele with the close-up sign, which means "close
up entirely; leave no space."

The close-up sign by itself looks like this:

⌒/   p͡roofreading

In combination with the dele, the sign looks as shown in Figure 2-B.

∫

FOR SEVERAL YEARS, a number of health spe-
cialists have had grave reservations about the   simp̶i̶m̶p̶le and compound interest   ∫
practice by which multinational drug firms sell prod-
ucts abroad by overstating the benefits and under-

∫   Her yearly postage bill is about   ∫
                                                          $200.

If it is not exact̶i̶c̶a̶lly right, it is wrong

∫   Avoid prolix̶f̶i̶xity!   coordinating, U.S. leadership and interest in the   ∫
                                   FAO has declined, perhaps less precipitously than
                                   in the U.N., as the interests and control of the poor-
                                   est states have grown. Although the FAO was active

Figure 2-B. Use of delete-and-close-up sign

Note that the close-up sign is used both around the dele in the
margin and around the cancel(s) or the crossthrough in the text.
In text, use two cancels or a crossedthrough for two characters.
Use a crossthrothrough for more than two characters.

Distinguishing Between Deletion and Deletion With Closing Up

You must distinguish between deletion and deletion with closing up,
and you must make the two marks accurately.

Mark to delete (never to delete and close up) when you want characters taken out but space left beside and around remaining characters. Use the dele alone to mark characters at the beginnings or
ends of words and to delete whole words, phrases, lines, or passages. Here is the rule:

- Mark only to delete

  - characters at either end of a word, or

  - a whole whole word.

Always mark to delete and close up when you want characters taken
out and remaining characters moved next to each other. Use the
delete-and-close-up sign for characters in the middle of words or
in the middle of groups of adjoining characters, such as letters
and punctuation. Here is the rule:

- Mark to delete and close up

  - characters in the middle of a word, or

  - characters in the middle of a group.

Think what could happen if you mark wrong:

Wrong mark	Wrong "correction"
either end of a word	eitherendof a word
a whole whole word	a wholeword
a word	a wo rd
a group.	a group .

No close-up sign is needed when you mark characters at the beginning or end of a line for deletion.

Normally, do not try to mark for the other spacing changes deletion
will cause. Leave the respacing to the typesetter or typist.

Deletion of Space

Use the close-up sign to de̲lete space in a line when no deletion
of characters is involved. To delete space between lines or in
other circumstances, see the instructions in the next chapter.

For practice in marking deletion and deletion with closing
up, turn to Exercise 2 in the Workbook. Always return to
this manual after finishing an exercise in the Workbook.

Insertion

"Insert" means "add." Insertion differs from replacement, which
is discussed later.

<u>Outs</u> (omissions, anything left out) are marked for insertion.

In-Text Marks

In text, use the caret (∧) for any insertion. Place the in-text
caret in the exact place the insertion must be made,∧the bottom of   *at*
a line pointing up, never at the top, never pointing down. Extend
one line of a caret when necesȧry. See Figure 2-C for examples of
marked outs.

Marginal Marks

The marginal mark indicates the matter to be inserted. (Never
write an insertion in text above the line.) In the margin, write
<u>short outs</u>--from one character up to seven words, or about one
line--horizontally (never vertically) on the page.∧ Take great   *Print if your*
care to write legibly in an easy-to-read size. Use the proper   *handwriting is bad.*
signs for punctuation marks (these are shown in the next chapter).
Distinguish carefully between lowercase and capital letters. Be
sure to group together characters that form words and to leave
space between words.

Control

Richard L. Eldredge, CAE, Executive
Director of the National Pest Association,
reports that in two-and-a-half years his
association's mailing costs almost doubled. Certainly, this is the same problem

York City, the ambassador said, as
he has in the past, that he has the
support and encouragement from the
White House.
   "The Pesient has encouraged me
to discuss things . . . It's amazing
that he has known instinctively what
I was trying to say even when the

r/d

New church panned

Sunny with a few cloudy periods today
and Thursday, which will be followed by ∧
Friday. Details on Page 5.

There were also tin-plated iron roofs.
They were first used in Canada in the
18th century. Thomas Jfferson put a
tin-plated iron roof on Monticello. The
tin was painted with a red oxide or
green pant; the later to imitate cop-
per's patina.

ℓ

rain

e

i/t

Figure 2-C.   Insertion

is that plain words

If the side margin lacks room, write the insertion at the top or bottom, and run a guideline from the caret to a side margin to the insertion. This is one of the few times a guideline is permitted; for example:

> The first rule of construction should be taken to
> mean what they say.

Insertion With Close-Up Hooks

Always mark to close up an insertion that must adjoin a group of characters. Put close-up hooks on the marginal mark, to the left if the insertion belongs to the character on its left, to the right if it belongs to the character on its right. Here is the rule:

cf
ic

- At either end of a word

ce/ic   - mark to close up an insertion.

Think what might happen if you mark without the close-up hooks:

Wrong mark	Wrong "correction"
clos up	clos e up (or) clos eup
an nsertion	an i nsertion (or) ani nsertion

e
i

Do not use hooks for insertions in the middle of words. Normally, do not try to mark for other spacing changes insertion will cause. Leave the respacing to the typesetter or typist.

For practice in marking insertion with and without hooks, turn to Exercise 3 in the Workbook.

Long Outs

How you mark <u>long outs</u> (more than seven words or about the width of one line of type) depends on whether the person making the corrections will have the dead copy to refer to.

When you are certain the typist or typesetter will have access to the dead copy, first, write in the live copy's margin, "Out. See copy p. x," giving the page number where the matter to be inserted can be found. Second, flag the page in the dead copy (see the section on how to make a flag in Chapter 9). Third, mark the appropriate passage in the dead copy by circling it or marking a bracket at its beginning and one at its end, preferably in color, and write (set) at the beginning. An example of this treatment is shown (without the flag) in Figure 2-D. In this figure, three lines have been dropped in typical fashion: The typist's eyes have skipped from the word "which" at the end of a line to the same word on another line.

Dead Copy

Live Copy

(set) When in the Course of human Events,
it becomes necessary for one People
to dissolve the Political Bonds which
[have connected them with another, and
to assume among the Powers of the Earth,
the separate and equal station to which]
the Laws of Nature and of Nature's God
entitle them, a decent Respect to the
Opinions of Mankind requires that they

When in the Course of human Events,
it becomes necessary for one People
to dissolve the Political Bonds
which ˄the Laws of Nature and of
Nature's God entitle them, a decent
Respect to the Opinions of Mankind
requires that they

(out, see
copy p.26)

Figure 2-D. Typical long out

When you are unsure that the typist or typesetter will have access
to the dead copy (and this is often the case in a typesetting shop),
type the out on a separate piece of paper. Attach the paper face
up at the top of the galley or page. Use masking tape across the
top of the paper, or use Scotch Post-it® notepaper, which adheres
securely with an adhesive strip yet removes easily. In the margin
of the galley or page, write "insert attached." If several long
outs occur on a page, key them A, B, and so forth and write "insert
A attached" and "insert B attached."

Insertion of Space

To insert space, you will often use the <u>octothorp</u> or <u>space mark</u> (#);
for example: Proofreading˄Manual. However, marks for insertion
of space are often more complicated. The next chapter gives details.

Replacement

"Replace" means "make a substitution here." Wrong characters,
words, or passages are marked for replacement with correct ones.

In text, cancel or cross through the wrong characters or words.
Be sure to mark no more and no less than what must be replaced.

In the margin, write the correct characters or words.

a
be/dd Cancel ¢ single character standing alone or one or two characters
at the ᵽeginning, the miᵭᵭle, or the enᵽ of a word. (See Figure 2-E for examples.)   d

AFTER THE SHOTS — Police help hostage Nellie Gurrath get
out from beneath the car, where she took refuᵴe Wednesday after
a police shootout with her captor.

t
Inᵮerior Decoration   random or does not exist at all. Func-
tional autoᵽomy seems to prevail. (3)   n

Figure 2-E. Replacement

beg Use the crossthrough only for whole words or for three or more char- *ds*
acters at the ~~lab~~innings or en~~tity~~ of words. Never cross through
characters in the middle of a word to mark for replacement. When
three or more characters in the middle of a word must be replaced,
cross out the entire incorrect word in the text and write the entire correct word in the ~~monfin~~. *margin*

The number of characters or words marked in text need not match the
number written in the margin; for example:

s
est   He who mark~~eth~~ last
marks b~~igger than others.~~

Think in terms of replacement. Do not mark the same spot first
to delete and next to insert; mark such problems for only one
operation--replacement; for example:

hi   abcdefg/jklm/rstuvwxyz   *nopq*

Marking an entire word for replacement can be the clearest and
most efficient way to handle certain problems. For example, this
is often a good way to mark when more than two characters are sur-
beginning plus at the ~~begbeginning~~ or ~~endord~~ of a word (instead of marking *end*
for deletion). This is always the best way to mark a word contain-
several ing ~~averele~~ errors.

When Not To Use Close-Up Hooks

To mark economically, do not use close-up hooks for <u>replacements</u>;
reserve hooks for <u>insertions</u> at either end of a word or for cases
when they are clearly needed; for example: G/ orge Washington.   *⌐e⌐*
Here are the rules:

- At either end of a word

m   - do not /ark to close up a replacemen/   *t*

- In the middle of a word

- do not mark to close up an insert/on, and   *i*

- do not mark to close up a repl/cement.   *a*

Nothing bad will happen if you mark to close up any kind of a
replacement or to close up an insertion in the middle of a word,
but you will have wasted time and effort, used more space in the
margin than you needed to, and made the copy look dirtier than
it really is.

Defective Characters

⊗ In the text, ring a <u>defective character</u>--bro(k)en, (d)irty, too l(i)ght, *⊗ ||| (set)*
or too (d)ark--and write a ringed <u>x</u> (⊗) in the margin. If you are
an inexperienced proofreader, use this mark cautiously. You must

distinguish between a genuinely defective character and a bad
machine copy or a poorly printed proof.

Do not mark too many (X)'s on a page; if many defective characters
occur, mark one or two and write a general comment; for example,
"Many defective e's throughout chapter, such as those marked in
first paragraph."

Spelled-Out Forms

To replace an abbreviation, numeral, or symbol with its spelled-
out form, ring it and write (sp) for "spell out" in the margin;
for example:

Instruction To Spell Out	Corrected Copy
(sp) (3 in.)	three inches
(sp) 5¢	5 cents
(sp) (N.J.)	New Jersey

It is always a good idea to draw a ring around "sp." With the ring,
the typist or typesetter understands that "sp" is an instruction
rather than the actual letters to be typed or set.

When there is the slightest risk that the spelled-out form is unfamiliar, treat the problem as a simple replacement; for example:

To replace a spelled-out word with its shorter form, write the abbreviation, numeral, or symbol in the margin; for example: ~~ten~~.   *10*

Long Replacements

On a separate piece of paper, type in their entirety extensive replacements that require resetting more than one line of type. Tape
the paper to the galley or page; key each separate passage by letter
(A, B, and so forth); and mark the margin of the final copy with the
key; for example, "Insert B, attached." Where the make-up has been
seriously disarranged, attach a new layout. In general, use any
means to ensure clarity.

For practice in marking replacement, turn to Exercise 4 in
the Workbook.

Incorrect Word Division

Mark incorrect word division character by character as a combina-
ation of insertion, deletion, and replacement; for example:

Delete-and-close-up plus insert:

reset incorʃ-
⌒⌣   ⌃ect word division   ʃ

Insert plus delete:

reset inco-
ʃ   ʄrect word division   ⌒

Replace plus delete:

reset incorreʄ
ʃ‖   ǂ word division   et

In these examples, a replacement is not hooked, but an insertion at
the beginning of a line is.

For practice in marking incorrect word division, turn to
Exercise 5 in the Workbook.

Transposition and Transfer

"Transpose" means "change the place." Characters, words, lines,
and passages set in the wrong sequence are marked to be transposed
or transferred to the right position.

Traditional Marks for Transposition

Simple transpositions of adjacent letters or words may be marked
in the traditional way--in text with a continuous double loop extending above one word or character and below the other, and in
the margin with the abbreviation "tr"; for example:

You can transpose more than two characters or words if the groups
are adjacent, for example:

However, never use a loop to mark transpositions of words that are
not adjacent. This kind of mark is strictly reserved for editors.
Mark such problems as replacements; for example:

Hurrah for the ~~blue~~, white, and ~~red~~!   red / blue

It is a good idea always to draw a ring around "tr" for the same
reason as around "sp."

A space and a character can be transposed; for example:

Proofreaders are galle/y/slaves

A better way to mark the same problem follows:

Proofreaders are galle⌣yslaves   ɔ/#

Complex word transpositions should always ~~in the marked be~~ *be marked in the* clearest way possible.

Transposition Marked as Replacement

Some styles of marking, including U.S. Government Printing Office (GPO) style, reserve the double loop for adjacent words; transposed adjacent letters must be marked as replacements; for example:

ro   p/r/ofreading

Figure 2-F shows this style.

When no style is specified, you may use either the loop or the replacement style; either will be clear. Complex letter transpositions should always be marked in the clearest way possible. *clearest* Replacement is often the ~~celaerst~~ way.

---

ei The 37-year-old Hartz reportedly is pleased with a chance to pursue a more liesurely lifestyle with his wife and three children in Washington

American delegations, at larger public conclaves, such as the World Food Conference, tend to be large and unwieldly.   *ld*

"The value of the prequisites accorded the rank was underscored when a junior White House aide jokingly referred to 'splash privileges' in Ford's new pool.   *er*

am This is just one more exmaple of the supervisors exhibiting their inefficiency.

Figure 2-F. Transposition

When you see a transposition of more than two adjacent letters, it is often easiest to mark for replacement of the entire word:

tration for a professional envoy, not ~~antoehr~~ political crony.   *another*

Traditional and Replacement Styles Compared

Here are examples of the two styles of marking for simple transposition of two or more letters in a group.

Wrong Word	Correct Word	Traditional Mark		Replacement Mark	
fried	fired	fried	tr	f‡ed	ir
lien	line	lien	tr	li‡	ne
bread	beard	bread	tr	~~bread~~	beard
angle	glean	angle)	tr	~~angle~~	glean
grin	ring	grin)	tr	~~grin~~	ring
anger	range	anger)	tr	~~anger~~	range

Transfers

"Tr" may mean "transfer to another line" or "transfer to another page (or galley)." Mark a line or paragraph to be moved to another place on the same page or galley with a bracket plus the instruc-tion "tr." (This is another exception to the rule that guidelines are unacceptable.) Here is an example:

The difference between a word that is right
ference between the lightning and the light-
and a word that is almost right is the dif-
ning bug.

                              --Mark Twain

One more exception to the rule against guidelines when part of a line needs to be transferred (is sometimes made) to an adjacent line.

To move (transfer) a line or paragraph to a different page or gal-ley, for example, to transfer a line from page 1 to page 3, mark the line to be moved with a bracket and the instruction "tr to p. 3," and on page 3 mark the place for the insertion with a caret in text and "tr from p. 1" in the margin. Do not use guidelines.

Never fully ring characters, words, or passages to be transposed or transferred. Mark around only partially, as shown above, to prevent the ring from being understood as a signal not to type or set the matter.

Run Over and Run Back

A whole word or two misplaced at the beginning or end of a line adjacent to the line where they belong may be marked with a short guideline (no caret) extending to a marginal instruction: "run over" means to move to the line below; "run back" means to move to the line above. The following headings, marked to be reset to "break for sense," are examples:

run back   ANOTHER DAY, ANOTHER
            DOLLAR--/ANOTHER DEADLINE

            PROOFREADER HANGED\BY DANGLING
            PARTICIPLE   run over

Here is a way to help you remember the difference:

run <u>back</u> means "<u>Back</u> up ↑ a line."

run <u>over</u> means "Put d<u>own</u> ↓ a line."

For practice in marking for transposition, turn to Exercises 6 and 7 in the Workbook.

For practice in marking for deletion, insertion, replacement, and transposition, turn to Exercise 8 in the Workbook.

QUESTIONS FOR STUDENTS

1. Write the names of the following marks:

ℐ _____   ⟩ _____

_____   ◡ _____

∧ _____   / _____

2. For what three purposes is the slash used in the margin?

3. When is a ring drawn around a marginal notation?

4. How many words are there in a short out?

5. What do you do with a long out when you know the dead copy is available to the typist or typesetter?

6. What do you do with a long out when you're not sure the dead copy will be available to the typist or typesetter?

7. What are three exceptions to the rule against guidelines?

Chapter 3

Additional Marks

The proof-reader's position is not an enviable one. When he does his best and makes his book correct he does no more than his duty. He may correct ninety-nine errors out of a hundred, but if he misses the hundredth he may be sharply reproved . . . for that negligence.

--The Practice of Typography,
Correct Composition
Theodore DeVinne
Oswald Publishing Company
New York, 1916

CHAPTER OVERVIEW

This chapter describes proofreader's marks for punctuation and symbols, for typographical changes, and for errors in spacing and positioning. Marks that differ for typed and typeset copy are discussed. Some alternative proofreader's marks are shown. A list of standard marks ends the chapter.

MARKS FOR PUNCTUATION AND SYMBOLS

Commas, Apostrophes, and Quotation Marks

In the margin, upright and reversed carets are used to distinguish between commas, apostrophes, and quotation marks.

comma:

apostrophe:

quotation marks:

Note that without the caret, it would be impossible to tell whether a , means a comma or an apostrophe.

In typeset copy, opening and closing quotation marks are different. Be sure to distinguish between opening and closing quotation marks by putting a little ball on the marginal mark: . You can remember which is which by thinking of openers as 6's and closers as 9's.

Superscript and Subscript

Superscript (superior) characters are printed or typed above the baseline of the type; for example: superscript[1]. Footnotes are often referenced with superscripts.

<u>Subscript</u> (<u>inferior</u>) characters are printed or typed below the line; for example: subscript$_1$. Mathematics and chemistry often use subscript characters.

Upright and reversed carets are used to place a character at the superscript or the subscript position. Note that the caret points toward the baseline.

```
superscript
            baseline                    V
subscript                        _____
                                      /\
```

The pointing carets are used to place any character above or below the line; for example:

Operation	Proofreader's Mark	Corrected Copy
Make correct baseline character subscript	$\land$2 H$_2$O	H_2O
Make correct baseline character superscript	2$\lor$ E = MC2$\lor$	$E = MC^2$
Insert superscript	2$\lor$ E = MC$_\land$	$E = MC^2$
Insert subscript	$\land$2 HSO$_4$	H_2SO_4
Replace wrong baseline character with correct subscript	$\land$4 H$_2$SO$_4$	H_2SO_4
Replace wrong baseline character with correct superscript	3$\lor$ 3^2 = 27	$3^3 = 27$

Note that the caret always encloses the marginal mark. The caret encloses the in-text mark only when the character is the correct one but its position in relation to the line is wrong. Use a cancel for replacement when the character is the wrong one.

Do not confuse the caret used for insertion with the symbols used for scripting. Use an upright (not inverted) caret in text for insertion both of subscript and superscript.

The subscript and superscript carets may be used together, for example, to insert a comma between superscript footnote references 2 and 3:

   Footnotes $^{2}{}_{\land}{}^{3}$

The combination of subscript and superscript marks is often used in mathematical copy; for example, to indicate that superscript 2 has the subscript <u>a</u>:

	Corrected
Mark	Copy

X 2 $\widehat{a}$ $x^2 a$

Hyphens and Dashes

This section describes how to mark hyphens, long dashes, and short dashes in typeset and typewritten copy. Here are the main rules for their use:

- Use the hyphen

  - to divide words at the end of a line (to divide words)

  - to join words to make compounds (great-uncle, self-confident),

  - to substitute for a short dash in typewritten copy and some typeset jobs.

- Use the short dash (en dash) in high-quality typeset copy

  - to act as a break between figures and letters (B-17, Section II-B-4-C)

  - to indicate continuing or inclusive numbers (pp. 2-10, 1942-45)

- Use the long dash (em dash)

  - to mark a pause for a sudden change of thought or a further explanation (The galleys—where are they?)

- Use the extra-long dash

  - to indicate an omission (To h —— with it!).

If you have the smallest doubt about how to use these punctuation marks, take the time now to read about them in Chapter 14 of this book or in a style manual. You must mark these symbols correctly. It is indefensibly wrong, for example, to mark for an en dash to divide a word at the end of a line; a hyphen is required.

Hyphens

A hyphen has the same marginal symbol in typeset and in typewritten copy--a double line followed by a slash (=/).

Dashes

Separate characters for a hyphen, a short dash, and a long dash are available to a typesetter. Only one character for all three symbols is available to a typist.

● Typeset copy

- The <u>short dash</u>, in high-quality typeset copy, is an <u>en</u>
  <u>dash</u> (a dash one en* wide). Its symbol is this: $\frac{1}{N}$

  In some typeset jobs (and in all typewritten copy), the
  hyphen is used instead of the short dash.

- The <u>long dash</u> (sometimes called a <u>full dash</u>), in typeset copy, is an <u>em dash</u> (a dash one em* wide). Its symbol
  is this: $\frac{1}{M}$

- An extra-long dash, in typeset copy, is marked with the
  number of ems width ($\frac{2}{M}$, $\frac{3}{M}$).

Examples

The next paragraph shows eight hyphens (rank-in-the-man,
sub-stantive, mili-tary, rank-in-the-job), one en dash (between the figures 2 and 3), and one em dash (between the
words "system" and "fully").

   Thus, the rank-in-the-man system is not a panacea for all personnel
in the foreign affairs community. It is a device to be used sparingly
for the specific purposes for which it is best suited. For example, with
average tours of 2–3 years, it wreaks havoc with many Washington
headquarters assignments where the need is strong for greater sub-
stantive depth, continuity, and bureaucratic skill. Aside from the military, most of the Government and all of the private sector use rank-
in-the-job systems—fully 96% of the U.S. labor force.

● Typewritten copy

- The short dash, in typewritten copy, is typed with the same
  character and marked with the same symbol as a hyphen: $=/$

- The long dash, in typewritten copy, is represented by a
  double hyphen; most people like it closed up to the characters before and after--like this. Its symbol is this: $--/$
  (It is also sometimes marked as for typeset copy: $\frac{1}{M}$).

- A longer dash, in typewritten copy, is marked with the
  number of closed-up hyphens needed (two hyphens equals
  one em). For example, to mark a two-em dash, write $----/$
  or $=////$ or $=/\,\text{(4x)}$ or $\frac{2}{M}$.

Summary Table

The following table summarizes the correspondence of typeset and
typewritten hyphens and dashes and their marginal marks.

_____

*Ems and ens are units of printer's measure. They are explained
 later in this chapter.

Typeset Copy		Typewritten Copy	
Character	Proofreader's Marginal Mark	Character	Proofreader's Marginal Mark
hyphen	=/	hyphen	=/
en dash	$\frac{1}{N}$	short dash, same as hyphen	=/
em dash	$\frac{1}{M}$	long dash, two hyphens (closed up)	--/
2-em dash	$\frac{2}{M}$	four hyphens (closed up)	----/ or = ⫽⫽ or =/④x⃝ or $\frac{2}{M}$
3-em dash	$\frac{3}{M}$	six hyphens (closed up)	------/ or = ⫽⫽⫽ or =/⑥x⃝ or $\frac{3}{M}$

Parentheses, Brackets, and Braces

When parentheses and brackets are marked in pairs on a line, mark
a slash between the opener and the closer, as shown below:

Enclosure	Dead Copy	Live Copy Marked for Insertion	
parentheses	where (and why)	where∧ and why∧	(/)
brackets	where [and why]	where∧ and why∧	[/]

When the marginal mark for a closer appears alone or as the
first mark in a line, it follows the slash; for example:

/) where (and why∧

/] where [and why∧

(/ The opener alone is marked in the normal way∧ preceding a slash).
These rules also apply to braces.

The three kinds of enclosure are usually shown in lists of proofreader's marks like this:

parentheses*   (/)

brackets   [/]

braces*   {/}

---

*Parentheses may be called fingernails, toenails, or crotchets.
Braces may be called curly brackets.

Other Punctuation

In the margin, circle all periods and follow other small punctuation marks with a slash to make them more conspicuous:

period ⊙

colon :/

semicolon ;/

Distinguish your mark for a question mark* from your mark for a query with the word "set"; for example:

question mark: Who ∧ (set) ?

query: Who Whom /?

Give an exclamation point* the same treatment, with the word "set"; for example: Oh ∧ (set) !

Mark a virgule (slash) with the abbreviation for "shilling," the printer's traditional name for the symbol; for example: and ∧ or. (shill)

Mark diacritical marks in the margin with the letter they accompany, not with the accent alone; for example:

garçon ç

señor ñ

entrée é

Schönberg ö

Special Symbols

Use proofreader's marks to identify a symbol whenever possible; for example:

asterisk (astrik): ✷/

ellipses (four types):

- periods (points) with spaces:

  - typewritten: ⊙#⊙#⊙#⊙

  - typeset: ⊙□⊙□⊙□⊙

---

*A question mark may be called a note of interrogation, an interrogator, a fishhook, or a query; it may be read by a copyholder as kwes, hay, or huh. An exclamation point may be called a note of admiration, an astonisher, or a baseball bat and read as bang, shout, or 'sclam.

- periods (points) without spaces: ⊙ ⊙ ⊙ ⊙
- asterisks: ✳ ⁄⁄⁄⁄
- dashes:

  - typewritten: ⁻ ⁻ ⁻ ⁻ ⁄

  - typeset: $\frac{1}{N}$ ⁄⁄⁄⁄

leaders, two types:

- periods: ⊙⁄⁄⁄⁄
- dashes:

  - typewritten: ⁻ ⁻ ⁻ ⁻ ⁄

  - typeset: $\frac{1}{N}$ ⁄⁄⁄⁄   or ⟨dash line⟩

Write out the names for symbols that have no special mark; for example:

Greek character, as noted: ∝ ⟨Gr. alpha⟩

reference marks: †⟨dagger⟩

mathematical, scientific, or technical symbols: R⟨reluctance⟩

ampersand: & ⟨ampersand⟩

bullet: •⟨bullet⟩ or • ⟨bold ctr dot⟩

For practice in marking punctuation and symbols, turn to Exercise 9 in the Workbook.

TYPOGRAPHICAL MARKS

Although correcting errors in the choice of type is a form of re-placement, only the mark for lowercasing one or two capital letters is the same as that for ordinary replacement. To lowercase one or two letters, cancel them in text and Write out the abbreviation ⟨lc⟩⁄⁄ for lowercase (lc) in the margin.

⟨lc⟩ To lowercase more than two successive letters, cancel the first and overscore the REST (one marginal mark will do); this makes it much easier for the typist or typesetter to see what letters are to be changed than would a series of cancels or one cancel through a word's first letter. (Some editors do this: LOWERCASE; or this: LOWERCASE.)

To capitalize a single letter, you may (1) underscore it three times in text and write "cap" in the margin, or (2) underscore it three times in text and write the correct letter (a̲̲̲, b̲̲̲, c̲̲̲), with the triple underscore in the margin.

A/B/C

For practice in marking punctuation, capitals, and lower-case, turn to Exercise 10 in the Workbook.

In marking typeset copy, use a single underscore to mean "set in italics," a double underscore for "set in small caps," a triple underscore for "set in capitals," and a wavy underscore for "set in boldface." The corresponding marginal marks are abbreviations; for example:

Marginal Mark	In-text Mark	Corrected Copy
ital	Set in italics	*Set in italics*
sc	Set in small caps	SET IN SMALL CAPS
caps	Set in capitals	SET IN CAPITALS
bf	Set in boldface	**Set in boldface**

Note that, to a typesetter, an underscore means "set in italic." A straight horizontal or vertical line under, over, or beside matter is called a rule; a typeset underscore is called a baseline rule. Baseline rules are rarely used for emphasis in typeset text, but underscores often appear in typescript (typewritten copy) where italics may not be available. To mark a missing underscore in typescript, draw it in text and write "score" in the margin; for example:

score

The word typescript means typewritten material.

You may sometimes need to use several typographical marks together; for example:

Marginal Mark	In-text Mark	Corrected Copy
bf ital	Set in boldface italics	***Set in boldface italics***
bf Caps	Set in boldface caps	**SET IN BOLDFACE CAPS**
C + sc	SET IN CAPS AND SMALL CAPS	SET IN CAPS AND SMALL CAPS
clc	set in caps and lowercase	Set in Caps and Lowercase
clc	SET IN CAPS AND LOWERCASE	Set in Caps and Lowercase

Cap I

①In small size type, when there is no room for three underscores, use a ring for the in-text mark.

To change italic type to roman, ring the italic type in text and
mark "rom" in the margin. To change boldface to lightface, ring
the boldface in text and mark "lf" in the margin.

When a character is upside down (this can occur in letterpress
printing or careless cut-in corrections), ring it in text and
mark in the margin with the turnover (invert) symbol--a whirl,
like a finger describing a clockwise motion (↻); for example:

> hand, and with musick sounding before
> them:) then follows one of the whifflers
> with a great bowl of white wine and sugar
> in his right hand, and his whifflers staff
> in his left: then follows the eldest steward,

"Wrong font" means that a different typeface or type size has been
set by mistake; mark *it* as shown. (To recognize wrong font characters you must know something about the variables in type design.
Chapter 10 discusses this subject.)

GENERAL SPACING AND POSITIONING MARKS

Individual characters, whole words, lines, or blocks of type can become misaligned in a crooked cut-in or paste-up. For example, the
following quotation's last line goes uphill:

> A proofreader should scrupulously avoid giving
> himself over to choler, to love, to sadness, or
> indeed yielding to any of the lively emotions . . .
> Especially should he shun drunkenness.
> --Jerome Hornschuch (1608)

Mark horizontal misalignment with a horizontal double bar in text
   and the word "straighten" in the margin. Mark vertical misalignment with a vertical double bar and the word "align" in the margin.

(Turn pages upside down if you are a beginner; you might catch misalignment and other spacing problems better when you are not dis-
tracted by reading words.)

Brackets are used both in text and margin to move matter in the
direction needed. In text, a right, left, up, or down bracket
should "push" or "pull" the badly spaced matter approximately
to the correct position; for example:

⊓   move up (roughly, to the horizontal line)

⊔   move down (roughly, to the horizontal line)

⊐   move right (roughly, to the vertical line)

⊏   move left (roughly, to the vertical line)

Never use a caret in text to correspond with a marginal move-right or move-left bracket; the caret could be interpreted to mean "insert bracket."

One way to indent or to remove indention is with the appropriate brackets. (A paragraph indention is better marked with ⊄ or, as explained later in this chapter, with the amount of indention wanted.)

Mark a bracket at each end of a line to be centered horizontally (in this case, do not try to show the correct position), and mark paired brackets in the margin; for example:

⌉PROOFREADING WITHOUT TEARS⌊   ⌉⌊

Use sideways brackets to center vertically; for example, for a small typeset bullet (a centered dot): ⊙ .

Justified copy is typed or set with each line the same width; every line of text is full measure   (except indented lines at the beginnings of paragraphs and short lines at the ends of paragraphs). To justify copy, space is put in or taken out be-tween words. Most books, magazines, and newspapers are set jus-tified. This paragraph has been justified.

⒡⒧ ⌈Flush is a marginal mark used with in-text brackets; it means "at the margin." Flush left (fl) begins at the left margin; flush right (fr) extends to the right margin. Justified copy is set full out--flush left and right (fl&r). Flush left is the term used for lines that do not have to be justified--for example, short lines, such as subheads or a paragraph's last line, or normal type-written copy. Flush left always results in ragged right; in fact, the specifications "flush left" and "ragged right" mean the same thing. Flush right (uncommon but possible) results in and means the same as ragged left.

Flush inside and flush outside refer to the inside and the outside margins in a two-page format; which margin is inside or outside depends on whether the page is a righthand page or a lefthand page. Figure 3-A illustrates flush copy.

Spacing marks include the close-up mark (which is the same in text and in the margin) and the delete-and-close-up sign. Closing up--setting characters with no space between them--is called bumping. The close-up sign may be called the bump sign, the delete-and-close-up sign, or the delete-and-bump sign. Except with the delete-and-close-up sign, close-up hooks do not belong above and below any marginal mark. If you must mark to close up at both the right and left, put the hooks both right and left; for example: G orge.

A break is the place where a line begins or ends. To indicate a paragraph break (a new paragraph) or to move matter to the speci-fied paragraph indention, use a caret in text and the paragraph

```
XXXXXXXXXXX
XXXXXXXXXXXX

XXXXXXXXXX
XXXXXXXX
XXXXXXXXXX
XXXXXXXXXXX
XXXXXXXXX
XXXXXXX
```

Flush left

```
XXXXXXXXXXX
 XXXXXXXXXXX

 XXXXXXXXXX
  XXXXXXXXX
     XXXXXX
 XXXXXXXXXXX
 XXXXXXXXXXX
 XXXXXXXXXXX
```

Flush right

```
XXXXXXXXXXXX    XXXXXXXXXXXX
 XXXXXXXXXX      XXXXXXXX
 XXXXXXXXXX      XXXXXXXXXX
    XXXXXXX      XXXXXXXXXX
XXXXXXXXXXX      XXXXXXXXXXX
  XXXXXXXXX      XXXXXXXXXXX
```

Flush inside

```
XXXXXXXXXXXX     XXXXXXXXXXXX
XXXXXXXXXXXXXX   XXXXXXXXXXXX
XXXXXXX               XXXXXXX
XXXXXXXXX              XXXXXX
XXXXXXXXXXXX     XXXXXXXXXX
XXXX            XXXXXXXXXXXX
```

Flush outside

Figure 3-A. Flush copy

sign (¶) in the margin. To indicate a line break (not necessarily a paragraph), you may use the run-back and run-over marks described in the earlier section on transposition, or the in-text <u>break sign</u>--a Z-shaped sign--with the marginal instruction "break." The following list is an example:

Aquarium, Department of Commerce Building,
   14th St. between Constitution Ave. and E St., N.W.
Botanic Garden, 1st and Maryland Ave., S.W.
Dumbarton Oaks,
   1703 32nd St., N.W.
National Arboretum,
   Bladensburg Rd. and R St., N.E.
Zoological Park
   3000 Block of Connecticut Ave., N.W.

When a paragraph has been mistakenly begun, use a caret in text and the instruction "no ¶ " in the margin.

In lists and other instances where a break is wrong but "no ¶ " does not apply, you must draw a connecting line from the break to the beginning of the next line and write the instruction "run on" or "run in" (they mean the same thing). The following list is an example:

Los Angeles, California. Population: 2,817,323
(city); 9.7 million (metropolitan area). Area: 463.7
square miles on the Pacific Ocean.

run on New York City, New York.
Population: 7,895,563 (city); 16,133,500 (consolidated
area). Area: 300 square miles at the mouth of the
Hudson River.

Blocks of hyphens ending lines, or blocks of the same word ending or beginning consecutive lines, are undesirable. The num- *break up*
ber of lines considered bad style varies among printers and publishers and depends on how wide the line measure is (frequent division is hard to avoid in short, justified lines). A common
standard requires resetting if there are four or more consecutive
lines making up a block.

Avoid combining the dele with the space mark; the resulting instruction is imprecise. To take out all space, use close-up signs. To ◯
take out some, but not all, space, write a caret in text and
less # "less #" in ∧ the margin. To delete a character and replace it
with a space, simply mark it for deletion (if you wish to be certain a replacement will be made, write the space mark in the   #
margin).

FL
run on You may write any instruction applying to
every line of a passage once only. This
paragraph is an example.

MARKS SPECIFICALLY FOR TYPESET COPY

Many marks used on typeset copy produced by any form of <u>composition</u>
(typesetting) or any method of printing are based on a traditional
vocabulary. The terms come from <u>letterpress</u>, the method that pre-
vailed for five centuries of printing with <u>hot type</u> (type cast
from metal) from a <u>relief</u> (raised) surface. Some of these marks
are described in the following paragraphs. A more detailed description of the terms is given in Chapter 10.

Leading

The material used between lines of metal type is called <u>leading</u>
(pronounced, and sometimes spelled, ledding). The word "leading"
has been adopted for use in other forms of typesetting. When space
must be added between lines, mark the place with an extended caron
(——————<) and write "ld," the abbreviation for "lead," in the
margin; when space must be decreased or taken out, mark the place
with an extended caron and write "ʃ ld", the abbreviation for "delete lead," in the margin. This is illustrated in Figure 3-B.
Proofreaders usually need not specify how many <u>points</u> or <u>picas</u>
(units of printer's measure) of leading must be inserted or deleted.

Immigration and Customs: You will be traveling through Canada and Alaska on your Princess Tour; identification may be required by Immigration officials such as a passport, birth certificate, voter's registration card or naturalization papers. Non-U.S. or Canadian citizens should consult the local consulate for proper documents.

Customs Inspection: All baggage is subject to inspection by U.S. Customs when you return to the United States. Under most circumstances, passengers are allowed a duty-free exemption of $100 per person, including one quart of alcoholic beverages. Specific information can be obtained from any U.S. Customs office.

10th Day: Skagway — Inside Passage. Today enjoy a sightseeing tour of Skagway. Your motorcoach will pick you up at your hotel. In 1898 Skagway was a city of gold mad prospectors. Ruthless exploiters. Painted dance hall queens. False fronted bars and false fronted gaiety. That's the way it was. The bars are still here. They're quieter now. Like the unpaved streets. You may stroll the wooden sidewalks past turn-of-the-century frame buildings and conjure up images of lustier days. A Trail of '98 Museum helps with the image making — and a Gold Rush Cemetery up on the hill. Following your sightseeing tour, transfer to the pier to board your cruise ship. Tonight you begin a thousand mile voyage along the Alaska and British Columbia coastlines.

Figure 3-B. Adding and deleting leading

Quads and Spaces

The spacing material used in a line between words, sometimes between letters, and for indention has two names--quads and spaces. To understand the difference between quads and spaces, you must know the terms em and en. An em is a unit of printer's measure equivalent to the square of the size of type in use (originally the size of the capital M); an em in 10-point type is 10 points wide and 10 points deep. An en is half the width of an em (originally the size of capital N); an en in 10-point type is 5 points wide and 10 points deep.

The noun "quad" denotes a piece of spacing material 1 en wide or wider. Em quads have their own proofreader's symbol, a small square: □. When an em quad is set, a block of white space is left on the page, for example, at the start of the first line of the following paragraph:

In this section, we will present our findings with respect to the general questions listed above. We will present the distribution of documents across

Use the em-quad and en-quad symbols to mark typeset copy for indention or spacing (most commonly for paragraph indention or lists and
for alignment of text or tabular matter) as shown:

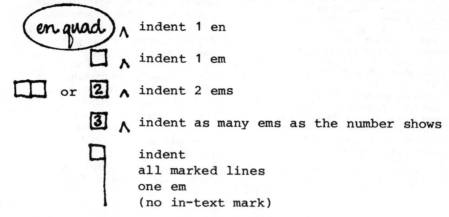

indent 1 en

indent 1 em

or indent 2 ems

indent as many ems as the number shows

indent
all marked lines
one em
(no in-text mark)

Quad marks should not be used to mark typewritten copy for correction because there is no such space unit on the typewriter.

<u>Spaces</u> vary from the width of a hairline to any width less than
one en. A space has its own special symbol, the <u>octothorp</u> (#).
This symbol is used as follows:

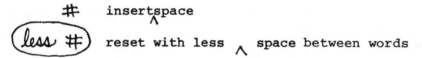

insertspace

reset with less space between words

equalize space; space evenly between words or characters where indicated with check marks; for example:

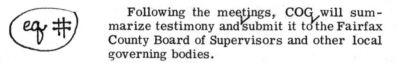

    Following the meetings, COG will sum-
marize testimony and submit it to the Fairfax
County Board of Supervisors and other local
governing bodies.

insert <u>hair space</u> (a very thin space); for example:

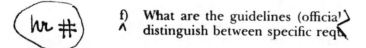

    f) What are the guidelines (official)
        distinguish between specific requ

The distinction between quads and spaces is disappearing in computer composition. All are called spaces--em spaces, en spaces, and
smaller spaces. The word "quad" is retained as a verb meaning to
fill out a short line with spaces, for example after the last word
in the last line of a paragraph.

Figure 3-C shows some examples of spacing and positioning errors.

A woman who works in this rather small office loves to gossip. I really don't trust her because she seems to have so much to say about everybody. I've often wondered what she

that state had shown healthy sales increases during the first four months of this year. Baxter directs Veedercrest Vineyards. Fetzer's winery in Medocino County carries the family name.

There is no organizational solution to this problem that does not incur concurrent costs. Some

A reputation for promptness is one of the things that a good printer is always striving for. He will have gained a great advantage when it comes to be said of him that he always gets work out on time, and it will pay him to endeavor to secure such a reputation by every means in his power.

Whitely—one of the movers behind the restoration of the Union Square historic district, a once decaying neighborhood near downtown Baltimore—says the university has misrepresented its intentions for the house fronting on Union Square and has violated the conditions of August Mencken's will.

But Alice Blondell, who has lived next door to the Mencken house for more than 40 years and knew the Mencken family, is certain Baltimore's most famous writer wouldn't like people meddling with his brother's will.

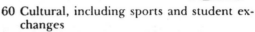

Cho pup 2 to 3 tomatoes, 1 small onion, ½ green pepper. Mix together. Dress with oil, vinegar, and hot sauce.

35 Arms Expenditures
40 Territorial Rights including Border Disputes
41 Diplomatic Recognition and Independence
42 Espionage
43 Fishing Rights
50 Use of the United Nations
51 Use of other International Organizations

60 Cultural, including sports and student exchanges
61 Scientific Research and Exploration
62 Joint Work on Construction Projects
63 Travel and Communications
64 Trade and Investments
65 Diplomatic

Data of this sort cannot be easily obtained from a cross-sectional survey. Longitudinal surveys are a more satisfactory source. In these surveys, characteristics of those who divorce are

Figure 3-C. Spacing and positioning errors

Letterspacing

Letterspacing is the insertion of spaces between the letters of words; for example, the word revenue appears, when letterspaced, as r e v e n u e . It is the designer's or editor's responsibility to provide specifications to the typesetter on letterspacing. Proofreaders must know how much, if any, letterspacing is specified.

See Chapter 12 for details on when a proofreader should instruct a typesetter to letterspace.

Rewriting to Space

Some kinds of spacing problems in typeset copy can best be solved by rewriting--adding or deleting words. This normally is an author's or editor's option; a proofreader only points out the problem or sometimes offers a solution in the form of a query (a question to the author or editor asking if the suggested change is acceptable) with the appropriate explanation, as shown in the following.

add to justify a word or words of?

To avoid resetting many lines when a correction involves deletion or insertion, add nearby∧approximately the ~~approximately the~~ same number of characters as must be deleted, or delete the same number as must be added. ⌡

Eliminating Widow Lines

A <u>widow line</u> is a short line at the top of a page--such as the last line of a paragraph--or at the bottom of a page--such as the first line of a paragraph (a page-bottom widow is sometimes called an <u>orphan</u> or a <u>club line</u>). (See Chapter 12 for a discussion of widows.)

There are several ways to eliminate a widow line or to <u>balance</u> (equalize the length of) facing pages or adjacent columns when one is shorter than the other: (1) Space may be adjusted above or below heads, tables, or illustrations; (2) A line may be <u>saved</u> (eliminated), or a line may be <u>made</u> or <u>created</u> (added), as follows:

- Space between words may be adjusted and several lines may be <u>spaced in</u> (<u>squeezed</u>, contracted) or <u>spaced out</u> (<u>spread</u>, expanded).

- Characters may be letterspaced to expand a line or, with some typesetting equipment, the space between letters may be reduced to crowd a line to fit its measure. (These are poor solutions for eliminating widows in good quality typesetting.)

- Rewriting may be done, as described below.

Rewriting may be the most desirable solution to eliminate a widow. The procedure is similar to that for rewriting to avoid resetting an excessive number of lines when deletion or insertion is required:

- To save (eliminate) a line, do the following: Look for a paragraph with a short final line and delete a word near its end, or <u>change words</u> to <u>decrease</u> the number of char-acters.

  rewrite ~~change words~~/? reduce ~~decrease~~/?

  change to ↑ save a line

- To make (add) a line, do the following: Look for a para-graph with a long last line and add a word that must be set in a new line, or mark a break on or within the final⌐word.
  ∧

  make a line/?

Ligatures

A <u>ligature</u> is a single character formed of two or more letters linked together. The following combinations should be ligatured in many kinds of typeset copy: ff, fi, fl, ffi, ffl.

Without Ligature	With Ligature
ff, fi, fl	ff, fi, fl
ffi, ffl	ffi, ffl

You have to know whether ligatures are available to the typesetter; some fonts lack them. When ligatures should be set, mark in text with the top hook of the close-up sign and in the margin with the hooked letters and "lig"; for example:

Missing Ligatures

Corrected Copy

 His rifled office files
baffled the sheriff.

His rifled office files
baffled the sheriff.

Other ligatures are rare, although old books or printing simulating the old typefaces may use ligatures for AE, ae, OE, oe, ct, and other combinations.

Push-Down-Space Mark

Most lists of proofreader's marks include the push-down-space symbol--a representation of a finger pushing down metal spacing material: ↓. Use this symbol only when you are reading proofs from metal type (and metal type is rapidly disappearing from use) and only when you find the particular defect the symbol represents.

In metal type, the characters that will pick up ink are raised above the leading and spacing material. If a lead or a space works up too high, it will pick up ink and print. Such a defect is marked to tell the typesetter to push the offending piece of metal back down so it will not print a black mark. Here is an example:

↓   mainly on diesel

MARKS SPECIFICALLY FOR TYPESCRIPT

In typescript, use the octothorp (#) to indicate spacing made with the typewriter's space bar as well as with the line spacer:

space (with space bar) between words or characters   #

\#⟩————— space (with line spacer)
              skip a line where caron points

Because the carriage moves over one space each time the space bar is struck, indention may be marked with exact numbers:

→5 indent number of spaces marked and type
      on the next space
   ⎤ indent
5 ⎟ each line
   ⎟ the number of spaces
   ⎦ indicated

General instructions may be used:

less #	less ∧ space
1st]	move to first indention specified in formatting
2nd]	move to second indention specified in formatting
¶ ∧	move to specified paragraph indention

Mark typed copy extending into the specified margins as shown in this paragraph, with a line showing the margin and the word "margin" in the margin itself; for left, right, and bottom margins, mark only at the bottom of the page, not at the line at fault.

The setting of the line spacer determines whether typescript is single spaced (ss), space and a half (1-1/2#), double spaced (ds), triple spaced (ts), or double double spaced (dds):

ss	1-1/2#	ds	ts	dds
xxxxxxxxxxx	xxxxxxxxxxx	xxxxxxxxxx	xxxxxxxxxx	xxxxxxxxxx
xxxxxxxxxxx				
	xxxxxxxxxxx			
xxxxxxxxxxx		xxxxxxxxxx		
xxxxxxxxxxx	xxxxxxxxxxx		xxxxxxxxxx	
		xxxxxxxxxx		xxxxxxxxxx

(ss) Proofreaders should reserve the abbreviations ss, 1-1/2#, ds, etc., for instructions involving more than one line. For line spacing errors involving only one or two lines, when the symbol # (for skip a line) is not sufficient instruction, the abbreviation "CR" for "carriage return" is used. "CR" assumes that one carriage return will begin a new single-spaced line. The instruction 2CR is equivalent to double spacing; it means "set line spacer to single space, skip a line, and type on the second line." 3CR means "skip two single spaced lines; begin to type on the third line"; it is the same as triple spacing. Line spacing marks are used in conjunction with carons or brackets. An example is shown later in this chapter.

PRECAUTIONARY MARKS

To prevent problems--

- Always close up insertions at the beginnings and ends of words:

t⁀ He will plan∧his garden today.

⁀t He will plan∧his garden today.

a⁀ She had∧cute appendicitis.

a⁀ He fought∧bout 10 years ago.

margin | | margin

● Use space marks when you need them:

He fought∧bout 10 years ago.   # a #

⌐ ⋔ # so   Be it eve∧humble, there's no place like home.

For practice in marking spacing problems, turn to
Exercise 11 in the Workbook.

CORRECTION OF WRONG PROOFREADER'S MARKS

The editor's mark "stet" for "let it stand; ignore the marked correction" is also used by proofreaders. Cross out the marginal cor- *ing* (stet)
rection; put dots in the text under the correction to be ignored.

Written-Out Instructions

When dealing with knowledgeable typesetters or typists, do not substitute written-out instructions for standard proofreader's marks:

᾿   Right: Wrong:

             proofreader∧s mark   no proofreader∧s mark (insert apostrophe)

However, the two most important things in proofreading are, first,
that you catch the errors and, second, that the person making the
corrections understands your instructions. If you do not know how
to mark something, write out the instruction. If you forget the
proper mark and have no time to look it up, write out the instruction. It is better that you look like an amateur than that your
marks be wrong. Never invent marks on the spur of the moment.

For example, if combining subscript and superscript carets is too
hard to figure out, write out an instruction and mark a ring
around it:

Proofreader's Mark		Corrected
Margin	Text	Copy
(2∧3 set super comma)	notes^2∧^{3}	notes^{2,3}
(X$_2$a set super a on sub 2)	x∧	x$_2$a

Write out and ring instructions (and draw a symbol) under the following circumstances:

● When the character designated is the same as a proofreader's symbol:

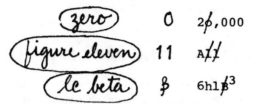

number sign # #4 and ∧5

shill / either ∧ or

equal sign =/ 2 + 2 ∧ 4

- When marks might be confused with another character; for example, to distinguish between a zero and a letter O, between a typewritten lowercase letter el (1) and the numeral one (1), or between capital B and lowercase Greek beta:

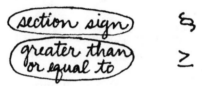

zero O 2Ø,000

figure eleven 11 A//

lc beta β 6h1β³

- When an infrequently used character has no special proofreader's symbol:

section sign §

greater than or equal to ≥

- When an instruction to the printer cannot be made with standard marks. In such a case, you can often use generally accepted abbreviations in the instructions:

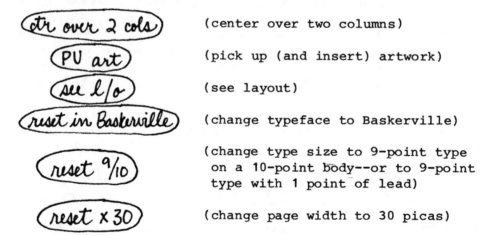

ctr over 2 cols (center over two columns)

PU art (pick up (and insert) artwork)

see l/o (see layout)

reset in Baskerville (change typeface to Baskerville)

reset 9/10 (change type size to 9-point type on a 10-point body--or to 9-point type with 1 point of lead)

reset x 30 (change page width to 30 picas)

A one-page list of standard proofreader's marks is provided at the end of this chapter.

For a review of proofreading marks, turn to Exercise 12 in the Workbook.

ALTERNATIVE PROOFREADER'S MARKS

Some of the standard marks in the list at the end of the chapter were chosen from among several alternative marks for these reasons: they are simple, quickly written, and specific; they are required by the U.S. Government Printing Office (the largest printing office in the world; they would be understood by anyone using the marks approved by the American National Standards Institute or those listed in the Merriam-Webster dictionaries, the American Heritage dictionary, the University of Chicago Press Manual of Style, and most American textbooks on printing.

Most other standard marks are recognizable variations of those listed in this chapter. For example, the sign for a hyphen: =/ may be drawn as /=/ or with close-up hooks, ⁀=⁀. The sign for an em dash: 1/M may be written 1/em or 1.

There are dozens of ways to make a dele. This sign derives from the Greek delta (δ) used by early printers. All variations retain the loop and most retain the tail, although few now look like the delta otherwise. Editors often like to use a simple loop (ℓ) but this is a poor choice for proofreaders because it could be mistaken for a lowercase e; if you use a loop, put a tail on it (ℓ) or turn it upside down (ə). Other forms of the dele include the following:

There are many ways to mark an ampersand (the "short and" sign):

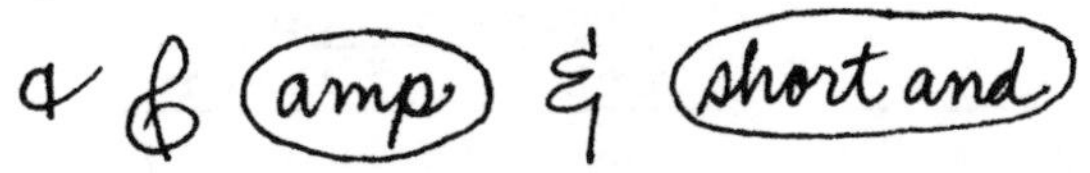

The close-up sign may be used vertically instead of ⌠ld or less #; for example, to take out the extra space between the following lines:

adjectives
adverbs

conjunctions

For typists and typesetters who want to decide for themselves how to correct a wrong word division, the proofreader writes out the whole word, putting a hyphen wherever a hyphen would be correct:

wrong ~~divisi-~~ di-vi-sion
~~on~~

~~maginary~~ ~~i-~~ imag-i-nary

There are often alternative ways, equally correct, to mark the same error, for example, to mark transposition in the following quotation:

Dead copy: Be sure of it; give me the ocular proof.

Live copy: Be sure of it; give me ~~proof~~ ocular the. ⌠/tr/proof
Be sure of it; give me proof ocular ~~the~~. the/tr/⌠

Slight variations of standard marks will not be misunderstood by a
typesetter, but uniformity in one person's work or in all work on
the same job is highly desirable. To change lowercase to capitals,
any choice from the following examples is clear; but the first is
preferred and the last is undesirable:

1. capital letters   3. capital letters

2. capital letters   4. capital letters

Other alternative marks are shown in the next chapter.

For practice in using standard marks, turn to Exercises
13 and 14 in the Workbook.

QUESTIONS FOR STUDENTS

Mark the examples in the following chart. Note that leading goes
between lines of typeset copy, space between lines of typed copy.

Instruction	Typeset Copy Text	Margin	Typewritten Copy Text	Margin
insert short dash (en dash) between figures	pp. 1 3		pp. 1 3	
insert long dash (em dash) between words	yes no		yes no	
insert lead between lines	abcdefghi nopqrstuv		(not applicable)	
insert space between lines (skip a line)	(not applicable)		abcdefghi nopqrstuv	
take out lead between lines	abcdefghi nopqrstuv		(not applicable)	
take out space between lines	(not applicable)		abcdefghi nopqrstuv	
indent first line 1 em	abcdefghijklm nopqrstuvwxyz		(not applicable)	
indent first line 5 spaces	(not applicable)		abcdefghijklm nopqrstuvwxyz	

STANDARD PROOFREADING MARKS

Basic Marks
(delete, insert, replace, transpose)

- delete 1 character
- delete more than 1 character
- delete and close up entirely
- inset from 1 character up to 7 words
- insert more than 7 words

out, see copy p.x

- insert and close up at left, at right
- replace 1 character

than replace more over 1 character

to// et transpose (words adjacent) or letters (or) letters

Marks for Punctuation and Symbols

- < inferior, subscript
- > superior, superscript
- apostrophe
- :/ colon
- comma
- ! exclamation point
- =/ hyphen
- period
- *set?* question mark
- quotation marks
- ;/ semicolon
- *shill* virgule (slash, shilling)
- () parentheses
- [/] brackets

Special Marks

- *stet* ignore marked correction
- *to/?* query at author
- make same correction as many times as slashes
- spell out (abbrev), numeral, or symbol
- correct wrong word divi-sion
- correct wrong word div-ision
- do not set ringed explanation in type

Marks for Spacing and Positioning

- *eq #* equal / space needed
- *run on* no new line
- *break* break. Begin new line
- carry over *to run over* next line
- *run back* carry back to previous line
- new paragraph
- *no* no new paragraph
- move right
- move left
- move down
- move up
- *straighten* align horizontally
- *align* align vertically
- center horizontally
- center vertically
- close up entirely
- # insertspace
- *less #* less space

Typographical Marks

- *ital* italic
- *sc* small caps
- *caps* all caps
- *bf* boldface
- *c+sc* caps and small caps
- *lc* lowercase
- *S/L/C* single-letter caps
- *Clc* caps and lowercase (as in a head)
- *Clc* CAPS AND LOWERCASE
- *x* defective character
- *wf* wrong font
- *lig* use ligature (as in off)
- *rule* use rule

Marks for Typewritten Copy Only

- # skip a line
- 2CR 2 carriage returns; skip a line, type on 2nd line
- 3CR 3 carriage returns; skip 2 lines, type on 3rd line
- *ss* single space
- 1½# space and a half
- *ts* triple space
- *dds* double double space
- 5 indent 5 spaces, type on 6th
- 5 indent 5 spaces
- *1st* indent to 1st specified indention
- *2nd* indent to 2nd specified indention
- =/ hyphen or en dash; type closed up
- --/ 2 hyphens closed up, equivalent to em dash
- *score* underscore

Marks for Typeset Copy Only

- 1-en dash
- 1-em dash
- inverted letter
- protruding spacing material
- *ld* insert lead
- *ld* take out lead
- indent 1 em or insert 1-em quad
- indent 2 ems or insert 2-em quad
- indent number of ems shown

General Rules

Mark every error twice--first in the text to show where the error is, next in the margin to show what correction is needed.

Use both left and right margins, according which is closer to the error.

Slash to separate multiple marginal marks.

Chapter 4

Interpreting Author's and Editor's Marks

At one side is the author's and editor's work and at the other is
the typesetter's work. My work goes between the two. I'm the
cheese that goes between two slices of bread to make a sandwich.

--Proofreader

CHAPTER OVERVIEW

This chapter discusses and demonstrates the differences between editor's marks and proofreader's marks, lists standard editor's marks,
and shows some of the many variations of editor's marks you may
encounter.

DIFFERENCES BETWEEN PROOFREADER'S AND EDITOR'S MARKS

To read manuscript against the live copy, proofreaders must be able
to interpret author's or editor's marks. Editor's symbols may be
the same as proofreader's, but they are used differently simply
because setting type is different from correcting it. When every
character is being set, marks are made only in the text; marginal
marks are unnecessary and confusing. Editor's marks should look
something like this:

The combinations possible from the 26 letters of the alphabet, if

each is used only once, number 620,448,491,733,238,439,360,0600.

Proofreaders mark both in the text and margin because a typist or
typesetter cannot be expected to search the entire text for occasional corrections. Proofing marks for the same passage look
like this:

The combinations possible from the 26 letters of the alphabet, if
each is used only once, number 620,448,491,733,238,439,360,0600.

Another reason for the proofreader's system of text-margin marks
is that, unlike the double-spaced copy editors usually work with,
copy to be proofread seldom has space between the lines for insertions and replacements.

When editors work with single-spaced typewritten copy, they resort
to proofreader's marks or to a combination of editor's and proofreader's marks.

Figures 4-A, 4-B, and 4-C show, in sequence, dead copy with standard editor's marks, live copy marked by a proofreader against the
edited dead copy, and new live copy corrected from the proofreader's
marks.

In J. T. Buckingham's edition of Shakespeare (1814) is, at page 915, an remarkable note, apologizing for a few "trifling errors," and adapting as an excuse a quotation from an advertisement "from the first edition of Reed, 1793":

He, whose business it is to offer this unusual apology, very well remembers to have been sitting with Doctor Johnson when an agent from a neighbouring press brought in a news proof sheet of a republication, requesting to know whether a particular word in it was not corrupted. "So far from it, sir," (replied the doctor with some harshness,) "that the words you suspect, and would displace, is conspicuously beautiful where it stands, & is the only one that could do the duty expected of it by Mr. Pope."

single spaced quotation FℓL

Figure 4-A.   Dead copy with editor's marks

In J. T. Buckinham's edition of Shakespeare (1814) is, at page 915, a remarkable note, apologizing for a few "trifling errors, and adopting as an excuse a quotation from an advertisement "from the first edition of Reed 1793":

He, whose business it is to offer this unusual apology, very well remembers to have been sitting with Dr. Johnson, when an agent from a neighboring press brought in a proof sheet of a republication, requesting to know whether a particular word in it wasnot corrupted "So far from it, sir," (replied the doctor with some harshness,) "that the word you suspect, and would displace, is conspicuously beautiful where it stands, & is the only one that could do do the duty expected of it by Mr Pope."

less #

Figure 4-B.   Live copy marked by proofreader against Figure 4-A

In J. T. Buckingham's edition of Shakespeare
(1814) is, at page 915, a remarkable note, apologizing
for a few "trifling errors," and adopting as an excuse
a quotation from an advertisement "from the first
edition of Reed, 1793":

> He, whose business it is to offer this unusual
> apology, very well remembers to have been sitting
> with Dr. Johnson, when an agent from a neighboring
> press brought in a proof sheet of a republication,
> requesting to know whether a particular word in it
> was not corrupted. "So far from it, sir," (replied
> the Doctor with some harshness,) "that the word you
> suspect, and would displace, is conspicuously
> beautiful where it stands, and is the only one that
> could do the duty expected of it by Mr. Pope."

Figure 4-C. New live copy corrected from proofreader's marks in 4-B

STANDARD EDITOR'S MARKS

(Marks not listed are same as proofreader's, although they are used
in text only.)

Basic Marks

deletej character

delete ~~delete~~ word

delete and close up

close up entirely;
   change to one wor d

close up part way;
   use less   space

insert word or character

connect insertion to the
character at its left:
   sing low (for sings low)

connect insertion to the
character at its right:
   sing low (for sing slow)

replace a character or ~~characters~~

transpose; (order change)

Punctuation and Symbols

comma

period

change comma to period

change period to comma

hyphen

apostrophe

inferior

superior

(continued)

<u>Spacing and Positioning</u>

insert⌗space
(or) insert/space

xxx. ¶Begin paragraph
(or) xxx. ⌐Begin paragraph...

xxxxxxxxxxxxxxxxxx.⌐
⌐xxxxxx. run on same line

]center[

[move left

]move right

<u>Typographical Marks</u>

/lowercase character

/LOWERCASE word

cap character

cap word

set in italic

set in boldface

set in caps and small caps

<u>Special Marks</u>

retain hyphen, as in bell‑
   like (used at ends of
   lines)

delete hy/
   phen and close up
   (used at ends of lines)

spell out ringed matter
   (change ③ oz. to three
   ounces)

use figure, symbol, or
   abbreviation for ringed
   matter (change three
   ounces to 3 oz.)

end (or) 30 (or) ⌗ (end
   of copy)

A list of abbreviations frequently used in editorial work is
given in Chapter 14.

ALTERNATIVE EDITOR'S MARKS

Authors and editors do not always use the marks in the foregoing
list. Variation of standard marks or nonstandard marks may be
used. Sometimes proofreader's marks are used incorrectly (⋃ for
move down). Sometimes marks seem to be original inventions (U/S/
for spell out). You may see a great variety.

You should have no problem interpreting variations of standard
marks:

Mark	Standard	Variation
circles or carets may be used instead of slashes	w/ard	w/ard (or) w/ard
the proofreader's ring or slash may be omitted	Ⓧ =/	X =
different use may be made of caps, periods, ampersands, plus marks, or abbreviations	wf clc fl	W.F. C+lc F.L., FlL

Mark	Standard	Variation

The symbol may be turned or drawn differently:

A different sequence may be followed:

Transposition may be marked with numbers instead of with the standard sign:

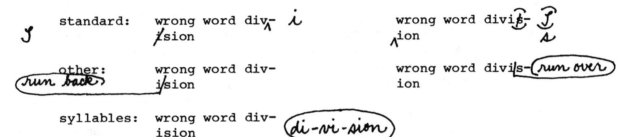

standard: change ~~words~~ (of order)∧ *words*

numbers: change words of order
　　　　　　1　　4　　3　　2

Word division may be marked differently, or the syllables may be separated for the typesetter to choose the division:

standard: wrong word div-∧/sion　　　　　wrong word divis-/ion

other: wrong word div-i/sion　(run back)　　wrong word divi/s-(run over) ion

syllables: wrong word div-ision　(di-vi-sion)

Other variations may include those listed below:

Standard		Variation
em dash	$\frac{1}{M}$	$\frac{1}{em}$ (or) |$\frac{1}{M}$| (or) |$\frac{M}{}$| (or) $\frac{1}{}$
2-em dash	$\frac{2}{M}$	$\frac{2}{em}$ (or) |$\underline{2}$|
en dash	$\frac{1}{N}$	$\frac{1}{en}$ (or) |*en*| (or) |$\frac{N}{}$| (or) —
em quad	▯	
2-em quad	▯▯ (or) ☐2	
en quad	*en quad*	▯ (or) ▢
spell out	(sp)	S.O. (or) W.O. (write out)
equal space (in margin)	eq #	√∧ (or) ∧∨
(in text)	e∨qu∨a∨1	e^qu^a^1 (or) e/qu/al
center	][	⌐¬
move left	[	⌐ (or) |←
move up	⌐¬	↑
caps	*Caps*	U.C. (uppercase)
paragraph	¶	N.P. (new paragraph)

	Standard	Variation
virgule (slash)	*shrill*	⊘
question mark	*set* ?	?
asterisk	✳	☀
horizontal mis-alignment (in margin)	*straighten*	═══
vertical mis-alignment (in margin)	*align*	‖ (or) ⧸ (ragged margin)

The difficulty comes with marks that have different meanings to different markers; you may have to figure out which interpretation is sensible:

ℐ#	delete space (or) delete some type and then insert a space to replace what was deleted	xx ⌢ xx	less space (or) close up
xx ⌢ xx	less space (or)	⊢⊣	em dash (or) hyphen
x ⌣ x	use ligature	⌐	paragraph (or) move left

Punctuation is often marked with great individuality. Although standard editor's marks include the ring to change a comma to a period (⊙) and the inverted caret to change a period to a comma (⋀), some editors ring any punctuation mark that should become a period and place an inverted caret over any mark that should become a comma. You may see redrawn marks, delete signs over part of an unwanted mark, and many other techniques to indicate a change in punctuation; for example:

	Editor's Symbol	
Original Punctuation	Change to Period	Change to Comma
comma	⊙	
period		، ⋀ ⋀
colon	⋌ ⊕ ⊙	⋌ ⋌ ⋀ ⋀
semicolon	⋌ ⊕ ⊙	⋌ ⋌ ⋀ ⋀
exclamation	⋌ ⊕ ⊙	⋌ ⋌ ⋀ ⋀
question	⋌ ⊕ ⊙	⋌ ⋌ ⋀ ⋀

Figure 4-D shows an example of a well marked edited page.

A careful editor will mark unusual usage or spelling to prevent mistaken "correction" or unneeded querying in one of several ways:

William Shakespere   *folo copy*

The medium is the massage   *C.Q.*

"Hello! How it goes?" he said.   *stet*

MariAnn ✓

pom-[pon] girls

In the phrase "follow copy," "copy" means the dead copy. "C.Q." means "It is correct as is." "Stet," of course, means "Let it stand." A checkmark means "I have checked this." The box means "Correct as written."

Newspaper copyeditors (sometimes called copyreaders) and people who have taken journalism courses may underscore a handwritten lowercase u and overscore an n:

Some journalists underscore a u and overscore an n

Some people also underscore w and a and overscore m and o:

Some journalists underscore a, u, & w and overscore m, n and o

Some authors, editors, and typemarkers distinguish a letter O from a zero by marking a diagonal line through the zero: letter O--O; zero--ø. The slashed zero is typed or typeset in certain technical material and also appears on copy from some typewriters or word processors; for example: a daily circulation of 240,000.
You may see the letter Z crossed through to distinguish it from numeral 2: Z--Ƶ; 2--Ƶ. You may see numeral 7 crossed through in the European manner: 7̸. And you may see numeral 1 with a beak: 1 or with a beak and a base: 1.

For practice in proofreading against edited copy, turn to Exercise 15 in the Workbook.

QUESTIONS FOR STUDENTS

1. Explain the difference between editor's marks and proof-reader's marks. Why are they different?

2. Why do you need to know nonstandard editor's marks?

VIII. LETTERS

Stationery

Use VPS letterhead paper for formal letters and memorandums sent outside the office.

Copies

Each division determines the number of carbon copies needed *it* for its purposes.

If a letter is prepared in answer to a regional representative's request, *prepare* one "courtesy copy" on blue manifold bearing the seal of the company is prepared for the regional office.

If the letter is in a foreign language, an English translation, including address, salutation, and complimentary close, is prepared. *A typed copy of the* The translation is typed and attached to the official record with copies of the letter.

If the letter is to be signed by an official in another division or department of the agency, forward, with the original and a prepared envelope (see X. ENVELOPES AND MAILING STICKERS), one yellow and four white carbon copies.

If carbons are to be routed to other persons than the addressee, this information may be added to the original, at the writer's discretion. Type four lines below the signature line the symbol "cc:" flush left, followed by a colon and the names or titles of the additional addressees. If the copy addresses are not to appear in the original, but only on the copies, *remove the original and* type instead the symbol "brc" (blind ribbon copy) followed by a colon and the names or titles of the addressees.

Figure 4-D. Sample of a well marked edited page

Chapter 5

General Procedures

A reader . . . should be a man of one business--always upon the alert--all eyes--all attention. Possessing a becoming reliance on his own powers, he should never be too confident of success. Imperfection clings to him on every side. Errors and mistakes assail him from every quarter. His business is of a nature that may render him obnoxious to blame, but can hardly be said to bring him any very large stock of praise. If errors escape him he is justly to be censured--for perfection is his duty. If his labours are wholly free from mistake--which is, alas! a very rare case--he has done no more than he ought, and consequently can merit only a comparative degree of commendation, in that he has the good fortune to be more successful in his labours after perfection than some of his brethren in the same employment.

--The Printer's Grammar
Caleb Stower, 1808

CHAPTER OVERVIEW

This chapter describes the basic procedures proofreaders should follow to (1) prepare for reading; (2) mark corrections on galleys, page proofs, and typewritten camera-ready copy; (3) aid the printer in making up pages from galleys; and (4) record who did the work. It goes on to describe the steps in reviewing, checking, revising, and re-proofreading. It ends with instructions for proofreading references.

PROOFREADING PROCEDURES

Whether you are working with typewritten or typeset copy, you should follow these procedures in all proofreading.

Preparatory Steps

Before you begin to read, take these steps:

1. Carefully read or reread your contract, specifications, instructions, or job order. Ask questions if necessary.

2. If there is more than one set of proofs, mark one "Master Proof" and number the others.

3. Make sure you have all the proper portions of the copy with matching sets of live copy and dead copy.

4. Make sure all the pages of the dead copy are numbered and in order. Do the same for the live copy.

5. Scan the dead copy. Check for attached memos. Check tops
   of pages, corners, and margins for notations and specifications on typeface, type size, justification, leading, and
   indention. If there is a dummy, make the same kind of
   preliminary check.

Marking and Querying

Corrections

Proofread as follows:

1. Following specifications and instructions, compare the live
   copy with the dead copy word for word and, where necessary,
   character for character. Mark the live copy for the correction of printer's errors (PE's)--any errors resulting from
   a typesetter's or typist's deviations from the dead copy,
   from specifications, or from good typesetting, printing, or
   typing practice. Use the proofreader's marks described in
   this manual or in special instructions for the job.

2. Query or mark for correction--whichever is required--each
   misspelling.

3. Pay special attention to be sure the last line of each galley or page reads properly into the first line of the next.

4. Verify all specified measurements. Use a line gauge and a
   ruler (provided in the Workbook); don't rely on your eyes.

5. When reading is interrupted, mark the place in both dead and
   live copy; go back a sentence or two when you resume reading.

Galleys and page proofs may be made by an unskilled operator on a
copying machine or on cheap paper on a hand-operated press. Do
not expect to see the quality of printing or paper of the final
product. Do not expect reproductions of photographs in page proofs
to be of good quality. Do not expect galleys or page proofs to
contain the margins specified for the finished product; wide margins are usually provided for the benefit of the proofreader.

Marks for Page Make-up

Matter that is set or prepared separately from the running text--
such as footnotes, artwork, and sometimes tables--does not appear
in its proper sequence in galleys. On galleys, proofreaders must
transfer from the dead copy to the margins of the live copy any
instructions needed for the make-up of pages. (Make-up is the
term used to describe the steps of assembling and spacing typed
matter and illustrations to fit the specified space.)

1. Spacing instructions relevant to paging (dividing copy
   into pages) when specifications or the dead copy provide
   them. For example, to indicate a new page or a new
   righthand page:

Sink 12 picas new RH page

CHAPTER TWO

(Sink means to leave a top margin of the indicated depth.)

2. Footnote callouts (reference marks); for example:

Jones's theory contradicts this.*

This is discussed fully in Brook's treatise.[1]

3. Callouts (first references) to tables; for example:

Table A-1 follows.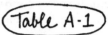

4. Callouts for artwork (note the size if it is specified);
   for example:

Figure 9 demonstrates this point.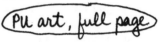

The following graph shows these trends.

(PU stands for "pick up.") *PU art, full page*

Procedures with Page Proofs, Repros, and Typewritten Camera-Ready Copy

Instructions may or may not specify re-proofreading at the page
proof stage. If re-proofing is not done, follow the procedures
described later in this chapter under Steps in Revising.

Whether or not re-proofing is done in page proofs that have been
made from galleys, it is especially important to be sure that
each page leads properly into the next, and that all elements of
each page (for example, captions, heads, footnotes) are properly
placed.

In page proofs, repros, and typewritten camera-ready copy, verify
that the space left for artwork agrees with the art's actual size
plus the specified white space around it. If the copy includes the
artwork, verify that the number of cuts (photographs or artwork
provided separately from the text) on a page is correct and that
each cut is right side up. Watch for callouts. Be sure the
called-out matter follows its callout as soon as possible: footnotes must begin on the same page and column as their callouts;
artwork and tables must appear as soon as enough space is available. Insert page numbers in jump lines, also called continued
lines (lines reading "continued on page x"), and in the table of
contents. Where required, insert page numbers in cross references.

Queries

Prepare queries as you proofread, following the instructions in
Chapter 7 or special instructions for the job. At the very least,
be sure to call attention to questions in the dead copy that apparently went unanswered before the live copy was typeset or typed.
When you see an unanswered query, you may write "See query in draft,

p. x"--citing the dead copy's page number--or quote the query; for example:

query in draft: "is spelling OK?"

Initials and Page Numbers

Initial (in pencil) each page or galley of live copy as you finish proofreading. Use the upper right corner in most cases. If the copy should not have marks on it, initial the backs of the pages. If required, at the bottom of each galley or page proof write the numbers of the beginning and ending pages of dead copy correspond-ing to the galley or page of live copy.

If instructions call for <u>mark-off</u>, the reader with the live copy says "mark-off" after the last word of every page or galley. The other reader then marks the place in the dead copy and writes two numbers in the margin--that of the page or galley ending at the marked place and that of the following page or galley; for example:

a galley's final word⟍first <u>word</u> on next galley $\frac{20}{21}$

If required, mark the dead copy as it is read with a diagonal line from the lower left corner to the upper right corner, and write the initials of the person who held the dead copy in the top right corner.

Review

Review your work as described in the following paragraphs. Part-ners may divide this work. Review should take no more than one-tenth of the time taken in all previous steps.

1. For pages, verify that <u>folios</u> (page numbers) listed in the <u>front matter</u> (table of contents, lists of tables and fig-ures) are accurate; if any folios are missing, fill them in.

2. Verify <u>line measure</u> (the width of the type line) and, for pages (not galleys), the <u>type page depth</u> (the total depth of all the type on the page). Verify leading (type size plus space between lines) by measuring from baseline to baseline of the type. (A line gauge and a leading gauge are provided in the Workbook.) For typewritten copy, verify paper size, margins, and line spacing.

3. Review all heads, including <u>running heads</u> (those across the tops of pages, usually repeating book and chapter titles) for overlooked typos.

4. Verify that each galley or page reads properly into the next.

5. Where charts, tables, and so forth are continued, check jump lines for accuracy.

6. Check for consistent placement of <u>folios</u> on each page. (Folios can--but should not--vary as much as an inch from the correct position.)

7. Review your marks and queries for appropriateness, clarity, and correct placement. Reread any line where a mark or query has been made plus two or three lines before and after it to be sure there are no other overlooked errors. (Errors often occur in groups; it is easy for proofreaders marking one error to overlook a second or third nearby.)

8. Verify all sequential numbers and letters of the alphabet. Items to be verified include folios; footnote callouts and footnotes; list items; references and bibliographies; tables, figures, and other illustrations; and the printer's code for insertion of camera-ready copy or artwork.

9. Reread the first galley or the first page or two. Then read the first paragraph a third time. For reasons we cannot fully explain, proofreaders have a tendency to overlook errors in the beginning of jobs--just where they are most noticeable and embarrassing later.

10. Be sure that all pages in dead and live copy are in order and right side up. Account, when possible, for all pages. Insert paper labeled "blank" for pages that will be blank in final copy. Insert labeled pages to explain any other missing pages in the dead and the live copy (for example, "pulled for graphics," "returned earlier"). The supervisor may have to help with this step.

STEPS IN CHECKING

All proofreaders eventually overlook something in their work. Checkers frequently discover such lapses. Ideally, the checker is not one of the job's initial proofreaders; a fresh eye is highly desirable. A checker should be a superior proofreader, preferably someone with full knowledge of the relevant editorial and production methods, style, standards, and specifications. (These topics are discussed in Part II of this manual.)

Checking should normally take no more than one-third of the time the proofreading took.

The following steps are recommended:

1. Read in full the following:

   ● Entire first and last paragraphs of each section, looking for typos

   ● First and last lines or sentences of each paragraph, looking for typos and checking that no paragraphs are repeated

● First and last lines of each page or galley to be sure each reads properly into the next

● Headings, including running heads

● Boldface, italic, and all-caps portions

● Passages in type smaller than the text, such as footnotes

● All lines in which an error or query is marked, plus two or three lines before and after.

2. Check the sequence of all numerical and alphabetical listings, including the printer's code for camera copy or artwork. When possible, check footnotes and their callouts for sequence and proper placement. Check folios for sequence and position.

3. Check spacing as follows: In page proofs, check page length and space between paragraphs and around heads. In a two-column page, check alignment of columns at top and bottom. If specifications call for modular leading (exact alignment of lines of type from one page or column to another), check accordingly.

4. Skim the entire job, checking for missed typos and repeated lines.

● Check for inconsistencies in items you noted earlier or in your overview of the whole job (for example, if you or the proofreaders noted a compound word hyphenated only part of the time, keep an eye out for more such inconsistencies).

● Check for obvious deviations from the specified style.

● Check for improper word division. (In galleys and page proofs, one word consistently divided wrong should probably be left alone. Check with the supervisor.)

5. Check for general appearance, looking especially for any of the following that may have been missed:

● Misalignments

● Broken letters and other evidence of poor type quality (This problem cannot always be detected in copy that isn't camera-ready.)

● Deviation from format (improper indention, line length, spacing, or leading; in typescript or page proofs, violation of image area and margins).

6. Check proofreader's markings as follows:

- Marks in text and margin--be sure proper symbols have been used; make sure no proofreader has changed the meaning of a sentence

- Queries and questions--try to answer or eliminate as many as possible and to see that those you retain are clear, relevant, grammatical, and correctly spelled. When given authority, turn queries into AA's (as described in Chapter 7).

7. Re-proof (against the dead copy) the following, where errors are most likely to go unnoticed in an initial proofreading:

- Last one or two columns in tables and last few entries in all columns

- Chart formats

- First page of the job.

8. Label proofs as required. A common system uses these categories: OK, OK a/c (OK as corrected), OK w/c (OK with corrections), or "Show revised proofs."

9. Give feedback, either directly or indirectly through proper channels, to the proofreaders about their work. An example of feedback is shown in Figure 5-A.

STEPS IN REVISING

Revising is proofreading revised page proofs (sometimes first page proofs), revised galleys, or corrected--not retyped--typescript. It is not normally re-proofreading.* This stage generally involves nothing more than ascertaining that all marked corrections have been made properly and that no new errors have been introduced in the correction process. (In many cases, a typist or typesetter makes two new errors for every one corrected--or may not correct clearly marked errors at all.)

Corrections of significant length--more than two lines--should be proofread by a two-person team if at all possible.

Revising Typeset Copy

Put dead copy and live copy side by side. Read each line that has a correction marked in the dead copy, comparing the dead copy with the live copy. Be sure the correction has been made and that no new error has been introduced in the resetting of the line. Read one or two lines above and below the corrected line to be sure the corrected line has been inserted in the proper place.

---

*Some publishers may use this step as a second proofreading.

TYPOGRAPHICAL ERRORS

It does not appear that the earliest printers had any method of correcting errors before the form was on the press. The learned correctors of the first two centuries of printing were not proofreaders in our sense; they were rather what we should term office editors. Their labors were chiefly to see that the proof corresponded to the copy, but that the printed page was correct in its Latinity; that the words were there, and that the sense was right. They cared but little about orthography, bad letters, or purely printers' errors, and when the text seemed to them wrong they consulted fresh authorities or altered it on their own responsibility. Good proofs, in the modern sense, were impossible until professional readers were employed men who had first a printer's education, and then spent many years in the correction of proof. The orthography of English, which for the past century has undergone little change, was very fluctuating until after the publication of Johnson's Dictionary, and capitals, which have been used with considerable regularity for the past 80 years, were previously used on the miss or hit plan. The approach to regularity, so far as we have, may be attributed to the growth of a class of professional proofreaders, and it is to them that we owe the correctness of modern printing. More errors have been found in the Bible than in any other one work. For many generations it was frequently the case that Bibles were brought out stealthily, from fear of governmental interference. They were frequently printed from imperfect texts, and were often modified to meet the views of those who published them. The story is related that a certain woman in Germany, who was the wife of a Printer, and had become disgusted with the continual assertions of the superiority of man over woman which she had heard, hurried into the composing room while her husband was at supper and altered a sentence in the Bible, which he was printing, so that it read Narr instead of Herr, thus making the verse read "And he shall be thy fool" instead of "And he shall be thy lord." The word not was omitted by Barker, the king's printer in England in 1632, in printing the seventh commandment. He was fined £3,000 on this account.

TO PROOFREADER OF TYPOGRAPHICAL ERRORS:

A fine job. More than 50 errors caught, only one missed:

	Lines
printing] More ⊙	28

Minor errors and our marking preferences

1. In-text mark missing: Printer (lc)   12 up
2. Inconsistent marks for replacement (please reserve caret for simple insertion). Your marks:

good:	earliest	1
inaccurate:	of	10 up
your marks:	Latinity	9
	king's	3 up
	and	4 up

3. Inconsistent marks for caps.
   your marks: Latinity
               king's
               and
   preferred: Latinity
              Latinity
4. Imprecise mark for word division: En-
   your mark: gland   2,3 up
   preferred: England
5. Kite strings (please avoid for normal proofreading marks)

your mark:	sc It does	
preferred:	sc It does	1
your mark:	L 3,000	
preferred:	L 3,000	

6. Transposition (please reserve for adjacent words)
   your mark: miss or hit   24
   preferred: miss or hit   hit/miss

Figure 5-A. Example of feedback

Watch for passages including more than two lines of corrections (not lines merely respaced). Re-proofread them, preferably with a partner.

When corrections have moved matter from one galley or page to another (for example, to make room for an inserted head or to correct spacing errors), check the sequence of all lines by <u>slug-ging</u> as follows: Fold under the margin of the dead copy and hold the folded edge against the live copy to be sure that the first word on every line is the same. In two-column pages, both columns must be slugged. When changes are found, take the following steps:

Galleys and Page Proofs

- Double check that no lines have been dropped and that each galley or page reads properly into the next.

- Check for new widows and new bad breaks or improper word division.

- Re-proofread the entire passage (one-person proofreading is usually satisfactory).

Page Proofs

- Check footnotes to be sure they are still in sequence and on the same page (or column) as their callouts.

- Check artwork to be sure it is still in proper position following first callout.

- Check the table of contents for the accuracy of folio listings.

- If indexing has begun, notify your supervisor of errors if corrections will involve page changes affecting the index.

- Check facing pages for alignment of top and bottom lines.

Revising Camera-Ready Copy

Unless an entire page of camera-ready copy has been redone (set, typed, or pasted up with new material), there is no new dead copy; the live copy itself is what has been corrected. Often a <u>cut-in</u> (splice) or a pasted-up passage indicates where a correction has been made. When material of any length has been cut out (to cut corrected material in) the cut-out copy should have been saved for you to check against the correction; otherwise you will have to return to the dead copy from which the live copy originally was made, as you will when corrections are pasted over errors. Read the new material plus a sentence or two before and after it to be sure the new material fits in properly.

RE-PROOFREADING

Re-proofreading (proofreading more than once, each time with a different reader or readers) is often done, especially for critical copy. The same techniques and procedures are followed, but pencils of different colors may be used for each reading.

Proofreading and re-proofreading of the same live copy must be done with the same dead copy. Never trust previously proofread material to serve as dead copy in the same stage of work; always use the dead copy the previous readers used.

SILENT READING

Checking is a proofreading function. Silent reading is an editorial function. When it is done, it is a last step after checking, and usually after revising. Silent reading is the term for a responsible reading of the entire live copy (without comparing it to the dead) for sense and policy (for example, to decide if the copy should be published as is). The reading may be done as a broad check on proofreading quality but not to nitpick. If the reader happens to see blatant errors, the errors are marked with proofreader's marks (not editor's marks).

HOW TO PROOFREAD REFERENCES

Copy with references poses special problems. The following sections summarize how to proofread such copy.

General Procedure. Proofread a footnote or endnote immediately after its callout in text. Be sure the callout or description corresponds in substance as well as to the number or letter that is called out. Be sure the numerical or alphabetical sequence is correct--nothing missing, nothing added.

Galleys. Mark callouts for footnotes in the margin. When the typesetter has not done so, mark also for insertion of illustrations and tables.

Pages. Be sure that what is called out follows its callout as soon as possible. Footnotes should begin on the same page and column as their callouts; tables and illustrations should begin as soon as there is space. If you know the artwork's dimensions but do not have the artwork itself, measure the space allotted to be sure it is correct. Check the sequence of the printer's numbering system for artwork to be inserted later.

Footnotes. If footnotes are in small type, read them a second time after you have finished the other proofreading (it is easy to miss errors in small type). If a footnote is continued, be sure two full lines have been set on the first page or column and that either the break comes in the middle of a sentence or the footnote is labeled "continued." Watch table footnotes for everything you would watch for in any other footnotes. If a table is continued, be sure footnote callouts are repeated when necessary.

    <u>Endnotes</u>. Do not confuse <u>footnotes</u>, which appear at the bottoms of pages, with <u>endnotes</u>, which appear at the ends of books or chapters. The difference affects proofreading. To help with page make-up, you must mark a galley's margin when a footnote is called out. You make no mark when an endnote is called out.

    <u>Source notes</u>. Learned journals often use numbers in brackets or parentheses in the text to refer to a numbered reference list at the end of an article. The first use of a source note appears with the author's name. Check to be certain the source note agrees with the reference list in notation and in the name of the author.

    <u>Acronyms</u>. For some jobs, you must query unfamiliar acronyms and abbreviations if they are unexplained at first occurrence.

    <u>Day and Date</u>. When the day of the week plus the date of the month are mentioned, be sure they correspond. Many telephone books and most almanacs contain perpetual calendars.

    <u>Bibliographies and Bibliographic References</u>. Be sure an author's name is treated the same every time it appears--same spelling, same use of initials. Be sure the names of publishers are correct (see the list in Part III). Watch for any inconsistencies in capitalization, punctuation, and spelling. Examples of two different styles are shown in Figure 5-B.

Style	Bibliography	Footnote
Library of Congress	Davidson, Roger H. The role of the Congressman. New York, Pegasus, 1969. 220 p. (Studies in contemporary American politics) JK1061.D32	Davidson, Roger H. The Role of the Congressman. New York, Pegasus, 1969, pp. 117-118 (Studies in Contemporary American Politics)
University of Chicago	Davidson, Roger H. <u>The Role of the Congressman</u>. Studies in Contemporary American Politics Series, no. 3. New York: Pegasus, 1969.	Roger H. Davidson, <u>The Role of the Congressman</u> (New York: Pegasus, 1969), pp. 117-18.

    Figure 5-B. Two styles for bibliographies and bibliographic references

---

QUESTIONS FOR STUDENTS

1.   What do you do if you find an unanswered query in the dead copy?

2.   What do you do if a page (such as a chart) must be taken from the dead copy and placed in the live copy?

3.   How much time should reviewing take for a job that took 10 hours to proofread?

4.   How much time should checking take for a job that took 12 hours to proofread?

5.   How do galleys compare in quality to the finished product? Why?

6.   If a footnote is called out in column 1 of page 2, on what page and in what column must the footnote itself begin?

7.   If a full-page illustration is called out on page 3, on what page should it appear?

8.   As if you were a checker giving written feedback, comment on the following proofreading job:

Dead copy

"Yes, words long faded may again revive;

And words may fade now blooming and alive,

If usage wills it so, to whom belongs

The rule and law, the government of tongues."

                              --Horace, Ars Poetica

Live copy

Yes, words long faded may again revive;

and words may fade now blooming alive,   and

If usage wills it so, to who belongs

the rule and law, the government of tongues

                              --Horace, Ars Poetica

period end quote

underline

Chapter 6

Methods of Proofreading

TO THE SCRIBES AT SAINT MARTIN'S MONASTERY AT TOURS, FRANCE:

Here let the scribes beware of making mistakes through haste. Let them distinguish the proper sense by colons and commas, and let them set down the points, each one in its due place, and let not him who reads the words to them either read falsely or pause suddenly.

--(Circa 782 A.D.)

CHAPTER OVERVIEW

This chapter describes and compares the two major methods of proofreading--one-person and two-person proofreading. It discusses the two-person method in detail. It also covers tape proofreading, proofreading live copy on a video display terminal (VDT), and "proofreading" without dead copy.

COMPARISON OF MAJOR METHODS

In comparing methods, keep in mind that a proofreader adept in one method may not adjust readily to the other and that proofreaders may have a strong preference for one method.

One-Person Proofreading

Sometimes called <u>single proofing</u> or <u>horsing</u>, one-person reading is done by a proofreader who places the dead copy and the live copy side by side and silently compares them. This is the slowest (in terms of elapsed time), the least expensive, and probably the most common method. In the hands of a nonprofessional, this method is undoubtedly the least accurate; outs and repeaters are likely to be missed. However, a good single proofer can do a remarkable job, and there are obvious advantages to scheduling and paying for the services of only one person. For certain material, such as the short takes in advertising copy and equations that must be compared character by character, it is often the preferred method.

Two-Person Proofreading

Sometimes called <u>double proofing</u>, <u>team proofreading</u>, or <u>partner proofreading</u>, two-person proofreading is the traditional method. Two people work together, one holding the dead copy, the other marking the live copy, one reading aloud to the other. This is the fastest (in terms of elapsed time) and the most expensive method. In the hands of nonprofessionals, it is the only method likely to produce acceptable results. It is the most accurate method for tables, long lists of figures, extremely hard-to-read dead copy, and hard-to-handle dead copy (such as index cards).

For clean, straightforward text, in the hands of experienced professionals, there are conflicting opinions about the accuracy of two-person proofreading compared with one-person proofreading. The arguments concern whether accuracy is decreased more by a single proofer's need to shift eyes constantly from dead to live copy or by double proofing's additions of the sense of hearing to the sense of sight, of a second person's input, and of interaction between two people. The great advantage of two-person proofreading is its speed.

Tape Proofreading

Proofreading in which the dead copy is read into a tape recorder and the tape is then used to compare with the live copy is in speed and cost midway between single and double proofing. Its advantages are that both dead and live copy need not be available at the same time (a machine duplicate of the dead copy can be read into the recorder), that two proofreaders need not be available at the same time, and that improved accuracy results when one person need not shift constantly from live to dead copy. However, if tape proofreading is not done with care, it is less accurate and less economical than team proofreading.

The table below compares the time needed to proofread and check 37,500 words by all three methods.

Hypothetical comparison of time needed
to proofread and check 50 galleys
(750 words each)

	One-Person Proofing	Tape Proofing	Two-Person Proofing
elapsed hours	10.0	12.5	7.5 team hours
total proofing hours	10.0	6.0 recording 6.5 marking	15.0 person hours
total checking hours	2.5	2.5	2.5
total workhours	12.5	15.0	17.5

ONE-PERSON PROOFREADING

A surface with a slanted top is less fatiguing for proofreaders to use but is seldom provided outside professional proofrooms. To single proof on a flat surface, clear enough space to move the two stacks of copy--dead and live--back and forth as you keep the same words approximately aligned.

There are several ways to keep your place in dead and live copy: you may use two straightedges, perhaps of different colors; you may

use a colored straightedge for the dead copy and the nonwriting end
of your pen or pencil for the live copy (choose a pencil without an
eraser that might catch on the paper); you may hold a page of the
dead copy in your hand, rolling it to follow the final copy line by
line; or you may use a typist's stand with a movable line marker.

The size of the unit that you read will vary. With straightforward
text and clean dead copy, you may read 10 or 20 words, perhaps two
full sentences, at a time. With unfamiliar technical language or
dead copy covered with editor's marks or written in hard-to-read
handwriting, you may read only one word at a time. It may help to
read difficult copy aloud.

Spend at least twice as much time with the live copy as the dead.
Be especially alert for outs and repeaters. Double check any lists
for omissions. Be sure each page reads properly into the next.

It's a good idea to follow all the procedures listed in Chapter 5 in
the section on Proofreading Procedures as well as all those listed
under Steps in Checking. (Some single proofers prefer to follow
comparison reading with a reading of the live copy only. Legal
text is sometimes checked one word at a time reading backward.)

TAPE PROOFREADING

There are two steps in tape proofreading: (1) the <u>recorder</u> reads
aloud the contents of the dead copy into the microphone of a tape
recorder; (2) the <u>marker</u> plays back the tape while following the
live copy.

For maximum speed and efficiency, marker and recorder should be the
same person. Second preference is for the marker to be someone
familiar with the material, such as the copyeditor.

Dictating equipment is ideal, but an inexpensive cassette recorder
will work, too, if it has a separate switch to start and stop play-
back instantly.

Most problems can be avoided by forethought. Erase every used tape
before recording. Be sure a battery-driven machine has fresh bat-
teries. Be thoroughly familiar with the equipment; know how much
time, if any, the equipment needs to run before your voice is recorded; know the optimum distance to maintain from the microphone;
and if your machine does not signal when the tape runs out, set a
timer with an alarm.

Do not overload a portable cassette recorder: a standard recorder
may be unreliable for tapes longer than 90 minutes (45 to a side);
a portable recorder may be unreliable for tapes longer than 60
minutes (30 to a side).

Keep a reel or a cassette in a box with a label identifying the
recorder, the job, and, for each side or track, the dead copy page
numbers. Record the same information at the beginning and the end
of every track or side.

A large part of the following section on two-person proofreading
pertains also to tape proofreading, particularly the descriptions
of verbal shortcuts and codes. However, the descriptions of signals
other than verbal ones are inapplicable; they should not be used.

TWO-PERSON PROOFREADING

General Description

The traditional proofreading team consists of a senior member
called a proofreader and an assistant called a copyholder. The
copyholder's duty is to read aloud from the dead copy as the proofreader follows the live copy. The proofreader is entirely responsible for the live copy and does all the marking and querying. The
copyholder must keep keenly aware of the proofreader's need for an
adjustment of speed or a pause to write a mark.

In some proofreading teams, often those in newspaper offices, the
proofreader (sometimes called the copyreader), with the live copy,
does all the reading aloud, marking, and querying. By this method,
the proofreader can regulate speed according to necessity. Proofreaders will occasionally make an intentional error to be certain
their copyholders are following accurately.

Another kind of proofreading team consists of two qualified proofreaders who share responsibility equally, who alternate reading
aloud, and who may alternate every few hours as holder (of the dead
copy) and marker (of the live copy). Whenever the draft is handwritten, extensively edited, or otherwise hard to read, the holder
should read aloud to the marker. When the draft is clean, whatever
works to produce fast, accurate proofreading with minimal fatigue
is acceptable. Partners may decide to alternate reading aloud
every paragraph, chapter, or hour; or the partner who reads significantly faster may do most of the reading. (Do not shift papers as
you change readers; one partner must act as holder and the other as
marker for at least several hours.) When copy permits it, some
proofreaders prefer to alternate reading paragraphs because this
keeps them alert and eliminates the need to identify a new paragraph each time one appears.

Agreement Between Partners

Partners new to each other must take the time to agree on all signals and shortcuts, and to find the highest rate of speed comfortable to both. When the person reading aloud is not marking, speed
and pauses must be adjusted to the marker's needs. For example,
partners may work side by side or directly across from each other
so that the movement of the marker's pencil is the signal to stop
reading aloud; or the marker may repeat the word where the reading
should stop and, when ready to resume, repeat the word again.

Vocalization

Although reading must be done intelligently, never automatically,
the normal, social speech pattern, with pauses for clarity and

emphasis for meaning, is far removed from a proofreader's read-aloud technique. In reading proof, vocalization is a rapid, steady, clearly enunciated near-monotone.

If you are not normally soft-spoken, try to become so when you proofread. The reduction in volume decreases fatigue and may well increase fluency and speed. Be aware that vowel sounds are those that most exercise (and tire) your jaw muscles; in American speech, they are the sounds that slow you down, and they are not always important to clear enunciation (compare the British pronunciation of "secretary" to the American). On the other hand, crisp consonant sounds make for precise speech. When consonants are not stressed, rapid reading aloud may become slurred and indistinct, especially in final consonant sounds such as the s in plurals and the ed in past participles.

What to Read Aloud

Read aloud words, punctuation marks, and all typographical descriptions such as changes in typeface, underscores, and capital letters. Read aloud all changes in spacing or indention in heads, paragraphs, lists, and anywhere else. Spell out or otherwise identify the correct spelling of proper names when there is the slightest possibility of error.

Certain shortcuts, code words, and signals are used to increase speed; many of these are described later in this chapter. Most are one-syllable "abbreviations" of the words for punctuation marks or typographical changes; for example: "com" for comma.

The following example demonstrates how a quotation from Milton would be read with one-syllable shortcuts (shown in parentheses) for punctuation marks and capital letters.

Copy (dead and live):

"As good almost kill a man as kill a good book: Who kills a man kills a reasonable creature, God's image; but he who destroys a good book kills reason itself."

                                                        --Milton

Reader:

flush left (quo cap) as good almost kill a man as kill a good book (cole cap) who kills a man kills a reasonable creature (com cap) God (pos s) image (sem) but he who destroys a good book kills reason itself (point close quo flush right dash cap) m i l t o n

Experienced proofreaders may omit some of the particulars; for example: the cap in standard proper nouns such as Milton, Chicago, Mr. Jones, or God; or the "point cap" at the end and beginning of sentences (when partners agree that a drop in voice or a pause gives the same information). An unusual usage repeated many times does not need to be signaled in full after partners learn it firmly; for example, after reading the abbreviation "BTU all caps, bumped" several times, partners may assume that when "BTU" is read it should be all caps and bumped.

When partners understand each other perfectly, any reasonable shortcut, code, or signal that increases speed is acceptable. However, some things are so often set or typed incorrectly they must never be omitted from reading aloud. These include possessive apostrophes, capital letters in Clc headings, and specification of different levels of heads.

People's Names

Proofreading teams who read directories, bibliographies, or other matter with frequent listing of people's names develop many short-cuts. Some of these follow.

Standard Spelling and Variants

Partners should agree on standard spellings and read them without spelling them out. The following might be considered standard: Brown, Clark, Cook, Smith, Ward, Elliott, Bissell, Russell, Thompson (with a p).

Read simple variants by describing the difference from the agreed-upon standard, for example: Browne (read as "Brown e"), Eliott (read as "Elliott one l"), Eliot (read as "Elliott one l, one t"), Thomson (read as "Thompson no p").

Spell out every letter in a variant of any complexity, for example: Brounn, Smythe, Tomsson.

Differences in Pronunciation

Careful pronunciation will distinguish between such names as Cohen and Cohan, or Anderson and Andersen. Some suggestions for other distinguishing pronunciations follow:

- Mc and Mac: Pronounce Mc as mick, and Mac as mack. (Read such names as Macmillan as "mack millan, m down").

- berg and burg: Pronounce the ending berg as bairg, and burg as boorg.

- Frederic and Frederick: Pronounce Frederic as Frederis, Frederick with a hard c.

- Katherine and Catherine, Karl and Carl: Pronounce Katherine and Karl normally, Catherine and Carl as Satherine and Sarl.

- Lewis and Louis: Pronounce Lewis as Lew is, Louis as Lou ee.

- man and mann: Pronounce the ending man with a short a (as in land), mann with a broad a (as in father).

- Stewart and Stuart: Pronounce Stewart as Stee wart, Stuart as Stoo wart.

- y and ey: Pronounce y alone as eye; for example: Myer (Mye er), Brownly (Brown lye), Brodsky (Brod skeye), Levy

(Lev eye). Pronounce ey as ee, stating that e is present; for example: Meyer (Mee yer), Brownley (Brown lee), Brodskey (Brod skee), Levey (Lev ee).

Abbreviations

Proofreading teams must agree when it will not be necessary for the person reading aloud to identify caps, periods, and other variations in abbreviations. Names of states, for example, would unquestionably be wrong in lowercase; there is no need to signal their capital letters. But usage in many other abbreviations varies for caps, periods, spacing, and symbols. For example: A.M., a.m.; sq. m., sq m, m^2; R.P.S., RPS, rps, rev per sec, r/s; LL.D., LL. D. If a particular style is not specified, a good memory--or a handy notepad--is needed to be certain that each partner understands the other and that the copy is consistent.

Some shortcuts for reading abbreviations are listed here:

1. If an abbreviation is pronounceable, do not spell it out but read it as if it were a word; for example: Ala., fig., Inc., min., oz.

2. If an abbreviation is pronounceable with a vowel sound added, and if that will save a syllable, read it so; for example: D.C. (dik), Mr. (mer), tsp. (tisp).

3. If an abbreviation is not readily pronounceable, even with the insertion of a vowel sound, or if no saving of syllables is involved, spell it out; or, if the marker knows what has been used before, sound the full word followed by "bree" (for abbreviation); for example: ft/lbs (foot pounds bree).

Here are some suggestions for reading abbreviations aloud:

a.m. (am)	f.o.b. (fob)	SC (sec)
Assoc. (a sock)	Jr. (jer)	S.D. (sud)
Ave. (av)	L.I. (lye)	Sept. (sep)
c.o.d. (cod)	Mr. (mer)	Sr. (ser)
Dec. (des)	N.C. (nek)	St. (stee)
D.C. (dik)	N.D. (nud)	U.S. (us)
Dr. (doc)	N.J. (nudge)	U.S.A. (usa)
e.g. (egg)	p.m. (pum)	Vt. (vit)
etc. (ets)	R.I. (rye)	Wm. (wim)

Intentional Mispronunciation

Some teams verify spelling by ear as well as eye by their exaggerated pronunciation of certain letters and syllables. This might include sounding out silent letters, such as corps (pronounced corpse) or indict (with the c sounded), and sounding syllables ordinarily dropped, such as quandary (pronounced quan da ry). It might also include reading soft c as hard, such as prophecy (pronounced propheky) as opposed to prophesy; distinguishing endings ible and able (pronounced ibble and able); and stressing normally

unstressed vowel sounds, such as accept and except (pronounced
ax ept and ex ept), capital and capitol (pronounced capi tall and
capi tole), analogous (pronounced anal o gous), and sanitize (pronounced san it ize).

Unfamiliar Words

Don't take the time to figure out or look up the correct pronunciation of hard or unfamiliar words. Read them aloud phonetically by the same principles as those used in intentional
mispronunciation.

Try to find pronounceable short words or meaningful letter groups
within long words:

    ar rhythm i a   extra po late

    di benzyl ethyl ene   dynamo meter

    pharma co graphy

Signals

Some proofreading teams set up audible and visual signals for typographic changes such as capitals, small capitals, italic, and
boldface. For example, to tap the table with a pencil simultaneously with the reading of a word could indicate a capital letter,
and to clearly enunciate a whisper could indicate italics. Some
proofrooms have developed elaborate sets of signals: one tap, two
taps, a stamp of the foot, a snap of the fingers, a raised index
finger, a sweep of the hand across the page, and so on. More than
one or two simple audible signals are not recommended to any but
highly experienced proofreaders in offices where many signals are
long-established practice.

Ad Hoc Shortcuts

Partners may invent shortcuts appropriate to a particular job or
kind of work. For example, when many legal cases are cited, the
word "case" could indicate two groups of italic (or underlined)
words with lowercase roman "v." intervening, as in Barton's Department Store v. Mildred Saddleman. In an extensive bibliography,
partners may decide (if the style lends itself to it) that a period
follows each entry and that only punctuation other than periods
will be read.

Reading Numbers

In copy with many numbers, partners may well decide that the like-
lihood of error requires a double check by reading every number
twice, the first time in characters, the next in words; for example:

Copy (dead and live): There are 4,020 students in 1,000 classrooms.
    Holder: There are four com oh two oh...
    Marker: four thousand twenty
    Holder: students in one com thou...

Marker: one thousand
Holder: classrooms

Syllable saving in an index entry's list of page numbers can be done by calling the first digit only once instead of repeating it for each entry in a series and not reading commas between page entries as follows:

Text	Verbalization
primitive tribes. culture: 109, 121, 138, 156, 198, 200, 242-245, 249; myths: 14	primitive tribes point culture cole one oh nine two one three eight five six nine eight two hun four two hy four five four nine sem myths cole one four

This shortcut also has the virtue of helping to keep reader and holder alert; they must think of and watch for something besides a simple sequence of numerals.

Reading Compound Words

Compound words take one of three forms--one word (solid), hyphenated (or hooked), or two word (open). When it is necessary to distinguish the forms of compounds, do as in the following examples:

- For _proof reading_ (two-word open compound), read "proof space reading," "proof reading ope," or "proof reading two words."

- For _proof-reading_ (hyphened), read "proof hy reading," or "proof reading hooked."

- For _proofreading_ (solid), read "proofreading sol," or "proofreading one word."

USEFUL CODE WORDS AND SIGNALS

Code	Meaning
pos	apostrophe
brack...clo brack	bracket...closing bracket
spot	bullet
cap, up, nonverbal signal (e.g., tap table)	single capital letter
caps	all capitals
three up	three words with initial capitals
nish	initial capital
click, cluck, c-l-c	capitals and lowercase
bumped	all capitals, no space or punctuation, as in USA
cen	centered
dit	ditto mark or same characters repeated on following line

Code	Meaning
cole	colon
com	comma
three dots	three ellipsis points (. . .)
bang, 'sclam, shout	exclamation point
hy, hook	hyphen
hyph	hyphen, in words with "high" as a syllable, as high-income
two hooks	two hyphens, as in day-to-day
indent, dent	indention
tal...rome	italic...back to roman type
dent three, in three	indented 3 spaces or 3 ems
blocked, dent all, in all	long indention, as in a set-off quotation
l-c, down, small	lowercase
l-c bumped	lowercase with no space or punctuation, as in rpm
pups	pp. (pages)
graph, pare, non-verbal signal (e.g., partners may switch reading aloud)	paragraph
pren, curve	parenthesis
pren...clo paren	open parenthesis...closing parenthesis
prens	parentheses
in the hole	single word or character in parentheses
dot, stop, point	period, decimal point
(vocal inflection: slight pause, dip in pitch)	period at end of sentence
kwes, hay, huh	question mark
quo...clo quo	open quotation marks...closing quotation marks
sem	semicolon
sing quo...clo sing quo	single quote...closing single quote
sco...ensco	underscore...end of underscore

Numbers

Code	Meaning
noom three, fig three	numeral 3
spell three	spelled out three
three five	35 (numerals)
thirty-five	spelled out thirty-five
thou	three zeros, or the word "thousand"
hun	two zeros or the word "hundred"
mil	six zeros or the word "million"
nought, oh (where no confusion with letter o is possible)	zero
super, soup	superscript
sub	subscript

Symbols and Diacritical Marks

Code	Meaning
cute e (or whatever letter is marked)	acute accent (é)
grahv e (or whatever letter is marked)	grave accent (è)
short and	ampersand (&)
elbow...end elbow	angle brackets: ≪ ≫
astrik, star	asterisk (*)
cut c	cents sign (¢)
soft c	cedilla (ç)
flex, doghouse	circumflex (^)
ball	degree mark (°)
doll, buck	dollar sign ($)
di, umlaut	diaresis (¨)
div	division sign (÷)
times, mult	multiplication sign (×)
pare sign	paragraph sign (¶)
balls	percent sign (%)
squiggle, sec sign	section sign (§)
snake	tilde (ñ)
short a (or whatever letter is marked)	breve (ă)
long a (or whatever letter)	macron (ā)

Lists

Code	List
a through d, prens	(a) (b) (c) (d)
four dots, nish, points	. Xxxxxx xxxx xxx. . Xxxxxxx xxxxxx xxxx. . Xxx xxxx xxxx xxxxx. . Xx xxxxxx.
one through four, points, nish, three sems, point	1. Xxxx xxxxxxxxx; 2. Xxxxxxx; 3. Xxxxxx xxxxx; 4. Xxxx.

COMMUNICATOR'S SIGNALS

The international communicator's alphabet and numbers, devised for optimum clarity in critical situations such as aviation radio, may be useful. For example, to answer such a question as "Did you say M or N?" the answer would be, "M for mike." These signals are especially helpful on the telephone.

alpha	India	Quebec	yankee	fife
bravo	Juliette	Romeo	zulu	six
Charlie	kilo	Sierra	zero	seven
delta	Lima (leema)	tango	wun	ait
echo	mike	uniform	too	niner
foxtrot	November	Victor	tree	
golf	Oscar	whiskey	fow-er (rhymes	
hotel	Papa	X-ray	with grower)	

One-Person Functions

Some proofreading procedures may be done more efficiently by one
person than a team. These single-person functions might be done
by one partner before or after the team's work is done, or they
might be divided between partners. Such functions include the
following:

- Verifying folio sequence, style, placement, and register

- Verifying the sequence of footnote, figure, and table
  numbers and their callouts

- Checking running heads

- Checking pages for general appearance: alignment, spacing

- Verifying word division

- Verifying format: margins, spacing, indention, headings

- Typing query lists

- Detecting widows

- Initialing and dating galleys or pages.

OTHER METHODS

Scamping

Word processing and computer composition reintroduce scamping--an
old way to revise without proving composition on paper. For hurried,
cheap printing, handset type could be corrected with the proofreader
reading from the dead copy as the typesetter followed along, reading
from the type itself and correcting errors in the metal. Using a
VDT, an operator can follow a proofreader, reading the screen and
correcting errors as they proceed. This method saves time and reduces cost, but it is unavoidably imperfect if a system of careful
checking is not set up: the operator is certain to miss some errors
and to introduce new errors when making corrections. The following
section describes a way to check the dead copy against the live,
corrected copy.

Direct Correcting

On VDT equipment, correcting copy is easy. For example, correcting a wrong character is often a matter of merely moving the electronic cursor to the character on the screen and striking the key for the correct character. It may take only a few minutes to learn to make simple corrections on this kind of machine. Proofreaders with a little typing skill can be trained as operators and can correct errors as they find them when comparing the dead copy with the display on the screen.

Proofreading done in this way is reliable only if a record is kept of corrections so they can be checked. Some equipment will display changes in a different typeface. Without such equipment, the proofreader can write a list of errors corrected, type or set a C (for correction) in the extreme margin whenever an operation is performed in a line, or mark the dead copy where errors in the live copy were found and add a checkmark in the margin at every line where a correction was made. Carets and underscores are the simplest way to mark dead corrected copy, as shown in the following chart. The checker then compares the dead copy either with a revised printout or with the image on the screen. It is not necessary to know precisely what the error was; it is only necessary to know that a correction was made at that point. The checker can then make certain that the correction did not introduce a new error.

Live Copy		Dead copy (marked to show that error was corrected)	
Error found by proofreader on screen	Corrected screen display or printout	Text	Margin
poofreading	proofreading	proofreading	✔
prooofreading	proofreading	proofreading	✔
pro ofreading	proofreading	proofreading	✔

"Proofreading" Without Comparing Live and Dead Copy

Sometimes both dead and live copy are available but only the live copy is read (this is called railroading). When this is done, you will need to go back to the dead copy occasionally--to check figures in text or tables, spelling of people's names, and anything puzzling.

When dead copy is not available, what you are doing is neither true proofreading nor copyediting, but something in between. With increasing use of word processing machines and computerized equipment that do not make more than one stage of a manuscript available, dry reading--without comparison--will become more common in the future.

Be sure you know exactly what is wanted. You probably will be expected to detect and mark typos, misspellings, and blatant errors in punctuation or grammar (see Chapter 7 on what constitutes a

blatant error). In some cases, normal querying and anything ap-
proaching rewriting may be unwelcome. In others, every error you
find must be queried rather than corrected.

Whether or not the dead copy is available, you should follow your
reading with the Steps in Checking listed in Chapter 5.

QUESTIONS FOR STUDENTS

1. Describe the kinds of copy best proofread by one person alone.

2. Describe the kinds of copy best proofread by two persons in a
team.

3. Spell out your last name in the words of the international
communicator's alphabet. Spell out your phone number.

4. The following quotation from <u>The Love Affairs of a Bibliomaniac</u>
by Eugene Field (Charles Scribners Sons, 1896) is written as if it
were being read aloud by a member of a proofreading team. Trans-
scribe it to appear as it would on a typewritten page. Note that
obvious capital letters, such as in the first person pronoun "I,"
after the period (point) ending a sentence, or in a proper name (unless there could be alternative capitalization, as in De Quincey),
are not voiced.

pare i have always thought that de quincey up d e space up
q u i n c e y pos s workshop sol would have given me great delight
point the particular thing that excited de quincey pos s choler
c h o l e r was interference with his books and manuscripts com
which he piled atop of one another upon the floor and over his desk
com until at last there would be but a narrow little pathway sol
from the desk to the fireplace sol and from the fireplace to the
door sem and his writing hy table dash gracious bang what a pelion
up p e l i o n upon ossa up o s s a of confusion it must have been
bang pare yet de quincey insisted that he knew quo just where
everything was com clo quo and he merely exacted that the servants
attempt no such vandalism as quo cleaning up clo quo in his
workshop point of course there would presently come a time when
there was no more room on the table and when the little pathway to
the fireplace and the door would be no longer visible sem then com
with a sigh com de quincey would lock the door of that room and
betake himself to other quarters com which in turn would eventually
become quite as littered up com cluttered up com and impassable
a b l e as the first rooms point pare from all that can be gathered
upon the subject it would appear that de quincey was careless in
his treatment of books sem i have read somewhere pren but i forget
where clo pren that he used his forefinger sol as a paper hy cutter
and that he did not hesitate to mutilate old folios which he
borrowed point but he was extraordinarily tender with his
manuscripts sem and he was wont o n t to carry in his pockets a
soft brush with which he used to dust off his manuscripts most
carefully before handing them to the publisher point

5. Read the following aloud while someone writes down what you are reading. Do not look at what is being written. Check the results to see what you missed describing:

Oliver Goldsmith wrote the following:
   Here's A, B, and C,
   E, F, and G,
   H, I, J, K, L, M, N, O, P, Q,
   R, S, T, and U,
   V, W, X, Y, and Z.
   And here's the child's dad
   who is sagacious and discerning
   and knows this is the fount of learning.

6. How might you read the following aloud to save syllables without misunderstanding?

   a. Geo. Brownly, Frederic Hoffmann, Louis McDonald, Meyer
       Thompson
   b. i.e., e.g., ibid., etc., et al.
   c. RPM, R.P.M., rpm, r/min
   d. bee keeping, bee-keeping, beekeeping
   e. 12 345 6^7 8$_9$
   f. Abc DE f gh--I
   g. At 9 a.m., on Wed., Nov. 18, Mr. Wm. Elliot, Jr., re-
       ceived a c.o.d. pkg. from his Dr. on L.I.
   h. $14.04, $14.25, $14.19, $14.54, $14.22, $14.37, $14.84
   i. 9,000; 27,000; 42,000; 436,000; 900,000

7. Practice reading aloud the following: a newspaper editorial, the table of contents of a current magazine, any page from this book.

8. Read the following aloud phonetically, using shortcuts but leaving no doubt how strange words are spelled: a page from a telephone book, a chapter from the "begats" in the Bible (try any of the first nine chapters of I Chronicles).

Chapter 7

Queries and Author's Changes

The proofreader is not permitted to change the author's copy or manuscript. However, he may query, or question, anything that he feels should be brought to the author's attention. The making of queries by the proofreader should be carried out with discretion and judgment, otherwise the author might ignore them entirely.

> --Proofreading and Copy Preparation
> Joseph Lasky
> Mentor Press, New York 1941

CHAPTER OVERVIEW

This chapter describes the difference between corrections and queries; tells you why, what, and how to query; and illustrates valid and invalid queries. It ends with a discussion of author's changes.

DISTINGUISHING BETWEEN CORRECTIONS AND QUERIES

Normally, you should expect to receive error-free dead copy and clear, detailed instructions. As a proofreader, you are employed to be sure the typist or typesetter follows copy, that is, reproduces the author's or editor's draft faithfully, according to the job specifications and good typesetting or typing practice. When typesetters or typists do not follow copy, you mark errors for correction. But you may also be required to catch errors in the author's or editor's draft; for example, incorrect facts, dubious grammar, obvious discrepancies, and inconsistencies in editorial style. You do not mark such matters for correction; you query them--write questions about them. Few jobs require you to query anything other than blatant--indefensible--errors.

Marks for correction are directed to typists or typesetters; only errors for which they are responsible are so marked. Queries are directed to authors and editors.

WHY QUERY?

Sometimes would-be proofreaders seem to have difficulty understanding that they must query--not correct--errors made in the dead copy (the editor's or author's draft) even when something is obviously wrong. There are several good reasons for this restriction:

First, proofreaders are seldom authorities in the subjects they deal with. Many a beginner has "corrected" something erroneously: diplomate has been changed to diplomat, corrasion to corrosion, adsorption to absorption. The exponent has been deleted from "10^3 gallons" because "there was no footnote 3," and "feet per second per second," the unit for measuring velocity, has been mistaken for a doublet. If you make such an error, you are responsible for harming a manuscript. If you make a valid query and it is discarded, the error is not yours. And if you make an ignorant query, no harm is done.

Second, authors and editors have the right to decide if any detail of their work should be changed. When you query, you give authors and editors a fair opportunity to see and correct the oversights you have found.

Third, proofreaders cannot authorize the money spent for corrections. The extra charges are often high when a typesetter or typist must correct other than their own errors. Even the insertion of a comma is costly--up to $30 in one organization. A change of one word often means a complete line must be reset. If the line then spills over (over-runs), a whole paragraph is involved. If the paragraph over-runs onto another page, an entire page must be reset, and so on.

When you make changes after copy has been set or typed, the cost of typesetting or typing can rise steeply. To instruct typists or typesetters to correct errors they did not make is to ask for free labor or extra charges for unplanned-for time. When you query, you put the decisions on expense into the proper hands.

Fourth, making unauthorized corrections is unprofessional. Querying is entirely professional. In fact, the ability to determine when queries are needed and to write them explicitly and briefly is a major characteristic of a first-class proofreader.

WHAT TO QUERY

You must always catch a misspelling (look up the word if there is the slightest doubt); if you are not authorized to correct it, you must query. You may almost always query errors that would seriously embarrass the author or confuse the reader--blatantly bad grammar, obvious errors of fact, and conspicuous illogic. When you have reasonable doubt of the exactness of dates, spelling of proper names or foreign words, or quotations, and when you have neither the time nor authority to resolve the doubt, you may query to suggest that verification is desirable.

Querying inconsistency in editorial style varies with the job. Some jobs have deadlines that do not allow for these fine points. To some writers or editors, consistency in certain points of style does not matter. (They may tell you, "Consistency is the hobgoblin of little minds." You can reply, "What Emerson wrote about was a foolish consistency and this isn't foolish if you want quality," but you leave the inconsistent style alone if they are not persuaded.)

The Proofreader's Checklist in Chapter 19 lists many possibilities
for errors to be queried and shows the different levels at which
querying may be required for different jobs.

Figure 7-A shows queries as they would normally be made on a galley
or page proof. Included are queries of fact, grammar, inconsistency,
unintentional ambiguity, and discrepancies in time and date.

REPORT ON NOVEMBER MEETING

The Board of Directors of the Association for Crosscultural Inter-
changes (AXIS) met at a working lunch at 12:00 p.m. on Wednesday,   *noon/? Tuesday/?*
5/? eight/? November 9, 1976. Only five of the 8 Directors were present. Vice   *per calendar*
President George Stephaney distributed the results of the demo-
graphic poll which each of the Board members with authority over
each...was/? a specific committee were asked in October to administer. A total
360/? of 36 of the 700 members--more than half--responded. Dr. Stephany   *ey/? see line 4*
arranged the results in the table form showing AXI's membership   *AXIS'a /?*
categorized/? broken down by age and sex.   *see line 2*

Figure 7-A. Example of querying directly on live copy

Why has the proofreader made these queries? Let's take them in
order:

- noon/? 12:00 p.m. is midnight.

- Tuesday/? November 9, 1976, was not a Wednesday. (Almanacs
  and some phone books contain calendars with which you can
  check the day of the week for any year.)

- 5/? eight/? The number style is inconsistent.

- each...was/? each...were is incorrect.

- 360/? 36 is not more than half of 700.

- ey/? Stephany is spelled Stephaney on line 4.

- AXIS's/? The possessive form of AXIS is surely not AXI's.

- categorized/? "broken down by sex and age" is unintention-
  ally comic.

FORMS OF QUERIES

On galleys, page proofs, or photocopies, marks for correction and
queries are usually written in different colors or with different
implements. Queries are written directly in the margins; checkmarks (or underscores, rings, or carets) are used in text, as shown
in Figure 7-A.

Many organizations expect proofreaders to ring queries; indeed, a ring is a safeguard against the setting or typing of an unanswered query. For example, the U.S. Government Printing Office specifies for a query on grammar that the correction be written with a query mark and enclosed in a ring.

If a proofreader knows that a checker or an editor will look hard at the work, rings around queries are undesirable, however. Here is the problem: If the answer to a query is yes, the ring has to be canceled; for example:

Text	Margin
12:00 p.m.	noon? OK

To avoid the problem, this book and its accompanying exercises teach querying without rings around queries. If the answer to a query is yes, only the query mark need be erased:

Text	Margin
12:00 p.m.	noon

Be sure you know your employer's policy. And always ring queries when you are not sure that someone will answer them.

Repro proofs and typewritten camera-ready copy require separate query slips or lists. On the copy itself, mark the location of the query in the margin with a ringed question mark written in a non-photo color. NEVER make an in-text mark for a query on a repro or on any camera-ready copy; there is no need to risk touching the type or marking too heavily (the hazards of using a nonphoto pencil are described in Chapter 9).

Query Slips

A pad of Scotch Post-it® notepaper, which adheres securely with an adhesive strip yet removes easily, is useful for query slips. A pad of 3" x 5" paper is next best; leave enough margin to fold the slip over the top of the relevant page and to attach a paperclip over the fold or drafting tape to the back of the sheet. If the query takes more than one or two lines, it is best to type it; otherwise, use a dark-colored pen or pencil, writing as legibly as possible. Label each query slip with a ringed question mark, ⑦ . Always list on every slip the live copy's page number (in case the slip falls off the page).

When you may not mark the location of the problem in the margin, cite the live copy's paragraph* and line** number. Cite the dead

---

*You may use the appropriate line counter (provided in the Work-book) to save time and eliminate counting paragraphs, but be sure the recipient of the query list also has a line counter.

**When a paragraph is cited, the line number is a subdivision of the paragraph; every paragraph begins with line 1.

copy's page, paragraph, and line number only when necessary to refer to the dead copy to answer the query (not when live and dead
copy are the same); for example:

    p 7, l. 14, draft p 4, l. 3   8 or 3/? draft illegible

Query Lists

Under almost all circumstances, a query list must be typed. Label
it "Query List" and give the name of the job and the date. Organize the list into columns, citing the final copy's section, page,
paragraph, and line number. An example of a typewritten query list
is shown in Figure 7-B; the same queries are made as in Figure 7-A,
but because the queries are not immediately adjacent to the text
as in Figure 7-A, they are more explicit. When a handwritten list
is acceptable, proofreader's marks may be used, as shown in Figure 7-C.

QUERY LIST   12/4/80
Report on November Meeting

Draft			Final				
Page	Par.	Line	Page	Par.	Line	Text	Query
not applicable			95		2	12:00 p.m.	noon? p.m. is midnight
						Wednesday	Tuesday? per calendar
					3	five.....8	5?...eight? for consis- tency.
					5,6	each...were	was? n. and v. disagree
					7	36	360? over half of 700
					3 up	Stephany	spelling OK? see line 4
					2 up	AXI's	AXIS's? see line 2
					last	broken down	categorized? otherwise seems like decrepit

Figure 7-B. Example of a typed query list

CONTENT OF QUERIES

Whenever possible, express a query as a question. Phrase the query
so that if the answer is no, the entire query can be crossed out
(or the query slip discarded); or if the answer is yes, and the

query is written in the margin, the question mark can be crossed out and the typist or typesetter can read what remains as an instruction; for example:

Text: manufacturers _is_   Query: are/?

Query List
Report on November Meeting   Query

Page # Line

95   2   12:00 p̶.m̶.   noon/? p.m. is midnight
               W̶e̶d̶n̶e̶s̶d̶a̶y̶   Tuesday/? per calendar
          3   five ... 8̶   5/? or eight/? for consistency
          5,6 each ... w̶e̶r̶e̶   was/? n. and v. disagree
          7   36ʌ   0/? over half of 700
          3 up Stephany   e/? as in line 4
          2 up AXI's   AXIS's/? see line 2
          last b̶r̶o̶k̶e̶n̶ ̶d̶o̶w̶n̶   categorized/? otherwise
                                    seems like decrepit

Figure 7-C. Example of a handwritten query list

Some queries, of course, do not lend themselves to a yes-or-no form; for example:

    sentence unclear/?

    no antecedent for "it"/?

If you question a statement of fact, an unusual spelling, or a quotation's accuracy, underline it and write "Author verify," ringed, in the margin; for example:

    In the United States, 1.045 boys   (Author verify)
    are born for every 1,000 girls.

A query must be absolutely clear and specific, and it must answer the following three questions:

1. Where is the problem? The place must be pinpointed. For queries made directly in the margins, make checkmarks or other marks in text. In query lists, cite page, paragraph, and line numbers and quote the text, as shown in Figure 7-B. In query slips, place a ringed question mark in the margin or cite paragraph and line number and quote a key word or two. Here is a good and bad way to query the same problem:

Text	Query Slip	Comment
Wynken Blynken and Nod	commas/?	too unspecific
	⋀ Blynken⋀/?	good

2. <u>What is the problem?</u> This can be shown in several ways:

- Proofreader's marks may be used in handwritten query lists as shown in Figure 7-C.

- The underscore may be used in typewritten query lists, as illustrated in several of the queries in Figure 7-B.

3. <u>Why is it a problem?</u> The greatest mistake proofreaders make in querying is failing to explain exactly why the question is being asked. Such phrases as "for consistency," "as previously," "per style sheet," and even "punc error" or "noun and verb disagree" are invaluable aids to the person who must decide what to do about queries. Unless you are certain that the reason for making the query is obvious (for example, when you have dealt with the same editor over a long period or when you have made the same query in the same job several times before), explain every query.

SPECIAL ABBREVIATIONS

Some editors are accustomed to seeing (G?) for questions of grammar and (F?) for questions of fact, as shown in the following example. Use these abbreviations only if you know they will be understood; for example:

(G? is) "Darien peaks" <u>are</u> the name given to experiences of revelation or discovery seeming to be as great as that of
(F? Balboa—
Keats got it
wrong) Cortez, when, as Keats described him, "with eagle eyes he star'd at the Pacific . . . upon a peak in Darien."

Queries may be addressed to the author (Au) or the editor (Ed); for example:

Q Ed: Is change in spacing OK?

SPEED IN QUERYING

Querying slows down proofreading significantly. Querying must be done efficiently, or the time loss is unacceptable.

Whether or not to query a point may be discussed between proofreading partners, but such a discussion should take no more than a few seconds; a quick decision is essential, or too much time is lost. When in doubt, query--and let the reviewer or the checker make the final decision.

When you do not immediately know how to word a query, do not take team time to figure it out. Postpone the problem by marking the final copy Ⓠ, writing a query slip or a query list item that says something like "problem here," and leaving it to be worded properly by the checker (or by you or your partner in your allotted review time).

RECURRING ERRORS

When the same problem is encountered many times throughout the copy, stop marking the problem each time in the text and make a separate query list; for example:

programming --
     one m only
     per GPO style/?   p 3
                                 9
                                 14
                                 22
                                 35
                                 96

If you are not sure the problem represents an error the editor will definitely want to have corrected, ask your supervisor before spending a lot of time noting the problem.

CAUTIONS IN QUERYING

Restrain your editing instincts. Do not rewrite. If a sentence is clear enough for you to know how to rewrite it, it should be left alone. For example, the following is an unacceptable query:

Text	Unacceptable Query
Of the approximately 30,000 foundations that exist in this country, most of the major ones number between three and five hundred.	There are three to five hundred major foundations among the 30,000 or so foundations in this country/?

If the text had read as follows, a query would be valid.

Text	Valid Query
Of the approximately 30,000 foundations that exist in this country, between three and five hundred.	fix incomplete sentence/?

In querying, there is no point in being a purist. Never gratuitously query which (that/?), will (shall/?), or want (wish/?). Be cautious of querying commas unless the comma's use affects meaning or you can back up a query with a rule from the specified editorial style guide, such as "insert serial comma per GPO style/?."

Query lightly, if at all (excluding unmistakable errors), when copy has been prepared by a professional copyeditor; if copy is technical, scientific, or mathematical; if copy is a legal or financial

document such as a contract, mortgage, or a transcript of testimony;
or if copy is quoted matter.

Never write a query that will change the meaning; for example:

> NASA leadership was concerned that European organizations
> were likely to be subsidized by their governments and thus
> might not purchase U.S. hardware, lent that of European ~~lent~~ *but* /?
> competitors instead.

"Lent" cannot be removed without changing the thought from "lend"
to "purchase." A valid query would for the same passage, might be
worded as follows:

> . . . purchase U.S. hardware, lent that of . . . *hardware,* ∧ *lent*   *when they are* /?

Use the dictionary to avoid querying perfectly good words used correctly; for example:

Kissinger's apparat∧   *cus* /?

> consciously written his farewell in the Sixth
> Symphony. However, while a concern with
> death <u>informs</u> this very original work, there is
> absolutely no evidence that Tchaikovsky in-
> tended to take his leave of the world when he
> produced it; there is, rather, every indication

permeates /?

Know your grammar. For example, the following query asks to change
good grammar to bad:

one...~~are~~ Space as a focus of foreign policy is one of those subjects
is /?   that <u>are</u> a direct result of technological advance.

The true antecedent of "that" is "those subjects," not "one." If
you turn the sentence around, this becomes clear: Of those subjects
that are a direct result of technological advance, space is one.

The following is an example of an unnecessary query:

> It is not only actors in the policy-making system
> who, when bureaucratic politics <u>works</u> badly, can   *work* /?
> narrow and delimit the President's choice . . .

Politics is a collective noun. Either a singular or a plural verb
is correct.

Query sexism when it could offend readers and embarrass the publisher. Suggest a graceful alternative when you can do so quickly;
for example:

> Every District Manager must turn in <u>his</u>   *a* /? *(sexist)*
> monthly equal opportunity report promptly.

> A schoolteacher's relationship to <u>her</u>   *ʃ* /? *(sexist)*
> students is critical.

Figure 7-D shows examples of valid queries.

For practice in querying, turn to Exercise 16 in the Workbook.

support the muscular ^ *dystrophy foundation* / ?
^

HELP YOUR DRYCLEANER
SUPPORT ✓ MUSCULAR DYSTROPHY ✓

Sunbelt women from Georgia to California here share with you their traditional beauty secrets. And to help you concoct your own off-the-kitchen-shelf cosmetics, see the chart of natural ingredients that follow.

chart ... follows / ?
^

⌐ /// ?

The advent of the automobile heightened the rise of the State police force. Earlier State police efforts had occurred in Texas ^ which organized Rangers ^ and Massachusetts ^ which appointed State constables.

SEAPINE CHESTS.

These beautifully crafted chests, in dark weathered finish, bound with antique brass bindings and handles will look as good in a land setting as it does on a luxury yacht. Perfect as an end

chests ...

they do / ?

"23-year-old... age 45"

23-year-old ʃ *employee* / ?

As he marched around the FTC building during the protest, Raymond R. Nuckles, a 23-year-old American Safety Razor employee declared: "That's my livelihood. If the plant closes down, I don't know what I will do. I've got to support my family (of four). Jobs are hard to find. You just don't go and find a job at age 45."

There are many possible ways to organize the United States government for the conduct of foreign policy. The choice between them will be influenced by the personalities of the President and his principal collaborators, but it should also reflect the nation's basic foreign policy priorities.

between among / ?

See ª *Goya* / ?
≡ ^

See ^ Goya
in the flesh
for about 85¢.

Figure 7-D. Examples of valid queries (assuming the live copy matches the dead copy)

lend /?

'Other show business personalities who <u>lending</u> their names to good causes are happy—and indeed inwardly content—merely to be listed on the notepaper and to make occasional speeches.'

ABC**HEATING** ^

#so it does not look like "cheating"/?

hold /?

With your right hand, take <u>ahold</u> of lever A.

3T's OK /?

8 p.m. (26) Bill Moyers' Journal. A look at the issues and consequences of last fall's prolonged teachers' strike at Levitttown, L.I., 40 miles from New York City.

Deterring crime: By failing to execute a convicted murderer do we risk prevention of other murders?

By Is /?

application...
~~have~~ has /?

Application of these methods in stores in San Diego and Houston <u>have</u> resulted in a 30 percent drop in robberies and a 50 percent decline in violence there, Sunshine said.

jeopardizing /?
~~do we risk~~

ecisions...
owledge...
sources...
ave
as /?

come specific and current. Even then, the momentum of earlier decisions, the greater technical knowledge, and the mobilizable resources of the operating agencies, has meant that State has relatively little independent leverage except in those issues for which it is able to mount a special and unusual effort. With regard to the direction of tech-

(prevention of murders would be a desirable risk)

two / are /?

Mr. and Mrs. Pieper have a family of five children, <u>one</u> of which <u>is</u> twins.

Ullmann /?
~~Ullman~~
anna /?
~~Annie~~

8 p.m. (22) The Critic's Place. Reviews of Liv Ullman in "Annie Christie" in Baltimore

Liv Ullmann, who opens this week in "Agatha Christie," asked several designers to submit sketches for a dress

anna /?
~~Agatha~~

Like his younger colleague, A. J. Casson, Carmichael had a fondness for portraying the characteristic stores, barns, and houses of rural Ontario settlements. During the 1930's, throughout the southern part of the Province and along the shore of Lake Superior, he found isolated dwellings or small villages from which he composed many watercolours, drawings and a few oils. ^

,/? as after barns in line 2 above

Figure 7-D.   (Continued)

Each of the diplomatic missions in the capital of the four countries was visited by a member of the project staff. The primary purpose of this visit was to interview those individuals who had authored the documents in our sample. In addition, the ambassador, the Deputy Chief of Mission and mission personnel from agencies outside the Department of State were interviewed. Annex D contains a list of the positions held by those individuals interviewed. A total of forty-seven interviews were conducted with approximate equal coverage of the four countries in the report.

[margin annotations: total ... / were was /? ○ly /?]

The interviewing schedule was based in part on the basic content of the documents selected. We also attempted to tap the producers attitudes toward foreign service reporting in general. (See Annex B) In order to elicit specific responses, we selected for each respondent a sub-sample of between five and ten documents that had been sent to the respondents' office. This small sample was intended to represent the range of topics and types of cables received in a given country office.

[margin annotations: producer's / producers' /? respondents /? tr /?]

The preliminary questions of the interview schedule were designed to investigate the relationship between the requirements of a respondent's job and his use of foreign service reporting. Each respondent was then asked a series of questions about each of the specific documents. These questions focused on the specific use that was made of each document, and why the document was written.

Using the selected sample documents, the respondents were asked to select what they considered the most and least useful reports and to suggest ways in which they might have been improved. Respondents were then given a list of other sources of information that may have been useful to them in preparing their reports. For each source of information, we asked whether or not it was used, how useful it was, and to what extent the source was utilized. Finally, the foreign service officers were asked for their general evaluation of the document routing and retrieval system and of foreign service reporting in general.

The responses by each producer were coded using the scheme outlined in Annex C. Subsequently, these data were compiled and analyzed. The results of our analysis are contained in the following sections.

TABLE 4.1.—PERCEPTION OF ROLE IN FOREIGN POLICY REPORTING SYSTEM

Role	# of Producers	% of Total Producers
Reporter	20	42.6%
Research Analyst	12	25.5%
Operational-Administrative	7	14.9%
Combination of Two of the Above	8	17.0%
	47	

[margin annotations: ○% / 4x /?]

Figure 7-D. (Continued)

DECIPHERING HARD-TO-READ HANDWRITING

The handwriting of authors and editors often presents problems. _I_ and _J_ may be mistaken for each other (*ʃ , ʃ*); it is often impossible to distinguish Jan. from June; and mistakes may arise when letters in a word are not connected and the word appears to be broken up into two or more words: *in ability   to ward*

It may be impossible to tell a capital from a lowercase letter:

the Telegraph Company

and some words or expressions may be quite unreadable.

The proofreader must often query such cases, but the following suggestions may help:

- Consider the context.

- Read on. Mark (or note) the place and see if same word or expression is used later.

- Use a magnifying glass.

- Count the humps. There will be more humps, for example, in portioning than in parting: *partiuuuug   pautiuy*

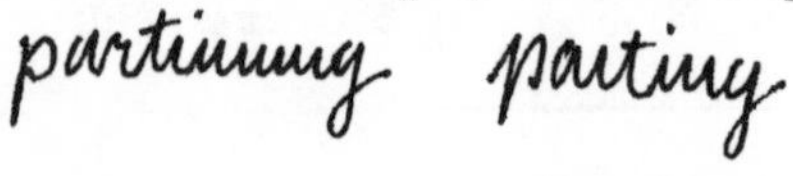

Do not yourself be guilty of ambiguous or illegible handwritten corrections and queries. Follow the instructions in Chapter 2 on writing out insertions. In your writing, take care to distinguish between cap I and J. Distinguish clearly between lowercase a and o; u, v, and w; r and n; n and m; e and the dele. Type anything longer than a few words on a slip of paper attached to the live copy and referenced to the live copy (with "insert A," for example). You can also type inserts right in the margin of a galley.

For practice proofreading and querying hard-to-read handwriting, turn to Exercise 17 in the Workbook.

AUTHOR'S CHANGES

A typesetter is responsible for correcting at no charge any unauthorized deviation from the dead copy or from the specifications.* Such a deviation is called a printer's error (PE). A typesetter is not responsible for correcting an error, such as a misspelling, that appears in the dead copy. In most jobs, when an error appears in the dead copy, the proofreader queries it and the author or editor decides whether to make a change. When a change of this kind is decided upon, it is called an author's alteration (AA) or sometimes an editor's alteration (EA). A copy error (CE) is one kind of AA--an obvious, unarguable error, such as a blatant misspelling or an omitted period. Some employers or customers like to distinguish CE's from other AA's. Some simply call both kinds of changes AA's.

Proofreaders may be required to catch and mark certain kinds of author's changes (CE's should always be caught, although you may need to query them instead of marking them for correction). When this happens, you must mark in a way that distinguishes PE's--which the printer pays for--from AA's (including CE's)--which the customer pays for.

There are different ways you may be required to do this: you may use different implements (pen and pencil), or different colors (usually dark blue for AA's and CE's, and red for PE's); you may label each correction PE, AA, or CE or you may write PE's in one margin and AA's (including CE's) in the other.

What if a proofreader misses a PE at an early stage of typesetting and catches it later? When does a PE become eligible to be charged as an AA? The answer depends on where the type shop draws the line.

Some production editors insist that PE's should be corrected at no extra charge up until the job is photographed (up through page proofs),

---

*Some small shops do not accept this responsibility.

and some type shops will oblige their customers to this point. However, corrections become more costly at every successive stage. Some shops accept PE's only through the galley stage, and many only through the first reading. Once a job is returned marked "OK" or "OK with corrections," further changes are charged as AA's.*

As a proofreader, you must know the policy for every job, because you must mark AA's as such. After the first round of reading, you may have to return to the original dead copy to discover when the error was first made.

The following quotation describes a small <u>literal</u> (a one-letter error) that, as an AA, cost the publisher the price of a new edition:

> I am reminded of an error that was made in setting up My South Sea Island, by W. Somerset Maugham, which we published. The whole edition--50 copies--had been printed when we discovered, to our chagrin, that Maugham's name was printed on the title page "W. Sommerset Maugham." We scrapped the edition and printed another.
>   --"Reading and Collecting"
>   Ben Abramson
>   September 1937

There are, of course, errors you can detect and some you cannot. Lawrence J. Hogan described at the 14th Annual Conference of the Society of National Association Publications an instance of each kind of error. An alert proofreader should have queried the literal in Hogan's first example:

> At one time in my life, I was editing a magazine and through a typographical error--just a little typographical error--the letter "e" was dropped off the word "care." So the story read that this man had been under the doctor's car for three weeks. Another little mistake occurred as a stenographer transcribed her dictation while I was editing the FBI employee magazine <u>The Investigator</u>. The story was supposed to say that the man was run down by his paramour, and it came out that he was run down by his power mower. Made sense, you know; it made sense. No proofreader is going to catch that.

---

*Included in a list of printing trade customs which "have been in general use in the Printing Industry throughout the United States of America for more than 50 years" is the following: "Printer regrets any errors that may occur through production undetected, but cannot be held responsible for errors if work is printed per customer's O.K. or if changes are communicated verbally."--<u>Trade Customs & Printing Contracts</u>, published by Printing Industries of America, Arlington, VA, copyright 1976.

QUESTIONS FOR STUDENTS

1. Define the following: follow copy; PE; AA; EA; CE; literal.

2. When must proofreaders query instead of mark for correction?

3. Why must proofreaders query errors made in the dead copy rather than mark them for correction?

4. Why can't you make a standard in-text mark for a query on a repro or other camera-ready copy? Does this ban also apply to a mark for correction?

5. Why must a page number appear on query slips? Does this rule also apply to correction slips?

6. When must a query cite the page, paragraph, and line number for the dead copy as well as for the live? Give two examples of the kind of problem requiring this.

7. Under what circumstances could you use the line counter provided in the Workbook? Under the same circumstances, should you also use the line counter for a correction list?

8. Assuming that the dead copy is the same as the live, write queries for the following as you would on a galley:

>   Marie had a little Lamb;
>   It's fleece was white as snow.
>   And everyone that Mary went
>   The lamb were sure to go.

9. Make a query list for the same problems shown in (8).

10. If you were given the authority to mark AA's for blatant errors and given instructions to mark PE's in blue and AA's in red, show how you would mark the following:

Dead Copy	Live Copy
The rule for making printer's errors only--to the exclusion of author's errors--was first recorded in 1608 by Jerome Hornisch of the Beyer printing office in Meiningen, germany. Writing of "a conscientous corrector, he said, "Never should he make changes in the text, even though he beleives it would be improved there by."	The rule for marking printers errors only--to the exclusion of author's errors--was 1st recorded in 1609 by Jerome Hornisch of the Beyer printing office in Meinengen, germany. Writing of "a conscientous corrector, he said, "Never should he make changes in the text, even though he believes it would be inproved there by."

Chapter 8

Tips and Cautions

If only one typo gets past you into print, it will be in a place
where everybody else catches it immediately.

—Laura's* rule

CHAPTER OVERVIEW

This chapter describes many of the circumstances when printer's and
proofreader's errors are likely to occur. It also details the physical care that should be taken in handling different kinds of
proofs.

WHERE TO WATCH FOR ERRORS

Watch for errors in prominent places, such as heads. Some proofreaders pin proofs on the wall, step back, and read the heads from
a distance. Some embarrassing uncaught errors in heads are shown
in Figure 8-A.

Intenational and Unintentional Modification of the Atmosphere

County Remapping

Parishoners Celebrate

DENIUM HATS

Save 100.00 now on this 12-foot x 12-foot patio, fully screened and covered with aluminum owning

Figure 8-A. Errors in heads

*Laura Horowitz, president of Editorial Experts, Inc., publisher of
this book.

**Finish President
To Meet With Ford**

Finnish President Urho Kekkonen is scheduled to arrive in New York today for a Bicentennial state visit.

**"The Bourgeios"
French
Restaurant**

10" VELECOPIDE
6⁸⁷
Compensation

**PAINTED
DAISES**

Flying Granny,
At 83, Soloes the
Atlantic Again

Bits & Peices

In the Prestigeous
VIENNA, VIRGINIA
AREA

PEWTER BANGEL BRACELET — engraved with three initials. Perfect for bridesmaids gifts, ushers gifts, graduation presents . . . any special occasion.

Salemen's
& Activities

Bookkeeping

Interested in producing your own honey? Two courses on beekeeping will be offered by the Beekeeper's Association of Northern Virginia in conjunction with the County extension service at

**WE STOCK BARGAGE DISPOSALS
FOR EVERY NEED
SO SHOP   FOR ALL
YOUR PLUMBING NEEDS.**

Figure 8-A.   Errors in heads (Continued)

Watch for errors in other prominent places, such as first lines and first paragraphs. Examples of errors in these places are shown in Figure 8-B.

* *

HOROWITZ-MARGARETEN FAMILY JOURNAL

SPECIAL NEW YEAR EDITION   September 1975 (5736)

PRESIDENTIAL INVITATION

In order to start the New York off right, we have arranged a social gathering for all members on the east coast, including visitors, to take place on Sunday, October 5th, 1975,

* *

Dear Friend,

As a fashion conscience American, this special edition of the new Quelle catalog is being sent to you.

* *

The Executive Woman

747 Third Ave. ▪ New York, N. Y. 10017 ▪ (212) 688-4601

Dear Friend:

You are invited to share and become part of a prestigious newsletter, The Executive Woman, created expecially for business and professional women.

* *

MARTIN LUTHER KING, JR.
CENTER FOR NON-VIOLENT SOCIAL CHANGE
671 BECKWITH ST., SW, ATLANTA, GEORGIA 30314

MRS. MARTIN LUTHER KING, PRES.

Dear Valued Friend:

Several weeks ago I traveled to Boston to speak out against the racism, violence and polarization that have tormented that city. I was deeply moved when one young white woman detached herself from a crows and said to me, "I never understood your husband when he was alive, but today I realize that we need his spirit more than ever before."

* *

Figure 8-B. Errors in first lines and first paragraphs

Watch for errors in any place they would be particularly embarrassing. The first embarrassing error in Figure 8-C appeared in a government report; the second, in a magazine renowned for quality; the
third, in a prospectus from a "quality" book club.

The transcript has been edited for the sole purpose of
correcting obvious typograhical and/or grammatical errors.
We regret that, due to time constraints, witnesses did
not have an opportunity to review their statements prior
to publication of this document.

> There has been a definite decline in edi-
> torial standards over the past twenty years
> or so, and it's apparent all up and down
> the line in the editorial process, beginning
> with the editor per se and going on though
> the copyediting and proofreading stages.

> The Society endeavours to remain an outpost of proper book
> production in an inflationary world, where inferior mass production
> processes are constantly driving out decent craftsmanship.

Figure 8-C.   Errors in embarrassing places

When you find one error, look for another. Errors often come in
clusters; where there is one, there are likely to be others nearby
(see Figure 8-D). The story of footnote 12, told in Figure 8-E,
demonstrates that errors flock together, that correction often
introduces new errors, and that proofreading is often imperfect.

(Independence Day
itself is set aside this year at Wolf
Trap for "picnicing and performances," the latter by the U.S. Air
Force Band, the Singing Sargeants,
and the Airmen of Note.)

The barriers
erected by race, culture and language
that divide the Vietnamese from their
adopted country are formidible.

**The hospital's plight, accord-
ing to Raleigh Cline, hospital executive vice president, is result
of its inability to raise its rates to
cope with losses suffered do to
declining admissions and the bad
debts of patients.**

With those questions in mind, Pei
becaomes skeptical about an architec-
tural cure that Henry Fored devised
for Detroit.
Pei says of that city's nearly complete, $350 million Renaissaince Cen-
ter: "I feel it's too big a dose of medi-
cine in one area. With all of that city's
ills, you'd think that the resources
could have been allocated elsewhere."

Figure 8-D.   Multiple errors

---

[12]Some confusion has been caused by Schlesinger also announcing the development of a new large warhead for the MI- *run over* NUTEMAN, a warhead which has some transient military use in attacking some military targets, such as Soviet hardened missile silos. (Its value is transient because improvement in missile accuracy is increasing missile effectiveness anyway without the need of larger warheads; improvements in accuracy also help make possible large reductions in collateral damage.) He has justified this proposal in terms of perceptions of the U.S.-U.S.S.R. strategic balance; the Soviet missile force has a much larger payload capacity and larger warheads than does the U.S. one. The proposed large warhead should, he has argued, be considered in the context of the Strategic Arms Limitations Talks, a context witin which we were trying to get agreement to reduce missile numbers and total payload. We were willing to trade away this addition to our counterforce capability in SALT, but we needed some currency to trade with. This warhead provided such coin. It had nothing to do with flexible options. Nevertheless, the collocation of these two policy pronouncements caused some confusion in press reporting and hostility among those opposed to nuclear flexibility anyway.

He argued that our strategic force should have some ability to destroy hard targets, even though he prefers to see both sides without major counterforce capabilities.

(1) Galley: incorrect word division marked

[12]Some confusion has been caused by Schlesinger also announcing the development of a new large warhead for the MINUTEMAN, a warhead which has some transient military use in attacking some military targets, such as Soviet hardened missile silos. (Its value is transient because improvement in missile accuracy is increasing missile effectiveness anyway without the need of larger warheads; improvements in accuracy also help make possible large reductions in collateral damage.) He has justified this proposal in terms of perceptions of the U.S.-U.S.S.R. strategic balance; the Soviet missile force has a much larger payload capacity and larger warheads than does the U.S. one. The proposed large warhead should, he has argued, be context of the Strategic Arms Limitiations Talks, a context witin which we were trying to get agreement to reduce missile numbers and total payload. We were willing to trade away this addition to our counterforce capability in SALT, but we needed some currency to trade with. This warhead provided such coin. It had nothing to do with flexible options. Nevertheless, the collocation of these two policy pronouncements caused some confusion in press reporting and hostility among those opposed to nuclear flexibility anyway.

He argued that our strategic force should have some ability to destroy hard targets, even though he prefers to see both sides without major counterforce capabilities.

considered in the

(2) First revise: word division corrected; new out
     introduced; typo discovered

[12]Some confusion has been caused by Schlesinger also announcing the development of a new large warhead for the MINUTEMAN, a warhead which has some transient military use in attacking some military targets, such as Soviet hardened missile silos. (Its value is transient because improvement in missile accuracy is increasing missile effectiveness anyway without the need of larger warheads; improvements in accuracy also help make possible large reductions in collateral damage.) He has justified this proposal in terms of perceptions of the U.S.-U.S.S.R. strategic balance; the Soviet missile force has a much larger payload capacity and larger warheads than does the U.S. one. The proposed large warhead should, he has argued, be considered in the context of the Strategic Arms Limitations Talks, a context within which we were trying to get agreement to reduce missile numbers and total payload. We were willing to trade away this addition to our counterforce capability in SALT, but we needed some currency to trade with. This warhead provided such coin. It had nothing to do with flexible options. Nevertheless, the collocation of these two policy pronouncements caused some confusion in press reporting and hostility among those opposed to nuclear flexibility anyway.

He argued that our strategic force should have some ability to destroy hard targets, even though he prefers to see both sides without major counterforce capabilities.

(3) Second revise: corrections made; another typo discovered

Figure 8-E. Footnote 12

Watch for new errors in corrected copy. Figures 8-F and 8-G show
how resetting can introduce new errors in spacing and word division.
Any kind of error can be introduced in corrected copy. Correction
frequently breeds new errors.

From the beginning, the civilian space program has included an important scientific research component. Though often adversely affected by budgetary needs of other program objectives, the scientific program has continued, with planetary probes, x-ray and other satellites, and with scientific experiments performed in connection with the manned space program. All of the applications programs as well as the manned space programs required research and experimentation prior to system design and deployment, so that research was an essential component.

(1) Wrong word
     division marked

From the beginning, the civilian space program has included an important scientific research component. Though often adversely affected by budget-ary needs of other program objectives, the scientific program has continued, with planetary probes, x-ray and other satellites, and with scientific experiments performed in connection with the manned space program. All of the applications programs as well as the manned space programs required research and experimentation prior to system design and deployment, so that research was an essential component.

run over

(2) Correction made; new
     wrong division introduced

Figure 8-F. Resetting introduces new wrong word division

Watch for errors in the following:

- Words that differ by only one or two letters; for example:

  alone, along   crowd, crows

  area, arena   labor, laborer

  chance, change, charge   morality, mortality

  clean, clear   of, or

  contact, contract   the, they, them, then

- Words with easily transposed letters; for example:

  autonomy   proportion

  board, broad   remuneration

  causal, casual   synonymous

  marital, martial   trail, trial

- Words with two or more vowels or consonants together; for example:

  advantageous   heterogeneous

  continuous   indemnity

  continuity   psychology

(continued)

In reexamining arms control concepts and rationales, a great number of issues and propositions are relevant. For example:

(a) The role of trust in arms control agreements. This is probably a false issue. No arms control agreement has been based on trust of the Soviet Union. Rather, negotiated or potential agreements have been supported on the basis that they involve mutual commitments which would be to the U.S. benefit if fulfilled, that our verification capabilities would enable us to know whether the agreement was being carried out by other parties, and that our defense posture unaffected by the agreement would assure our security if the agreement were to be violated or otherwise unsuccessful. It is unlikely that "trust" need have any larger role in future negotiations.

(1)   First proof: word division error marked

In reexamining arms control concepts and rationales, a great number of issues and propositions are relevant. For example:

(a) The role of trust in arms control agreements. This is probably a false issue. No arms control agreement has been based on trust of the Soviet Union. Rather, negotiated or potential agreements have been supported on the basis that they involve mutual commitments which would be to the U.S. benefit if fulfilled, that our verification capabilities would enable us to know whether the agreement was being carried out by other parties, and that our defense posture unaffected by the agreement would assure our security if the agreement were to be violated or otherwise unsuccessful. It is unlikely that "trust" need have any larger role in future negotiations.

(2)   First revise: error corrected; spacing error introduced

In reexamining arms control concepts and rationales, a great number of issues and propositions are relevant. For example:

(a) The role of trust in arms control agreements. This is probably a false issue. No arms control agreement has been based on trust of the Soviet Union. Rather, negotiated or potential agreements have been supported on the basis that they involve mutual commitments which would be to the U.S. benefit if fulfilled, that our verification capabilities would enable us to know whether the agreement was being carried out by other parties, and that our defense posture unaffected by the agreement would assure our security if the agreement were to be violated or otherwise unsuccessful. It is unlikely that "trust" need have any larger role in future negotiations.

(3) Second revise: everything correct

Figure 8-G.   Resetting introduces spacing error

extenu<u>a</u>ting   ster<u>eo</u>type

extran<u>eous</u>   thera<u>peu</u>tic

- Words ending in <u>ful</u> and <u>tion</u>, especially if they are long words; for example:

  accredi<u>ta</u>tion   inter<u>pre</u>tation

  demon<u>str</u>ation   ini<u>tia</u>tion

  deter<u>io</u>ration   ins<u>ti</u>tution

  disc<u>ri</u>mination   mindf<u>ul</u>

- Certain proper names; for example:

  Penns<u>yl</u>vania (often seen as Pennslyvania)

  W<u>a</u>lter (often seen as Wlater)

- Words spelled wrong because of the position of letters on the keyboard; for example: automovile (<u>v</u> and <u>b</u> are next to each other on the keyboard)

- Any word with <u>ship</u> in it (especially "leadership"); double check the <u>p</u> in these words to be sure it is not a <u>t</u>.

- In legal work, such words as--

  therefore = in consequence

  therefor = an exchange or refund

- Words, particularly of three or more syllables, divided at end of line (consti-tutionality).

Watch especially for word division errors in the following:

- Proper names (wrong--Kiss-inger; right--Kis-singer)

- Foreign languages. Division is sometimes very different from English; for example: Russian: Che-khov; French: bi-blio-thè-que; Spanish: in-te-rro-ga-ción; German: eu-ro-pä-i-sche

- Medical and pharmacological terms

- Scientific, mathematical, and technical terms.

Watch for the following typesetter's or typist's errors:

- Forgetting to follow instructions, especially with inserts; for example, forgetting to go back to pick up copy in the right place

- Not switching back to the right type size or correct font after type changes

- Creating widows at the top or bottom of a page.

Watch for the following editor's errors:

- Skipping or repeating numbers, especially for footnote callouts

- Omitting closing parentheses, brackets, or quotation marks

- Confusing double and single quotation marks

- Placing items out of order in alphabetical listings

- Crossing out words and failing to write in a change

- Writing in a change, but failing to cross out the superseded words

- Leaving out small words (such as a, an, the, or) when rewriting sentences.

CAUTIONS

On the first round, proofread everything. If you find a long section that must be reset or recoded because it is in the wrong font, proofread it. Unless errors are marked, they will not be corrected. If you do not proofread any material for any reason, mark it clearly "not read."

Take nothing for granted. Do not trust addresses, phone numbers, store hours, or any recurring material that has become so familiar you are tempted to accept it without reading.

Take special care with figures.

- If a dollar figure or number is both written out and given in numerals, be sure the two forms correspond.

- Watch prices for the following:

  - inconsistency (as when $30 is given for a price formerly listed as $20)

  - sense (as when a sale price is greater than the manufacturer's list price).

Take special care with legal and financial materials. They must be perfect.

Be sure the number of faces in a photograph matches the number of names in the caption.

Take special care at the start of a job or a section. Errors are often uncaught at the beginning of a proofreading stint.

Keep alert in the home stretch. Errors often slip by at the ends of tables, chapters, and sections.

Keep in mind that errors are likely to be found in the middle of long words and at the end of unusually long lines.

Be careful when there is any major typographical change. Errors are easier to miss in heads, all-cap lines, italic, boldface, or small type (as in footnotes).

Be careful when errors are frequent; the greater the number of errors, the greater the number of opportunities for you to miss errors.

If you wish to catch errors, do not become too interested in the subject matter. If you cannot help your interest and there is time, read the matter for pleasure first (perhaps on your own time) and then proofread it.

Do not trust yourself to catch all the errors in the live copy if you are the typist or the typesetter. When you have made the errors, it is hard for you to find them. Hold the dead copy while your partner marks the live copy.

Similarly, do not trust yourself to catch all the errors in the live copy if you are the writer or the editor. Hold the dead copy while your partner marks the live copy.

Do not misplace an in-text mark. Figure 8-H shows three examples of misplaced insertions. There are two possible explanations. Either the proofreader put the caret in the wrong place or the typesetter did not follow instructions precisely.

HANDLING COPY

Camera-Ready Copy

Handle camera-ready copy with great care. Unlike a galley proof or photocopy, a camera-ready page is a master, a repro proof; no other usable copy exists. You are responsible if you smudge the type or mar the image in any way that shows up in the final printed page.

Protect the pages from pets, children, rain, and snow.

Never put a cup of coffee or any liquid on the same desk or table as camera-ready copy. Touch the copy only with clean, dry hands, and be careful not to smudge the copy; fingerprints show. Do not wrinkle or fold the paper. Take care that paperclips or binder clips leave no depressions in the paper; the shadow of a groove or furrow can reproduce.

	Proofreader's Error	Misplaced Insertion	Typesetter's Error	
c	other ∧ infrations	nominal fines of $5 or $10. He stopped more cars than he ticketed, checking for these and otherc infrations of the D.C. hack rules.	other infrations ∧	c
ro	the ∧ andins	Prepare the ro andins with the crumbled sheets of paper, kindling wood and logs. Open the damper fully and a torch of crumbled newspapers should be held up to the damper. The draft should pull the flames upward and suppl⸺	the andins ∧	ro
private	one postal offic∧ial	Yet just over a year ago, this column reported that based on before-and-after salary comparisons of a majority of postal officials, only one person took a pay cut to go to work for the U.S. Postal Service. Most got raises of from $2,000 to $7,000 a year, and one postal offiprivatecial doubled his industry salary.	one ∧ postal official	private

Figure 8-H. Proofreader's or typesetter's error?

Use a tissue overlay or a pen or pencil with a nonreproducible color, marking lightly and neatly (marks that are too heavy make corrections difficult and may show up in reproduction), or use margin-only marks or a correction list. (See Chapter 9 for tips on marking camera-ready copy.)

If you are working with photocomposed, camera-ready material that has been processed on stabilization photopaper (S paper), you must keep it out of overly bright light. In some cases bright light can cause fading of type (loss of density). If photocomposed material has been processed on resin-coated paper (RC paper) or similar non-light-sensitive paper, this will not be a problem.

If you are a freelancer, and your negligence or carelessness makes camera-ready copy unusable, you may have to pay for retyping or re-typesetting and reproofreading the work.

When you work with camera-ready copy, remember that it is easy to paint something out. For example, if some items in a list have terminal punctuation and others do not, it is far simpler to achieve consistency by removing the existing punctuation marks than by inserting new ones. Query accordingly.

Photographs

Never use an ordinary pen or pencil to write on the image area or on the back of a photograph; the pressure of the implement can show through. (Some soft-tipped markers avoid this problem.) Do not put a paperclip on a photograph if the clip will extend onto the image area. Write instructions in the margin, on paper taped onto the back, or on an overlay of tissue pasted over the back and folded over the front (use a soft pencil lightly).

Cut and Paste

Never use scissors or paste on a draft or a proof. Editors may cut and paste a draft, but proofreaders may not. (An exception to this might occur if a proofreader is given the extra function of furnishing a dummy for page make-up; in this case, an extra set of proofs, never the printer's set, is used.)

QUESTIONS FOR STUDENTS

1. Write a correction list for all the heads in Figure 8-A.

2. Write a correction list for all the illustrations in Figure 8-B.

3. Find the errors in Figure 8-C.

4. Identify the errors in all the illustrations in Figure 8-D.

5. Describe the precautions to take with camera-ready copy.

Chapter 9

Modified Marking Techniques

Proofreading is my vocation and my obsession. I search for errors
on cereal boxes and in travel folders, mail order catalogues, and
greeting cards. I write proofreader's corrections on letters from
friends and query the instruction sheets that come with new appli-
ances. Some dark night I will take a can of red paint and a brush
to the nearby street sign that reads "Greenfied Rd." and paint a
caret between the e and the d and an l at the side.
--A professional proofreader

CHAPTER OVERVIEW

First, this chapter describes some of the adaptations of standard
marks that are needed for different jobs. Then it shows you how
to mark corrections on copy for typists who do not know proofreading marks. Next, to show you how to handle copy needing major modifications from standard techniques, it describes the following:

- How to mark typed or other camera-ready copy

- How to mark copy in the text only

- How to mark copy in the margins only

- How to write corrections in the text and checkmarks
  in the margin

- How to proofread without marking on the copy.

CAUTION TO PROOFREADING NOVICES

To avoid confusion, do not work the exercises as they are called
out in this chapter. For now, read the chapter only as supple-
mental, background information. When and if you work where modified marks or marking techniques are needed, re-read the applicable
section and then do the accompanying exercise as a starting point.

ADAPTING MARKS

You may sometimes need to adapt the standard marking techniques to
the preferences or needs of an employer or customer, to the typist
or typesetter, or to the particular form of copy.

Adapting Marks to the Employer or Customer

A list of marks may accompany a proofreading job. If a few of the
marks differ from those in Chapters 2 and 3, you will of course use

the marks requested.   There may also be special instructions, such
as the following:

- Mark for correction in one margin only (left or right, as
  specified).

- Mark in both margins but make multiple marks from <u>left to
  right</u> in the right margin and from <u>right to left</u> (beginning at the point closest to the text) in the left margin;
  for example:

f/m   Now is the ti*p*e *f*or all good men t*w*o come to aid. *the of their country*

- Distinguish among printer's errors, callouts, author's
  alterations, and queries (for example, mark printer's
  errors and callouts in red, author's alterations in blue
  followed by "AA," and queries in red).

For practice in adapting marks to a customer's specifications, turn to Exercise 18 in the Workbook.   Novices: See
caution on first page of this chapter.

Adapting Marks to the Typist or Typesetter

You must be certain the typist or typesetter understands standard
marks before you use them.   Even experienced manuscript and editorial typists and computer typesetters may not know all the marks
(we have seen ⅄ translated incorrectly to the word <u>in</u>, and *LOWER-
CASE* misinterpreted as "delete the marked word").   If you have the
smallest doubt of a typist's or typesetter's knowledge of standard
marks, ask for a list of marks that will be understood.   If that
is not available, make a list of the marks you use and submit it
with your work.

Stenographic and secretarial typists may know only a few marks.
When you doubt that standard marks will be understood, give explicit instructions as shown in Figure 9-A, which is an example of
live copy proofread against the dead copy in Figure 4-A.   Compare
these written-out instructions with the standard marks for the same
copy shown in Figure 4-B.

Adapting Marks to the Copy

The stage the live copy is in or the particular form the live copy
takes may require adaptation in marking.   Several kinds of adaptation are discussed in the rest of this chapter.

HOW TO MARK CAMERA-READY COPY

Always try to get a photocopy rather than the camera-ready original.
If you cannot, you must take special precautions in handling and
marking camera-ready copy.   Because this copy, when corrected, will
be photographically reproduced, your marks must not show up on the

change T to I
lower 1

add comma

In J. T. Buckingham's edition of Shakespeare   *add g*

(814) is, at page 915, a remarkable note, apologizing   *change to o*

for a few "trifling errors, and adopting as an excuse   *add close quotes*

a quotation from an advertisement "from the first

edition of Reed 1793":

> He, whose business it is to offer this unusual
>
> apology, very well remembers to have been sitting   *< less space*
> with Dr. Johnson, when an agent from a neighboring
> press brought in a proof sheet of a re-publication,   *take out hyphen*
> requesting to know whether a particular word in it   *and close up*
> *add space* was not corrupted, "So far from it, sir," (replied   *change comma to period*
> *cap D* the doctor with some harshness,) "that the word you
> *suspect* suspect, and would displace, is conspicuously
> *beautiful* beautiful, where it stands, (&) is the only one that   *spell out and*
> *take out do* could do the duty expected of it by Mr. Pope."   *change comma to period*

Figure 9-A. Written-out instructions

reproduction. Use a pen or pencil of a nonreproducing color (usually pale blue because the standard film used for reproducing black-
and-white copy is blind to certain shades of this color). Another
option is to use a tissue overlay as described later in this chapter.

For practice in writing out instructions for corrections,
turn to Exercise 19 in the Workbook. Novices: See caution
on first page of this chapter.

Use of Nonreproducing Pencil

Try to reach a happy medium between marks that are too light and
those that are too heavy.

- Do not mark so heavily that the paper is furrowed or that
  a press or copying machine will reproduce the marks.

- Do not mark so lightly that the typist can see the marks
  only by holding the paper close to the light.

Suggestions: Keep your pencil sharp. When you make a small mark,
put a slash after the mark to call attention to it. Pencils are
not of uniform quality. If you have a bad one, throw it out (or
try first to salvage it by moistening the lead).

HOW TO MARK COPY IN THE MARGINS ONLY

Some copy, such as certain reproduction proofs and photo material, can be marked only in the margins, because the risk of marks being reproduced or damaging type is too great. Photocomposition proofs are sometimes made with extra-wide margins; these are folded over so that the back side can be marked with margin-only marks.

Marking only in the margin takes a little getting used to; the trick is to maintain clarity while giving an instruction as tersely as possible. You must indicate where an error occurs in a line and then show what correction is to be made. You are, in effect, combining in-text and marginal marks.

Insertion and Replacement

To insert or replace one or two characters, write the entire word correctly in the margin, including a caret pointing to the specific change; for example:

Marginal Mark	Error in Text
insert ^	inset
replace ^	replece

To insert or replace an entire word, write the preceding word and, when necessary to avoid confusion, the following word in addition to the insertion or replacement, and point a caret to the change; for example:

Marginal Mark	Error in Text
an entire word ^	insert an word
an entire word ^	replace an whole word

Deletion

For deletion, write out the error in the margin. Using a combination slash and dele (or, when appropriate, the in-text sign for delete-and-close-up), show what to take out; for example:

Marginal Mark	Error in Text
deletee	deletee
del(e)ete	deleete

Figure 9-C is an example of copy with marginal marks only.

For practice in marking copy in the margins only, turn to Exercise 21 in the Workbook.

In
814

Reeds

Tn J. T. Buckinham's edition of Shakespeare

(814) is, at page 915, a remarkable note, apoligizing

for a few "trifling errors, and adopting as an excuse

a quotation from an advertisement "from the first

edition of Reed 1793":

He, whose business it is to offer this unusual

apology, very well remembers to have been sitting
with Dr. Johnson, when an agent from a neighboring
press brought in a proof sheet of a re-publication,
requesting to know whether a particular word in it
wasnot corrupted, "So far from it, sir," (replied
the doctor with some harshness,) "that the word you
susepct, and would displace, is conspicuously
beautifull where it stands, & is the only one that
could do do the duty expected of it by Mr, Pope."

Buckingham's

apologizing

errors,"

< less #

ref publication

corrupted

& and

Mr

was # not

Doctor

suspect,

beautifull

do

Figure 9-C. Copy marked in margins only

HOW TO MARK COPY IN THE TEXT ONLY

Some kinds of copy must be marked in the text only (this is never
true of camera-ready copy). When and why this is done are explained in the following paragraphs. There are two ways to do
this: by making corrections yourself and by using editor's marks.

Making Corrections Yourself

You may need to make the corrections yourself. For example, if a
typewritten draft will not be corrected by the typist before going
to a reviewer who does not know proofreader's symbols, you must
correct the errors right on the copy.

Do not use proofreader's or editor's symbols. Just make the necessary changes right on the copy as you go along. You will have to
use your judgment on how to do this neatly and unambiguously. Some
suggestions follow.

Insertion

If there is room, write the missing character right on the line;
there is always room for punctuation marks. If a missing character or word
falls at the end of a line, write it right on the line. If there
is no room, write a caret in the line and write the missing
charter(s) above the line; but if copy out is more than three or four

words, consult your supervisor: You may be asked to type the correction yourself and cut and paste it in place, or you may be asked to write a correction slip and return the job to the typist for this kind of correction only. Mark missing space between words with a straight line.

Replacement

Change punctuation by writing over the error; for example:

Period changed to comma: ,

Comma changed to period: .

Period changed to parenthesis: (

If necessary, use white opaquing fluid; for example:

Colon changes to period: . (the top is painted out)

Semicolon changed to period: (the top and part of the bottom are painted out)

Change wrong letters when it can be done neatly; for example:

c to d: d   o to b: b

When necessary, slash or cross through wrong letters and words and write the correction above the sign. Use your judgment on correcting lowercase and caps; for example:

r to R: R   L to l: ł

P to R: R   A to a: A

Deletion

Do not use the delete sign. Simply slash a character, cross through a word word or, when appropriate, use the in-text delete-and-close-up sign.

Transposition

Use the in-text curve for transposition.

Other Marks

To close up entirely, use two curves. To close up part way, use only the top curve. Do not worry about one extra space between words. Forget small mechanical imperfections; they do not matter so long as you can read a character or word.

Figure 9-D is an example of corrections made directly by a proofreader.

For practice in making corrections yourself, turn to Exercise 22 in the Workbook.

In J. T. Buckinham's edition of Shakespeare
(1814) is, at page 915, a remarkable note, apologizing
for a few "trifling errors," and adopting as an excuse
a quotation from an advertisement "from the first
edition of Reed, 1793":

He, whose business it is to offer this unusual

— < *less space*

apology, very well remembers to have been sitting
with Dr. Johnson, when an agent from a neighboring
press brought in a proof sheet of a republication,
requesting to know whether a particular word in it
was not corrupted. "So far from it, sir," (replied
the doctor with some harshness,) "that the word you
suspect, and would displace, is conspicuously
beautiful where it stands, *and* is the only one that
could do the duty expected of it by Mr. Pope."

Figure 9-D. Corrections made directly by a proofreader

Using Editor's Symbols

You may need to use editor's symbols (in-text marks only)--for example, if a clean typewritten draft is to go directly to a typesetter
without returning to a typist for correction. Professional typesetters are as familiar with editor's marks as they are with proofreader's. For the first typesetting, editor's marks are more efficient
(proofreader's marks are designed for revising copy). Editor's marks
are made as follows:

Write changes and corrections that won't fit on the line above the
line, never below. If a correction is too long to fit, a conscientious editor types it and inserts it in place by cutting and pasting;
proofreaders using editor's marks, however, must treat this problem
as instructed, perhaps by writing correction slips (described later
in this chapter).

Insertion

Use a caret for *marking the place an* and write *an* insertion above the line; use hooks on an
inserted character only when *on* necessary for clarity.

Replacement

To mark replacements, cross through or sl/sh the error and write the correction ~~over~~ *above* the line.

Deletion

Mark deletions with the editor's loop, horizontally for more than one ~~character~~ character, vertically for a single character. Use the delete-and-close-up sign where appropriate.

When a deletion or another mark is made ~~in error~~, stet it (mark dots or dashes under it and write <u>stet</u> in the text or margin) to indicate that the original copy should be restored.

Transposition

Mark transpositions boldly--As, both (transpositions)(simple) and (ones)(complex)(more).

Other Marks

Give typographical instructions with proofreader's in-text marks: <u>italic</u>, <u>small caps</u>, <u>full caps</u>, boldface. Use a slash (without the delete loop) for lowercase; put a "roof" on it for more than one CHARACTER.

Use the space mark to show where to insert space, the close-up sign to show where to take out space. Circle (abbrevs.) to be spelled out. Mark a new paragraph with the paragraph sign or a right angle (see below). When a line is to run into the next, show this with your pencil. Mark punctuation with care. You may be able to write some marks directly; you may need to use symbols for others, such as a comma's subscript and an apostrophe's superscript. To change a comma to a period, circle it. Mark dashes according to their length; for example, en (short dash)   April 5/6; em (long) dash: Q. Why?—-A.   I don't

know.   Make a double line mark for a hyphen.   Mark words divided

at the end of a line either to close up or to retain the hyphen;

for example:

>   . . . . . proof-
>   reading
>
>   . . . . . in=
>   text marks

Figure 9-E is an example of corrections marked with editor's
symbols.

For practice in marking with editor's symbols, turn to
Exercise 23 in the Workbook.

In J. T. Buckingham's edition of Shakespeare

(1814) is, at page 915, a remarkable note, apologizing

for a few "trifling errors," and adopting as an excuse

a quotation from an advertisement "from the first

edition of Reed, 1793":

He, whose business it is to offer this unusual
apology, very well remembers to have been sitting
with Dr. Johnson, when an agent from a neighboring
press brought in a proof sheet of a re-publication,
requesting to know whether a particular word in it
was not corrupted. "So far from it, sir," (replied
the doctor with some harshness,) "that the word you
suspect, and would displace, is conspicuously
beautiful where it stands, & is the only one that
could do do the duty expected of it by Mr. Pope."

Figure 9-E.   Corrections with editor's symbols

HOW TO WRITE MARKS FOR CORRECTION IN THE TEXT AND CHECKMARKS IN THE MARGINS

Some offices that produce copy with plenty of space between lines
have adopted a marking technique combining in-text corrections--the
same as editor's marks--with marginal checkmarks. Many computer
printouts adapt to this kind of marking technique. A few lines
from such a printout, marked for correction, follow:

0049   001   [EM]For the first couple of weeks ih April,   ✓

0050   002   domestic travel continued to run ''very

0051   003   strong, an industry spokesmen said.[QL]   ✓

Figure 9-F shows this system used in an example.

[/M] In J. T. Buckingham's edition of Shakespeare (1814) is at   ✓✓

page 915, a remarkable note, apologizing for a few "trifling   ✓

errors, and adopting as an excuse a quotation from an advertise-   ✓

ment "from the first edition of Reed 1793": [QL]   ✓

[//M] He, whose business it is to offer this unusual apology,

very well remembers to have been sitting with Dr. Johnson,

when an agent from a neighboring press brought in a proof

sheet of a refpublication, requesting to know whether a   ✓

particular word in it wasnot corrupted/ "So far from it,   ✓✓

sir," (replied the doctor with some harshness,) "that the   ✓

word you suspect, and would displace, is conspicuously   ✓

beautiful where it stands, (&) is the only one that could do   ✓✓✓

do the duty expected of it by Mr Pope."   ✓

Figure 9-F. Corrections in the text and checkmarks in the margin

---

For practice in writing marks for correction in the text
and checkmarks in the margin, turn to Exercise 24 in the
Workbook.

HOW TO PROOFREAD WITHOUT MARKING ON THE COPY

No proofreading marks are permitted on some repros, on direct-use typed copy such as letters and address labels, and on mimeograph stencils. How to prepare a correction list (handwritten or typewritten) or handwritten correction slips is described in the following paragraphs.

Another possibility is to use an overlay of tracing paper attached to the back of the paper and folded over the front. (A later section in this chapter, Special Techniques, discusses this overlay procedure.)

Correction Lists

When preparing a correction list, label it as such and with the name of the job. Organize the list in columns (on lined paper if handwritten) as shown in Figures 9-H and 9-I, which list the errors made in Figure 9-G. Cite the draft page, paragraph, and line number* only when it is necessary to refer to the draft to make a correction, as when copy is omitted or the draft is illegible. When draft and final copy are the same, there is no need to refer to the draft; do not take the time to do it.

Handwritten Correction Lists

Handwritten correction lists lend themselves to the use of standard proofreader's marks. The last two columns are headed "Error" and "Correction," as shown in Figure 9-H, and amount to almost the same thing as in-text and marginal marks. A proofreader has to make very little adjustment to write such a list. The main thing is to take the time to write very legibly.

For practice in making a handwritten correction list, turn to Exercise 25 in the Workbook.

Typewritten Correction Lists

Typewritten correction lists must be handled differently from handwritten lists. The last two columns are headed "Corrected Error" and "Correction to Make," as shown in Figure 9-I, and amount to spelling out the instructions.

For practice in making a typewritten correction list, turn to Exercise 26 in the Workbook.

---

*When a paragraph is cited, the line number is a subdivision of the paragraph; every paragraph begins with line 1.

Tn J. T. Buckinham's edition of Shakespeare
1
(814) is, at page 915, a remarkable note, apoligizing

for a few "trifling errors, and adopting as an excuse

a quotation from an advertisement "from the first

edition of Reed 1793":

He, whose business it is to offer this unusual

apology, very well remembers to have been sitting
with Dr. Johnson, when an agent from a neighboring
press brought in a proof sheet of a re-publication,
requesting to know whether a particular word in it
wasnot corrupted, "So far from it, sir," (replied
the doctor with some harshness,) "that the word you
susepct, and would displace, is conspicuously
beautifull where it stands, & is the only one that
could do do the duty expected of it by Mr, Pope."

Figure 9-G. Live copy to be proofread without marking it
             (dead copy appears in Figure 4-A)

Correction List for Proofreading Manual, Figure 9-G

| Draft | | | Final | | | | |
Pg.	Para.	Line	Pg.	Para.	Line	Error	Correction
				1	1	Tn Buckinham's	
					2	⌐¬814^ apoligizing	
					3	errors,^ and	
					5	Reed^ 1793	less # between lines
				2	1-2	re-publication	3
					4	wasnot	#
					6	corrupted⋌	⊙
					4 up	doctor	D
					3 up	susepct	tr
					2 up	beautifull	∫
						&	sp
					last	do do	∫
						Mr,	⊙

Figure 9-H. Handwritten correction list (corrections
             of errors in Figure 9-G)

Correction List
for Proofreading Manual, Figure 9-G

Draft			Final				
Pg.	Para.	Line	Pg.	Para.	Line	Corrected Error	Correction to Make
				1	1	In	change T to I
						Buckingham	add g
					2	1814	lower 1
						apologizing	change i to o
					3	errors,"	add end quotes
					5	Reed,	add ,
				2	1-2	--	delete space btwn lines
					4	republication	delete hyph and close up
					6	was not	add space
						corrupted.	change , to .
					4 up	Doctor	cap D
					3 up	suspect	tr p and e
					2 up	beautiful	delete l
						and	spell out &
					last	do the duty	delete extra do
						Mr,	change , to .

Figure 9-I.   Typewritten correction list

Correction Slips

Correction slips are notes on small pieces of paper attached to
the relevant pages. You can use Scotch Post-it® adhesive slips,
which come in several sizes, or you can use sheets from a small
(perhaps 3" X 5") pad, attached with paperclips or with drafting
tape.

yuk — never

To write a correction slip:

1. Use a dark-colored pen or pencil (never use light green
   or nonphoto blue; these colors do not photocopy and are
   hard to see). *amen*

2. Write very legibly. *amen*

3. Cite the final copy's page number on each slip. (Cite *amen*
   the draft page number only when the typist or author
   must refer to the draft--for example, when copy has
   been omitted.) *because the slip can fall off and often does*

4. Be concise, but remember that although brevity is important, clarity is paramount (the use of proofreader's marks often helps to achieve both, as the example in Figure 9-H shows).

5. Label the slip "Cx," if necessary, to distinguish it from a query slip (labeled Q). You might also use <u>different</u> <u>colors</u> of paper for correction and query slips. *great*

so write it out if in doubt over-explaining is better

Figure 9-J.   Correction slip (corrections of first three errors in Figure 9-G)

Comparison of Query Slips and Correction Slips

In general, query slips differ from correction slips in that question marks and explanations are added. For a description of query slips, see Chapter 7.

Text	Query Slip	Correction Slip
I found a million dollar baby in a 5 and ten cent store.	*five /?* *(for consistency)*	⑤ sp
Roses are red; violets are blue, sugar is sweet, and so are you.	*red ⸝ ↱ /?* *(like "blue," etc.)*	*red ⸝ ↱*
Invitation is the sincerest form of flattery.	*Imitation /?* ~~Invitation~~	*Imitation* ~~Invitation~~

Use of Line Counters

You may use the appropriate line counter (provided in the Workbook) to write correction lists or slips to save time and eliminate the counting of paragraphs, but only if you are certain that the recipient of the correction list also has a counter.

SPECIAL TECHNIQUES

Flags

Use flags when they would be helpful to call attention to errors. You may flag dead copy to help the typesetter find omitted copy, ← *vital* and you may flag live copy to help the editor find queries or, in a job in which very few pages have been marked, to help the typesetter find those few.

You can buy metal, plastic, or paper "signals" at office supply stores; the detachable kind that protrudes beyond the edge of a page is best. You can attach small Scotch Post-it® sheets so they act as flags. It's easy to make your own flags, however. Here's how:

1. Cut a sheet of paper (preferably bright construction paper) into 14 triangles:

   (a) Fold the sheet in half, again in half, and yet again in half, dividing it into eight rectangles.

   (b) Open up the folded paper, draw lines, and cut triangles out of each rectangle.

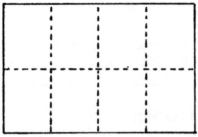

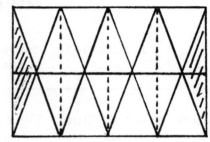

(a) Fold on dotted lines   (b) Cut on solid lines

2. Attach a triangle to the top of a page:

   (a) Make a fold about one inch deep at the base of the triangle. Place the fold over the edge of the paper with the triangle pointing down.

   (b) About an inch from the first fold, make a second fold so the triangle points up.

   (c) Fasten the flag with one or two ~~paperclips~~. *pieces of artist tape*

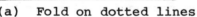

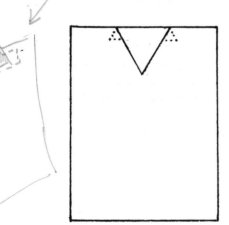

How about just magic tape on the back of the mms. pg

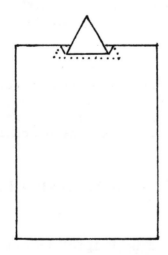

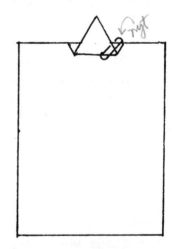

(a) Fold down   (b) Fold up   (c) ~~Fasten~~ *tape*

How to Mark Copy With No Margins

Three techniques are useful for proofreading typed or printed copy
with no margins:

1. Add a margin. If the copy is a galley or a photocopy, cut
a rectangular wing of paper and attach it to the back of the
copy with tape or adhesive (not staples). If the copy is
camera-ready, you must use drafting tape or masking tape
(because it is easily removable). Cut tape the length of
the page. Use a straightedge and draw a centerline down the
full length of the tape's sticky side. Holding copy type-
side up, place it on the tape with its righthand edge against
the centerline. Place the margin on the other side of the
tape. Gently rub your finger down the tape on both sides
to attach the tape securely. The following figure shows
the finished page.*

Copy . . .   . . . Added Margin

2. Use tracing paper. Take a sheet of tracing paper (or any
see-through paper) the appropriate size for the copy, and
make a half-inch horizontal fold across the top. Attach
the folded section to the back of the copy with masking
tape. Read the copy through the tracing paper and make
proofreader's marks right on the tracing paper. Be careful
with camera-ready copy; if you have a heavy hand, your marks
may leave dents that can be picked up by the camera. The
following figure illustrates the technique.

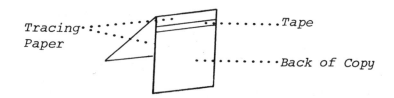

Tracing Paper · : · · · · · · · · · · · · · · · · · · Tape

· · · · · · · · · · Back of Copy

Not recommended. Bad for typesetter →

3. Write correction lists or slips as explained in this chapter.
Write query lists or slips as explained in Chapter 7.

To review the standard marking techniques, turn to Exercise 27 in the Workbook.

*You can buy ready-made "Add-A-Margin" sheets with adhesive edges.
Write Quill Corp., 3200 Arnold La., Northbrook, IL 60062 for their
catalogue.

4. Photocopy onto larger paper. Reducing size of type may be practical in some cases

5. Paste onto larger paper

QUESTIONS FOR STUDENTS

1.   Explain some of the variations from standard techniques a job might call for.

2.   When you are not allowed to mark on the live copy, describe three techniques that can be used to indicate what corrections must be made.

3.   For what kind of copy is light blue pencil used?

4.   For what form of correction should light blue pencil not be used?

5.   Mark list (1) as you would for a typist who knows no proofreading marks, list (2) as camera-ready typing, list (3) as repros to be marked in the margins only, and list (4) as copy to go directly to an author who does not know proofreading marks.

(1) proefreading	(3) proefreading
pro ofreading	pro ofreading
poofreading	poofreading
porofreading	porofreading
proofreadinga	proofreadinga
prooofreading	prooofreading
p^{ro}ofreading	p^{ro}ofreading
pRoofreading	pRoofreading
(2) proefreading	(4) proefreading
pro ofreading	pro ofreading
poofreading	poofreading
porofreading	porofreading
proofreadinga	proofreadinga
prooofreading	prooofreading
p^{ro}ofreading	p^{ro}ofreading
pRoofreading	pRoofreading

Part II
Specifications and Standards

In-text Marks

Use only underlines and carets. Do not touch the characters with
your pencil; they may not reproduce clearly if you do.

    Wrong: Now is the tame for all good prooffers
           to go to my aid   *i/J̃ come*

    Right: Now is the tame for all good prooffers
           to go to my âid   *i/J̃ come*

Marginal Marks

Use standard marks as described in Chapters 2 and 3, but keep your
marks minimal in size and length. If you must write an instruction
longer than a word or two, use a separate correction slip (as described later in this chapter). If the dimensions of the image
area or live matter area (the rectangle the camera will photograph)
are specified, or if the copy is marked to show the limits of the
image area, write the marginal marks outside the area. Initial the
copy on a back corner. Write all queries on separate query slips
or in a separate list (see Chapter 7).

Figure 9-B shows an example of marks on typewritten, camera-ready
copy proofread against the dead copy in Figure 4-A. Note that the
marks in this example are shown in black, the wrong color for the
purpose.

For practice in marking typewritten camera-ready copy, turn
to Exercise 20 in the Workbook.

I/g
U

        1   Tn J. T. Buckinham's edition of Shakespeare

(814) is, at page 915, a remarkable note, apoligizing   o

for a few "trifling errors, and adopting as an excuse   "

a quotation from an advertisement "from the first

    ◊̂   edition of Reed 1793":

        He, whose business it is to offer this unusual

                                                    —⟨ *less* #

apology, very well remembers to have been sitting
with Dr. Johnson, when an agent from a neighboring
press brought in a proof sheet of a re-publication,   J̃
requesting to know whether a particular word in it
   wasnot corrupted, "So far from it, sir," (replied
the doctor with some harshness,) "that the word you
susepct, and would displace, is conspicuously
beautifull where it stands, & is the only one that   Ⓐⓟ
could do do the duty expected of it by Mr, Pope."   ⊙

Figure 9-B. Marks on typed camera-ready copy (marks shown here
in black must be in nonreproducing color)

Chapter 10

Type and Its Specification

Have you noticed how picturesque the letter Y is and how innumer-
able its meanings are? The tree is a Y, the junction of two roads
forms a Y, two converging rivers, a donkey's head and that of an ox,
the glass with its stem, the lily on its stalks and the beggar lift-
ing his arms are a Y. This observation can be extended to everything that constitutes the various letters devised by man. Whatever
there is in the demotic language has been instilled into it by the
hieratic language. Hieroglyphics are the root of letters. All
characters were originally signs and all signs were once images.
Human society, the world, man in his entirety is in the alphabet.
Masonry, astronomy, philosophy, all sciences start here, impercep-
tible but real, and it must be so. The alphabet is a source.

A is the roof with its rafters and traverse-beam, the arch "arx",
or it is like two friends who embrace and shake hands. D is the
back, and B is a D on a second D, that is a "double back",--
bump; C is the crescent, is the moon, E is the foundation, the
pillar and the roof--all architecture contained in a single letter. F is the gallows, the fork, G is the horn, H is the facade
of a building with its two towers, I is the war-machine that
throws projectiles, J is the plough, the horn of plenty, K signifies one of the basic laws of geometry: the angle of reflection
is equal to the angle of incidence, L is the leg and the foot,
M is the mountain, or the camp within its tents, N is the door,
closed with a cross-bar, O is the sun, the porter P is carrying
a burden, Q is the croup and the tail, R signifies rest, the porter leaning on his stick, S is the snake, T is the hammer, U is
the urn, V is the vase (that is why U and V are often confused).
I have already said what Y signifies. X signifies crossed swords,
combat--who will be victor? Nobody knows--that is why philos-
ophers used "X" to signify fate, and the mathematicians took it
for the unknown. Z is the lightning--is God.

--Victor Hugo

CHAPTER OVERVIEW

To interpret specifications given to the typesetter and printer and
to detect substandard quality in typeset copy, proofreaders must
know some of the basic elements of typography. This chapter tells
you how to interpret typographic specifications, how to measure
type and spaces, and how to recognize typefaces. Some of the information will also help you understand typewriter type.

This chapter and those that follow introduce many terms from the
vocabulary of typography and printing. If you are a novice, do not
worry about memorizing all these new words; only the concepts are
important for you to understand. Use the index to come back to
these chapters when you need a specific definition or explanation.

INTRODUCTION

Specifications take several forms. One set of specs is the job order, spec sheet, or other instructions to the typesetter and printer. (See Example of Specifications to the Printer in Part III.) Proofreaders do not always see these specs. Proofreading is often detective work--deducing from the evidence what the specs are; this manual will help you become a better detective.

p. 345).

At any stage of production, the dead copy provides specs for the live copy. In the first proofreading, the dead copy's text with its editor's marks and typemarks serves as specs. You already know some of these marks--those that tell the typesetter to set caps, small caps, and italic, for example. This chapter will introduce you to other typemarks.

In proofreading revises, proofreading marks in the dead copy are specs for the live copy. When page proofs are made, a dummy (as described in Chapter 13) may serve as specs.

This and the next few chapters are a bare beginning to the subjects of typography and typographic specifications. As technology advances, thorough knowledge of the subject will become increasingly necessary for proficiency in proofreading.

Many experts expect computer-based phototypesetting and word processing machines to replace the typewriter eventually, as they are now replacing other typesetting equipment. Typewriter faces will give way to such faces as Times Roman and Univers. Typographers will design formats to be programmed into tapes, disks, or cassettes; a typist with a few hours training will be able to produce a page of the quality that used to require seven years of apprenticeship. (Although typists will not actually be "creating" the page, they will provide the keyboarding.)

Advanced technology will not eliminate the need for proofreading, but it will affect _how_ proofreading is done--what will be involved in the proofreading process--and in some cases _where_ it is done. (Eventually, proofreaders may have, in their homes, video display terminals [VDT's] on which to do their work. The VDT's will be linked, via telecommunication, to a central computer.)

WHAT TYPOGRAPHIC SPECIFICATIONS INCLUDE

Style is divided into two categories (which may often overlap):

- _Typographic style_--the selection and arrangement of type in text and display, and the arrangement of tables and illustrations. For typewriter copy, typographic style is synonymous with _format_.

- _Editorial style_--the rules followed for consistency in such matters as spelling, capitalization, punctuation, compounding, word division, abbreviation, use of numerals and symbols, and use of italic and underlines. Editorial style is discussed in later chapters.

Typographic style is specified in instructions for text, heads, and all displayed matter. The specs should include the following, to cover every line of type and white space:

- Typeface--in text and display matter

- Type weight and form

- Type size

- Capitalization of heads--for example: all caps, all small caps, caps and lowercase (Clc--important words capped), initial caps (only first letter and proper nouns capped), all lowercase, caps and small caps

- Letterspacing, if any (see Chapter 12) *p. 209*

- Vertical position--leading or linespacing for lines of text (primary lead), for spacing between paragraphs or blocks of type (secondary lead), and for display; sink (distance from top of page to first line)

- Line measure (column width), if copy is justified or set to a particular width or image area

- Margins (for typescript and mechanicals)

- Horizontal position--centered, flush left, flush right, indented, justified, ragged left, ragged right, or ragged left and right

- Special treatment--boxes, underlines, initial letters, ornaments, borders, rules, sidebars (short secondary stories that develop the minor facts of the major story, set off typographically), and so forth.

TYPE MEASUREMENT

Points and Picas

"Printer's measure" is a system called the point system. It has two units:

1. The point--approximately 1/72 inch--is used to express measurements such as type size or the thickness of leads and rules.

Figure 10-A illustrates rule sizes.

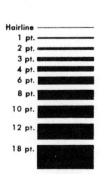

Figure 10-A. Rule sizes

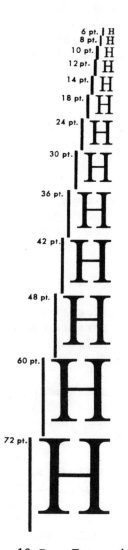

Figure 10-B. Type sizes

On Figure 10-B, which illustrates type sizes, the heavy vertical line shows the true size; the white space above and below the capital H_ represents the space necessary to accommodate the ascending and descending strokes in lowercase characters such as b_ and j_.

2. The pica (pronounced pike-uh)-- approximately 1/6 inch and equal to 12 points--is used to express larger measurements, such as line width, margin width, and column depth. Everyone working with type should know these equivalents:

        12 points = 1 pica
         6 picas = 1 inch
        72 points = 1 inch

(Actually, 6 picas equal .99648 inch in British, Canadian, and American usage, but for all practical purposes, 6 picas equal a full inch.) Figure 10-C shows the relationship between picas and inches.

Printer's measure is not normally given in decimals. For example, 13.9 picas usually means 13 picas, 9 points (not 13-9/10 picas).

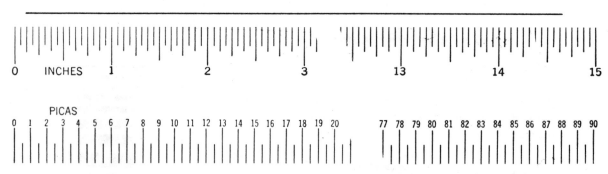

Figure 10-C. Pica and inch ruler

The Metric System

The following equivalents and conversion formulas may be helpful when conversion to the metric system is complete:

Inch-centimeter equivalents:	1 inch = 2.54 centimeters
	1 centimeter = .3937 inches
Inch-centimeter conversion:	inches X 2.54 = centimeters
	centimeters X .3937 = inches
Point-centimeter equivalents:	1 point = .351 millimeters
	(.0351 centimeters)
	1 centimeter = 28.57 points
Point-centimeter conversion:	points X .0351 = centimeters
	centimeters X 28.57 = points
Pica-centimeter equivalents:	1 pica = .4212 centimeters
	1 centimeter = 2.38 picas
Pica-centimeter conversion:	picas X .4212 = centimeters
	centimeters X 2.38 = picas

Type Size

Type size is measured in points. Type up to 14 points in size is usually used for text or body type. Larger type is usually used for display, as in heads.

You cannot easily measure the size of printed letters with a line gauge. Different faces of the same size fill different amounts of vertical space. Compare Cheltenham and Times New Roman, both in 36-point type:

abcde   Cheltenham

abcde   Times
        New Roman

To measure type, some typesetters may provide a transparent sheet of type samples, such as the one from which Figure 10-D is printed. Usually, however, you will use a line gauge and measure the depth of lines--type size plus leading.

Ems and Ens

Type and space may be measured in ems and ens.

The em is a variable unit; its size depends on the typeface being used. An em is a square the width and depth of the type size. For example, in 12-point type, an em is 12 points wide and 12 points deep; in 18-point type, an em is 18 points wide and deep.

The mark for an em quad (▢) or for multiple em quads (for example, ▭ or ▣) may be used to specify white space anywhere in

Helios
6E   7E   8E   9E   10E   11E   12E   14E   18E   24E   30E   36E

English
6E   7E   8E   9E   10E   11E   12E   14E   18E   24E   30E   36E

Oracle
6E   7E   8E   9E   10E   11E   12E   14E   18E   24E   30E   36E

Souvenir
6E   7E   8E   9E   10E   11E   12E   14E   18E   24E   30E   36E

Serif Gothic
6E   7E   8E   9E   10E   11E   12E   14E   18E   24E   30E   36E

Tiffany
6E   7E   8E   9E   10E   11E   12E   14E   18E   24E   30E   36E

Ronda
6E   7E   8E   9E   10E   11E   12E   14E   18E   4E   30E   36E

Avant Garde
6E   7E   8E   9E   10E   11E   12E   14E   18E   24E   30E   36E

Engraver's Text
6E   7E   8E   9E   10E   11E   12E   14E   18E   24E   30E   36E

Paladium
6E   7E   8E   9E   10E   11E   12E   14E   18E   24E   30E   36E

Holland Seminar
6E   7E   8E   9E   10E   11E   12E   14E   18E   24E   30E   36E

Original Script
6E   7E   8E   9E   10E   11E   12E   14E   18E   24E   30E   36E

Commercial Script
6E   7E   8E   9E   10E   11E   12E   14E   18E   24E   30E   36E

Figure 10-D. Type samples in different sizes

the text--paragraph indention (1 em is the standard indention),
space between columns, and so on.

An em dash is a dash line 1 em wide (marked $\frac{1}{M}$).

Some typesetters charge by the em measurement; for example, their
cost can be based on the price per 1,000 ems of type set.

An en is one-half the width of an em. For example, in 12-point
type, an en is 6 points wide (but 12 points deep).

Because a single digit or a fraction set as one character is, in
most fonts, 1 en wide, an en space is also called a figure space
or a fraction space. (An en space is the same thing as an en
quad.) Some leader dots are 1 en apart. An en dash (marked $\frac{1}{N}$)
is a dash line 1 en wide.

To be sure you are understood, you might follow the custom of
calling an em quad a mutton quad, an en quad a nut quad, an
em dash a Mary dash, an en dash a Nancy dash.

Note that in newer typesetting methods, the word "quad" as a
noun has been replaced by the word "space," as in "em space" and
"en space." In computer composition, "quad" is a verb: "to quad
left," for example, means to set characters flush left and fill
out the line with space.

Agate Lines

Until the point system was established, type sizes were designated
by name. Agate (5-1/2 points) is one of the names still in use.
(Another is pica and another nonpareil--a half pica.)

Agate lines are measurements used by newspapers and magazines, primarily in classified ads. They measure space, not type. There
are 14 agate lines to the column inch--that is, a newspaper space
1 column wide and 1 inch deep contains 14 agate lines. A space 2
columns wide and 1 inch deep contains 28 agate lines; the mark-up
for such a space might read, "14 agate lines on 2 cols."

Wordspacing

Most typesetting machines (and some typewriters) provide a way to
vary minutely the width of spaces between words. Because of this
spacing variability, a line can be justified and still have equal
spacing (or at least the appearance of equal spacing) between the
words in it.

To illustrate spacing variability, Figure 10-E shows the size of
spaces available to the typesetter of handset metal type. The
typesetter sets a line with a standard-size space between words.
When the line is too short, the typesetter adds or replaces spaces
in any combination that will justify the line and keep the appearance of equal wordspacing in that line.

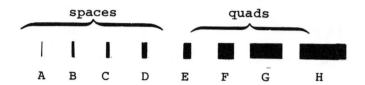

Key: A. Hair space   E. En quad
      B. 5-em (5-to-the-em) space   F. Em quad
      C. 4-em (4-to-the-em) space   G. 2-em quad
      D. 3-em (3-to-the-em) space   H. 3-em quad

Figure 10-E. Relative size of spaces and quads
              in 12-point handset type

Thick spaces (3-to-the-em) were for many years the standard size
used between lowercase words in roman text. Closer spacing then
became the custom, with 4-to-the-em and even 5-to-the-em spaces
(thin spaces) the standard, depending on the amount of leading
(wider spacing may be called for in leaded matter than in unleaded
matter).

Typesetting machines adjust wordspacing automatically to justify
a line. On many machines, fine adjustments of space are often
possible (54 units to the em is not uncommon in phototypesetting).
The terms "hair space," "thin space," and "thick space" are still
used, but their meanings have changed. For example, at least one
phototypesetting machine has a key labeled "thin sp" that sets a
3-to-the-em space; on some computers, the key labeled "thin space"
is used to _tie_ a space--to prevent it from stretching (for instance,
to prevent an apostrophe _s_ from being set as a separate word).

Linespacing (Leading)

Lines of type are often _opened up_ (aired) by inserting extra spacing between them.

In handset type, extra space between lines is created by inserting
strips of metal called _leading_ (pronounced "ledding").

A typesetting machine can be set so that each line includes added
leading or linespacing.

Lines of type are sized in two figures: (1) the type size and
(2) the type size plus added leading. For example, a line is called
"8 on 10" when 8-point type is set with 2 added points of lead (8-
point type set in a line 10 points deep).

In hot metal, leading is the space between lines. In cold type,
leading is the measurement from baseline to baseline, as shown
in Figure 10-F.

type line   --6 pt. lead } 12 pt. type
type line   } 12 pt.type } on 18 pt. body
type line

type line   } 12 pt. type
type line   } on 18 pt. lead
type line

Hot metal leading (12/18)   Cold type leading (12/18)

Figure 10-F. Leading in hot metal and cold type

Photocomposition may be minus leaded--that is, the space between
lines decreased rather than increased. Figure 10-G shows several
examples of leading.

10/9½	Among the many factors determining a typographer's choice of leading are the length of the line, the size of the type, and the x-height, set width, and comparative legibility of the typeface.
10/10	Among the many factors determining a typographer's choice of leading are the length of the line, the size of the type, and the x-height, set width, and comparative legibility of the typeface.
10/11	Among the many factors determining a typographer's choice of leading are the length of the line, the size of the type, and the x-height, set width, and comparative legibility of the typeface.
10/12	Among the many factors determining a typographer's choice of leading are the length of the line, the size of the type, and the x-height, set width, and comparative legibility of the typeface.
10/13	Among the many factors determining a typographer's choice of leading are the length of the line, the size of the type, and the x-height, set width, and comparative legibility of the typeface.
10/14	Among the many factors determining a typographer's choice of leading are the length of the line, the size of the type, and the x-height, set width, and comparative legibility of the typeface.
10/20	Among the many factors determining a typographer's choice of leading are the length of the line, the size of the type, and the x-height, set width, and

Figure 10-G. Examples of different leading for 10-point type

Leading may be specified as optical (opt or visual); the typesetter
will insert space to give the appearance of the amount specified.
Such insertion is done, for example, in the case of a line of

capital letters that will have a base of blank space (for the descenders of lowercase letters in the same font) beneath the baseline.

Narrow columns (14 picas wide or less) usually have less leading than wide columns (20 picas wide or more).

Normally, when you find unequal leading, you need not specify the exact size needed; mark only to add or to delete lead (with an extended caron in text and "ld" or "𝕵 ld" in the margin). Your eye should be good enough, however, to catch a line with a 1-point difference in leading.

TYPEFACE RECOGNITION

Names of Typefaces

A typeface may be named for its original designer (Baskerville; Bodoni, Garamond, Goudy); for its use (Times New Roman was designed for the London Times; Century and Avant Garde were designed for Century and Avant Garde magazines); for its characteristics (Excelsior and Paragon were designed for high legibility); or for its designer's fancy (Souvenir, Centaur, Perpetua).

Typefaces have generic names as well as brand names; for example, different manufacturers call Caledonia different names, including Caledo, Balmoral, Highland, California, Edinburgh, and Laurel.

Different manufacturers' versions of the same typeface differ slightly from each other. You can, for example, seldom interchange one manufacturer's 10-point Baskerville with another's.

Variables in Standard Typefaces

The differences among the hundreds of thousands of typefaces can be minute. An untrained eye cannot distinguish even gross differences. To identify type or recognize a wrong font, you must know what the variables are.

Basic Parts of Letterforms

A few basic terms for the parts of letterforms are illustrated in Figure 10-H.

Figure 10-H. Parts of letterforms

- X-height is the height of the lowercase letter x and of letters a, c, e, m, n, o, r, s, u, v, w, and z.

- Ascenders are the strokes of lowercase letters extending above x-height; letters b, d, f, h, k, l, and t have ascenders.

- Descenders are strokes extending below the baseline; letters g, j, p, q, and y have descenders, as does capital Q and, in many typefaces, capital J.

- The baseline is the bottom line (excluding descenders) of lowercase letters and most capital letters.

- Cap height is the height of capital letters. Depending on type design, caps may be taller or shorter than ascenders, or both may be the same height.

Serifs and Other Terminations

Serifs are the small strokes and crosslines at the ends of major lines. Figure 10-I shows a capital R with its serifs separated from its major lines. (Some typefaces, called sans serif*, do not have serifs.) The serif is often the most important identifying element in a type design. Serifs come in many varieties; Figure 10-J shows just a few.

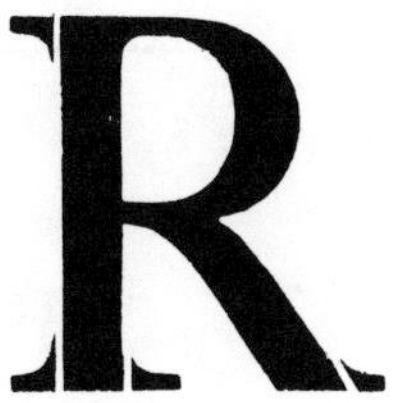

Figure 10-I. Serifs separated from main lines

Other terminations of letterstrokes, such as the hooks (tails) of many t's, the finials of such letters as f, j, y, and g, and the loop of the g are all identifiers. In fact, lowercase g alone often provides a clue to typeface identification. Figure 10-K shows a few identifiers.

Figure 10-J. Varieties of serifs

*"Sans," French for "without," in this phrase has a thoroughly anglicized pronunciation; "sans serif" rhymes with "Dan's tariff."

t ^{t} $_t$ t t $_t$ t g g g g g $_g$ g g

Figure 10-K.   Typeface identifiers

Thick and Thin Contrast

Letterforms vary in contrast between the thick and thin strokes;
Figure 10-L shows three typefaces to illustrate the difference,
the first with little, the last with great thick-thin contrast.

Distribution of Stress

Another variable is the distribution of stress through the swell-
ing and thinning of curved strokes; the B's and especially the
O's in Figure 10-M show how stress may be distributed at different
angles.

A monoline typeface has no variation in the thickness of line:

ABCDEFGHIJKLMNO abcdefghijklmno

abcdefghijklm

abcdefghijklm

abcdefghijklm

Figure 10-L.   Contrast in
thick and thin strokes

BOX   BOX

BOX   BOX

Figure 10-M.   Distribution of
stress in B and O

Type Weight and Form

Weight refers to how fat or thin a typeface is. A family of type
might include several of the following weights: extra-light, light,
semi-light, medium, demi-bold, bold, extra-bold, and ultra-bold.
Other terms may be used, such as book, heavy, or black. Figure
10-N shows several weights in one family.

Type form or proportion is the relative width of a typeface. Any
weight or size within a family of type might include several of
the following proportions: ultra-condensed, extra-condensed, condensed, semi-condensed, normal, semi-expanded, expanded, extra-
expanded, ultra-expanded. Other terms may be used, such as extended
or wide instead of expanded, or narrow or compressed instead of

condensed. Figure 10-O shows several forms in one weight of a type family.

In specifications, the term "normal" or "medium" is often omitted. "Futura" alone means not light or bold; "Cheltenham Bold" means not condensed or extended.

Futura Light
Futura Medium
Futura Demi Bold
Futura Bold
Futura Extra Bold

Figure 10-N. Five weights in the Futura family

CHELTENHAM BOLD COND.
ABCDEFGHIJKLMN abcdefghijklmn

CHELTENHAM BOLD
ABCDEFGHIJK abcdefghijkl

CHELTENHAM BOLD EXT.
ABCDEFGH abcdefgh

Figure 10-O. Three proportions in Cheltenham Bold

Apparent Size

Apparent size is one of the ways typefaces differ. A face with long ascenders and descenders will appear smaller than a face with short ascenders and descenders and a greater x-height. (See examples under Set Width below.)

Set Width

The set or set width (the average width of letters) varies from narrow to wide among typefaces of the same size, weight, and proportion. For example, here are two 18-point, normal weight, medium proportion faces:

Pack my box with five dozen

Pack my box wit

Set width is a major factor in copyfitting (choosing a typeface to fit a given space or figuring how much space copy in a given typeface will need).

Ligatures and Kerning

A piece of foundry type (for handsetting) whose face overhangs the body is kerned. For example, the top loop of the f in the adjacent figure overhangs the body and prints in the space of the adjoining letter; the part of the f to the right of the vertical line is a kern. (Because an f kern will not fit with another f, an i, or an l, ligatures for these combinations are supplied in foundry type.)

fox

Hot metal machine composition supplies ligatures but no kerned letters at all. Photocomposition makes kerning possible through reduction of the set widths of adjoining letters. Computerized photocomposition can be programmed for kerning.

Units and Groups of Type

An <u>alphabet</u> is a collection of characters including the letters from <u>A</u> to <u>Z</u>, numerals, and punctuation in one size and design. For example, one alphabet of 10-point Bodoni Book consists of lowercase roman; another alphabet, of roman capitals; another, of roman small caps; another, of lowercase italic; and so on.

A <u>series</u> of type is a complete collection of sizes in one design; for example, a series of Bodoni Book consists of 6-, 8-, 10-, and 12-point, up to 72-point, type.

A <u>font</u> consists of all the characters in one size and one design. For example, in handset foundry type, a font of 10-point Bodoni Book consists of all the roman caps and lowercase letters, figures, and punctuation marks. This is the definition used in proofreading. If 10-point Bodoni Book is specified for a page of printing, any roman character from another font (8-point Bodoni Book, or 10-point Bodoni Bold, for example) must be marked (wf) (wrong font). (A character mistakenly set in italic would be marked (rom).)

A <u>family</u> of type is a complete collection of all the related designs in one typeface; for example, roman, italic, bold, or condensed.

This is a sample of cap and lowercase <u>A</u>'s from a family of Univers:

Aa *Aa* Aa *Aa* **Aa** ***Aa*** **Aa** **Aa** Aa *Aa*
Aa *Aa* **Aa** ***Aa*** Aa Aa **Aa** **Aa**

A <u>library</u> is a collection of fonts and series available for one method of typesetting through one print shop or composition house.

A <u>character</u> is a single printed symbol produced from an individual piece of handset type or from one keystroke on a typesetting machine. <u>Alpha characters</u> are letters of the alphabet. <u>Figures</u> or <u>numeric characters</u> are numerals. <u>Pi characters</u> (a term introduced in computer composition; the word used to be <u>sorts</u>) are such symbols as stars, bullets, ampersands, dollar signs, and mathematical and technical symbols. Some pi characters are "font dependent" (dollar signs, for example); others are "font independent" (bullets, for example).

Categories of Type

Standard typefaces include the following:

- Roman, which can be divided into three subcategories:

  -small serif
  Examples: Baskerville   Bodoni   IBM Delegate

-strong serif
Examples: Clarendon , most typewriter faces.

-sans serif (Gothic, grotesk, block letters)

Examples: Helvetica   Optima   IBM Letter Gothic

- Italic

Examples: *Baskerville Italic*   *IBM Light Italic*

Special typefaces include the following:

- Text* (black letter, spire Gothic)
Examples: Wedding Text   Old English

- Written (script, cursive, handlettered, calligraphic)

Examples: *Park Avenue*   **Brush**   *Palace Script*

- Special display (decorative, novelty, ornamented)

Examples: *FOURNIER*   **BABY TEETH**

- Special purpose
Examples:

-optical character recognition (OCR): ABCDEFGhijklmnop

-magnetic: ABCDEFGHIJ

Roman Faces

A traditional classification of type divides roman text faces into three main groups: Old Style, with oblique stress and little thick-thin contrast, like the manuscript of medieval scribes who held a broad pen at an angle; Transitional, with stress moving away from the oblique to the vertical and with more thick-thin contrast; and Modern, with geometrical contours, vertical stress, and greater thick-thin contrast.
Examples: Old Style Cheltenham

Transitional Baskerville   Modern Modern No.20

Italic Faces

Italic is normally slanted. A true italic has been "cut" or designed as a separate face. True italic has hooked terminals that recall its origins in handwritten script, and its lowercase a and f differ from the lowercase roman a and f. Some so-called italics are actually slanted romans; phototypesetting equipment can create an oblique version of a roman face by "distortion."

---

*"Text" as used here means a classification of type.

The original italic was narrower than roman. Machine-set hot
metal, such as Linotype, cannot produce italic in a different set
width from roman. Photocomposition, however, can.

true italic: *abcdefg*   *abcdefg*   *abcdefg*

slanted roman: *abcdefg*   **abcdefg**   *abcdefg*

An italic may be designed to match a particular roman face, to
relate well to a particular roman, or to be unrelated to any
particular roman.

roman: Spectrum   Univers Light

matched italic: *Spectrum Italic*   *Univers Light Italic*

roman: Bodoni Book

related italic: *Bodoni Book Italic*

unrelated italic: *Arrighi*

Figures

Figures (numerals) fall into two main
groups. Old style (O.S.) figures are
like lowercase; some are x-height;
some have descenders; some, ascenders.

old style: 1234567890

lining: 1234567890

Lining (or ranging) figures are uniform in height and are usually
the same height as capitals.

A lining figure set among old style (nonlining) figures (or vice
versa) should be marked "wf."

Decorative Features

Typographic design may include any number of decorative features,
sometimes in color, such as typographic spots (dots, squares,
arrows, symbols, and small cuts); fleurons (printer's ornaments
and flowers); and decorative borders, rules, and dashes. The
variety is wide.

Ornamental initial letters are often used as a ceremonial opening
to a chapter, section, or story. They are specified by type size
and typeface, sometimes by the number of lines they will occupy
(3-L for three lines, 2-L for two lines).

Here are examples of two styles of initials:

- Sunken (also called drop or set-in): A_{FTER} had

- Raised (also called standing or stick-up): A few
    minister of e

Swash letters have extra curves and lines. In the following example, the R and the second A are swashed.

FIRST CATCH YOUR ELAND

Reverse type, or a reverse plate, is light on dark. In the example shown in Figure 10-P, the type is white on black. A negative that is meant to stay a negative is a reverse (also called a positive negative or a readable negative).

Distinguish between reversing and flopping--turning a negative to face the other way (for example, to show a person facing into the page instead of out of it). The example below shows what can happen if a negative is flopped by mistake.

ЯOꟼ

Our Proofreader GOOFED!
The price on our
PORTABLE BAR
should read
$39⁹⁵ each
This is *not* a price increase. It is strictly a proofing error. Please accept our apology.

Figure 10-P.   Reverse type

SPACING

Forms of Indention

In paragraph indention, the first line of every paragraph is indented, and the following lines align with the left margin. This is a form of reverse indention.

In positive indention, the lines following the first are indented. A hanging indention is a positive indention.

"Flush and hang" means to begin the first line at the margin (flush left) and hang the following lines at a specified indention. "Indent and hang" means to indent the first line and hang the following lines at a further indention.

Figure 10-Q shows some of the various forms of indention for paragraphs and heads.

A blocked indention may be specified by an em-quad symbol with a tail extending to each line to be indented. The mark for a 1-em blocked indention is shown here.

The mark for a blocked 2-em indention--a 2-em symbol with a tail-- is shown here.

Reverse indention
(regular paragraph
indention)

Positive indention

Hanging indention

Justified squared or
block indention--center

Block paragraphs
(ragged right,
flush left)

Pyramid

Inverted pyramid
(half diamond)

Lozenge

Ragged left, flush
right (ranged right)

Ragged left and right
(irregular)

Justified copy (flush
left and right)

Staggered (de-
scending stair-
steps, steplines,
droplines)

Ascending stair
steps

Left increase

Left decrease

Right increase

Right decrease

Figure 10-Q. Forms of indention

The first line of a new chapter or any first line of type follow-ing a white line (wide leading equal to the depth of the printed line) needs no indention. Full caps or small caps may be used for the first word or two of a chapter or section.

Levels of Indention

In quotations, lists, or outlines, several levels of indention may be needed.

In typeset copy, the first level of indention is often 1 em, marked with the paragraph symbol (¶) or the symbol for an em quad (▢); the second level then is 2 ems (▢▢ or ②); and the third, 3 ems (▢▢▢ or ③).

In typewritten copy, the paragraph symbol (¶) often indicates the first level of indention; the em-quad symbol should not be used. The number of spaces a typist indents depends on the specifications. The most common first-level indention is 5 spaces (with the first character typed on the 6th space). Second, third, and further levels may or may not be 5 additional spaces each; instructions should specify this. These levels may be marked with numbers indicating the spaces to skip (2), with numbers indicating the level (2nd), or simply "1st indent," "2nd indent," and so on.

MARK-UP

To specify typographic style, mark-up (copymarking, type specifying, typemarking, guidelining) is done, during or after copyediting, on the manuscript pages. A typemarker uses the standard symbols to mark spacing, indention, paragraphs, lowercase, italic, small caps, caps, and boldface. Other instructions to the typesetter, usually marked in the upper left corner of the first draft page of every chapter or section, include specs for typeface, type weight, type form, leading, and column width. The following paragraphs explain these specs.

Typeface, Weight, and Form

The name of the face and the particular alphabet (when other than medium or normal weight and form) are given for both body and display type.

Some typefaces are specified with a number--a manufacturer's series number, a printer's case number, or a number designating a particular font or lens setting. Here are examples:

    Times Roman Bold (28 Lf 10-12)
    Continental Clarendon 5 (2428n)

The name of the typesetting process or the manufacturer's brand name may be included; for example:

    Century Expanded (Linofilm)
    Univers 55 (Compugraphic)

Type Size and Leading

Type size is usually marked in combination with leading. The specification may look like a fraction; for example, 9-point type set with 1-point leading to make a line depth of 10 points is marked 9/10 or $\frac{9}{10}$. Ten-point type set in a 12-point line is marked 10/12 or $\frac{10}{12}$. Sometimes the type size is enclosed in parentheses: (9)/10 or (10)/12.

If type is set solid (unleaded), the two numbers are the same; for example, 8-point type set solid is marked 8/8.

Here are examples of the kinds of specs for typeface (including weight and form), type size, and leading you might see:

>   Times Roman 10/12 Bold (28 Lf 10-12)
>   Continental Clarendon 5, 9/10 (2428n)
>   Century Expanded 11/12 (Linofilm)
>   Univers 55 (Compugraphic) $\frac{8}{9}$
>   California (11)/12

You might also see leading specified in words rather than numbers. Common leading, single leading, and leading mean 2-point leading. Double leading is 4 points deep; triple leading, 6 points deep.

You may see specs for two settings for leading--the primary or line leading (between lines of text) and the secondary or paragraph leading (between paragraphs). One way such specs appear is with the type size in parentheses, the primary leading before a slash and the secondary leading after the slash; for example:

>   (9) 10/12

Line Measure (Column Width)

When galleys are to be set, the line measure (column width or type page width) is often marked as well as the typeface, type size, and leading; for example, here is one way to mark for 9-point Bodoni to be set on a 10-point line in a column 19 picas wide:

>   Bodoni 9/10 X 19

Sometimes "pica" is abbreviated "pi." Here are examples of specs for typeface (including weight and form), type size, leading, and column width:

>   Times Roman 10/12 Bold (28 Lf 10-12) X 22 pi
>   Continental Clarendon 5, 9/10 (2428n) X 18
>   Century Expanded 11/12 (Linofilm) X 21 pi
>   Univers 55 (Compugraphic) $\frac{8}{9}$ X 15
>   California (11)/12 X 30
>   Bodoni (9) 10/12 X 19

Justification Symbols

Some typemarkers use special symbols to specify justification. Here are two kinds of these symbols:

	Pointing Carons	Circles With Tails
flush left, ragged right	<	ᓚ
flush right, ragged left	>	ᓂ
justified: flush left and right	< >	ᓂᓚ
centered	> <	ᓂᓗ

Other Ways Type May Be Marked

Type specs are sometimes given in a diagram. Here are two examples of diagrams currently in use; the key to each is shown on the left, and an example is on the right:

type size	line measure
primary leading secondary leading	justification symbol

10	20
12 / 24	ᓂᓚ

justification symbol	line measure	special information
type size line leading paragraph leading	type-face	cap style

<	19	Footnotes 8/10
10/12 6 pt A	Times Roman	Clc

In newspaper and magazine advertisements, size is usually given in whole pages, half pages, and quarter pages; small ads are marked for depth in agate lines and for width in number of columns. Sometimes inches are specified. Here are some ways copy may be marked for newspapers or magazines:

    To specify 3 columns by 10 inches: 3 X 10
    To specify 150 agate lines by 2 columns: 150 X 2

TYPEWRITER FORMAT

Specifications for a typewriter (or word processor) format may include line numbers and tab settings. The numbering system includes the whole page, both white space and typewritten area.

Every line, blank or typed, has a number. Line numbers begin at the top of a page. With standard typewriters, the numbers are the same for single or double spacing and for elite or pica type. There are six lines to the inch; an 8-1/2" X 11" page is 66 lines long, and lines are counted from 1 to 66.

Margin or tab settings number the character spaces across a page from left to right. Across an 8-1/2" X 11" page in elite (12 spaces to the inch), there are 102 spaces--tabs 1-102; in pica (10 spaces to the inch), there are 85 spaces--tabs 1-85.

A format specifying 1-inch margins, with the page number below the bottom margin setting, on 8-1/2" X 11" paper, typed in elite, might read as follows:

```
Side margins:   12/90
Top line:       7
Bottom line:    60
Page number:    line 63 (1/2" up from bottom)
```

The line counter for single spacing and the typewriter character counter in the Workbook can be used to verify spacing with this kind of specification.

ARTWORK

Art and artwork are terms that refer to anything involving a different medium from typesetting or typing. Drawings, illustrations, cartoons, maps, photographs, graphs, and charts--figures of all kinds--are included. Tables and tabular material are not usually artwork; normally they are set or typed along with the text. Figures and tables are called display matter.

Illustrations are often called cuts. The words beneath a cut are often called a cutline and sometimes a caption, a legend, an underline, or a squib. Cutlines have different formats; for example, they may be centered, flush left, flush and justified, or indented right and left. Set full, they are in one block of type, known as a leg. When artwork is wide, the cutline may be set in two blocks or columns--two legs--or even three:

```
+-------------------+         +------------------------------------------+
|                   |         |                                          |
|                   |         |                                          |
|                   |         |                                          |
|      (cut)        |         |                  (cut)                    |
|                   |         |                                          |
+-------------------+         +------------------------------------------+

Xxxxxxxxxxxxxxx               Xxxxxxxxxxxxxxx        Xxxxxxxxxxxxxxx
xxxxxxxxxxxxxxx               xxxxxxxxxxxxxxx        xxxxxxxxxxxxxxx

One-leg cutline                    Two-leg cutline
```

Boldface, italic, or all-cap words that lead into a cutline are called lead-ins, catchlines, or kickers:

> PROOFREADERS AT WORK. The two people shown
> are employees of Editorial Experts, Inc.

When the catchline is set to one side of the cutline, it is called a sideline:

> PROOFREADERS   The two people shown are employees
> AT WORK   of Editorial Experts, Inc.

In the printing process, artwork falls into two categories: line art, which has no continuous tones (such as a simple black-and-white drawn cartoon), and halftones. Halftones are copy with continuous tone (photographs) or intermediate tones between black and white (drawings containing grays).

A dummy shows where artwork is to be placed and gives instructions necessary for reduction or enlargement and cropping.

Line art is simply enlarged or reduced to fit the space allotted for it in the dummy and then treated the same as the rest of the black-and-white text. Halftones, however, must be screened. In the screening process, a crossline screen or grating is used to break up the image into a regular pattern of dots of varying sizes. The dots give the illusion of lighter and darker tones. The placement of halftones is indicated by a key (often an "a" number; for example, 1a, marked in the empty space on the dummy and on the photograph to be placed there).

QUESTIONS FOR STUDENTS

1. How many points are there in 2-1/2 picas?

2. How many picas are there in a 6-inch line measure?

3. How wide is a figure space?

4. Why should the terms "thin space" and "thick space" be used cautiously?

5. Describe the typefaces in Figure 10-R in terms of the variables discussed in this chapter (they are all 24-point typefaces).

6. Clip an example of each of the following kinds of typeface from a newspaper or magazine: small serif roman, strong serif roman, sans serif, italic, script, special display, text (such as black letter).

7. Measure the column width, the type page's width and depth, and the leading (baseline to baseline of the type) for every block of type on one page of a magazine.

8.   Explain the meaning of the following copymarks:

Bodoni Bold 9-1/2 leaded
Avant Garde (11) 13/17

---

(1)   THE QUICK brown fox

(2)   THE Quick brown

(3)   *THE QUICK brown*

(4)   THE Quick brown fox

(5)   **THE QUICK Brown**

(6)   *The Quick Brown Fox Jumps over the*

(7)   **THE QUICK BROWN fox jumps over the**

(8)   **THE QUICK BROWN fox jumps over**

Figure 10-R.   Find the variables

Chapter 11

Composition

There's nothing static about proofreading. You have to adapt
continually to new processes and new machines, and with every
new one there's a period of chaos. Once the typesetters learn
what they're doing with new equipment, we proofreaders can begin
to learn what we're telling the typesetters to do to make corrections. In a couple of years, we're all comfortable (we get so
we can even tell who set a take by the kinds of typos we find).
Then they put in a new machine and the cycle starts again: we
see a lot of errors, including kinds we've never seen before,
then the errors decrease and we begin to learn our job all over.

                                        --Faye Hanson, proofreader

CHAPTER OVERVIEW

It is important for proofreaders to understand what their marks instruct typesetters to do. Typesetting and printing are changing
rapidly. New developments bring new kinds of problems for proofreaders to watch for and new ways for typesetters to correct errors.
But the older ways are still practiced, and understanding them is
helpful--indeed, basic--to adapting to the new ways.

This chapter discusses different methods of <u>composition</u>--the production of type arranged for printing--and the special problems each
presents to proofreaders.

INTRODUCTION

Before a page can be printed or reproduced, the image to be reproduced must be composed. The basic methods are "hot type" composi-
tion--with three-dimensional (relief) metal type, by hand or ma-
chine--and "cold type" composition--by various processes that
produce a two-dimensional (plane) image.

Be sure to distinguish between composition and printing; they are
two separate steps in the production process. Almost always, the
proofreading marks you make are directed to a <u>compositor</u> (typesetter), not to a press operator.

This chapter can help you begin to understand the different processes and the terms used. The important thing, however, is to
learn about the kind of composition you work with. The best way
to learn is to ask somebody in your shop to show you the details
of composition or--better--to let you act as a compositor long
enough for you to know exactly what you're telling the typesetter
to do to make corrections.

WHAT YOU'LL ENCOUNTER AT WORK

If you work in a typesetting plant, you will need to know only
the particular typesetting and printing methods your plant uses.
You will probably work on only one segment of a job (a take) at
a time. You may proofread the galleys for Chapter 2 of a book and
then not see that book again until Chapter 20 or until the page
proofs. You may spend an entire day doing a long take from one
job, but more likely you will work on many different jobs--galleys,
page proofs, dummies, and mechanicals--reading indexes, magazine
articles, pamphlets, directories, books, journals, newsletters,
and reports. You may be wholly immersed in a difficult job and be
interrupted for something "hotter." You may have as many as six
jobs on your desk at once.

If you work as a freelancer or as an employee of an organization
offering editorial services, you will need to know something about
every major kind of typesetting and printing process; you are
likely to see them all. But you will probably not be able to see
a job through from beginning to end.

METAL COMPOSITION

By Hand

To set type by hand, the typesetter assembles individual metal
characters and spaces (foundry type, each piece called a type)
in a receptacle called a composing stick, which holds about 10
lines of 10-point type. Equal spacing between words in justified
lines depends on the typesetter's skill. The block of type set
in the stick is transferred to a galley (a long, narrow, flat tray),
and other blocks of type are then set in the stick and transferred
to the galley. When the galley is full, a proof is taken of the
assembled matter; after proofreading, corrections are made. The
corrected type then is taken from the galley, divided into pages,
locked up securely, and placed on the press. The assemblage of
type locked up for the press is called a form.

By Machine

Typecasting machines include the following:

- Linotype, Intertype. The operator manipulates a keyboard
  that drives the machine to assemble matrices (the molds
  from which the type is cast) of individual characters. Interword spaces are set automatically by striking the spaceband key, which inserts a wedge into the line and adjusts
  spacing to equal width. After a line is set, the typecasting mechanism ejects a slug (a complete line of type)
  onto a galley. The process then continues as with handset
  type, or--more often--a plate (a one-piece form) to go on
  the press is made from the type.

- **Monotype**. The operator works at the keyboard of a machine that punches a coded tape. The tape is subsequently run through a second machine where individual characters are cast completely assembled into lines. The process then continues as with other typecasting machines. Interword spacing is equalized with an automatic spaceband.

- **Ludlow**. The typesetter sets the matrix by hand in a stick and places the matrix on a machine that casts a slug. This machine is used principally for display type; seldom are more than a few lines set Ludlow. Interword spacing in justified lines is, of course, manual.

The Proofs

Galley Proofs

A galley normally holds enough type to make up two or three book pages. Proofs taken from the galley are called galley proofs (shortened to galleys), and each proof is numbered to correspond with the number of the printer's galley (tray). Galley proofs vary in size but are usually about 8" X 20". They contain one column of type and have wide margins for marking.

Revised Galley Proofs

After the galley proofs are read, marked, and corrected, another set of proofs may be made. These revised galley proofs are sent to the proofreaders, who mark missed corrections and new errors.

Page Proofs

After corrections are made from the proofreader's marks on the galley, the compositor will physically move around the blocks of type to make the pages and then pull a new proof from the form. The page proof will have "holes" left for halftones. Proofreaders verify the corrections and check the arrangement of the pages (see Chapter 5 for details).

How Corrections Are Made

In handset type, corrections are made manually by adding, taking out, replacing, or transposing the individual types and spaces. When a correction is made, the spaces between words in justified copy must almost always be reset to restore equal spacing.

In Linotype or Intertype composition, any error in a line means that the entire line (or more) must be reset and cast. The line with the error is removed and the replacement inserted.

In Monotype composition, a simple correction can be made by hand, but a more complex correction requires resetting an entire line.

In Ludlow composition, after corrections have been made by hand in the matrix, the entire slug must be recast.

Special Problems

General

Here are cautions and problems that may apply to your work:

- Proofs are pulled on proof presses on cheap paper. The quality of printing is not what it will be in the final press run.

- A line of type may not rest flat in the galley. Such a line will print only the top or bottom of characters; this is called type "off its feet." An example is shown in Figure 11-A.

- Particles of metal or dirt may adhere to the bottom (foot) of a type and raise a part of the printing surface, causing it to print imperfectly or even to punch through the paper.

- A portion of a character may break off and the character may print as a broken letter.

Handset Type

Here are some problems to watch for:

- A character can be set upside down.

- Type can wear down after many uses. A worn lowercase <u>e</u>, for example, may produce a fainter image than other characters. This kind of problem can usually be solved by proper <u>make-ready</u>--the process by which a printer equalizes the height-to-paper of all parts of the form.

- Spacing material may work up in the form and protrude enough to pick up ink and print.

Machine Composition

Here are some cautions:

- Keep in mind that when a correction involves resetting a slug, the slug may be inserted in the wrong place and an entire line will be out of sequence. Do not be too hasty to mark "Out, see copy"; look further along to be sure the missing copy has not been shifted. In revises, check the lines before and after every line where a correction has been made to be sure the correct sequence has been maintained. A misplaced line is shown in Figure 11-B.

- Be cautious about marking "defective type." Broken type--characters with the line obviously bent or incomplete, or with white space showing in a break--should be marked. Recurring

The King spoke from a platform decked, in his honour, with fruits and flowers. He had arrived in the early afternoon, accompanied by General Joab, the Chief of Staff; Captain Lanaiah, Commander of the Royal Guard; and other high-ranking officers.

Figure 11-A. Type off its feet

Chances are, you've got one or two treasured prints that you would like to hang on your wall but you're turned off by the high cost decoupage. This fascinating craft from ancient France of framing. Why not try involves cutting out a picture of your choice, applying it to a wooden plaque and then coating it with a special finish.

Figure 11-B. Misplaced line

smudged, blurred, or faint type should not be marked repeatedly.

● Note frequent faint or blurred areas, but write only one instruction; for example, write "check for faint (or blurred) areas throughout."

● Do not mark slight vertical misalignment of type at the margins as an error. Type is not usually locked in the galley with side locks when proofs are taken. Do, however, mark misaligned columns in tabular matter.

Here are some problems to watch for:

● Slugs (lines of type) cast wider than measure must be sawed off. When too much is sawed off, part of the characters at the ends of lines is removed.

● Wide measure may require two adjoining slugs. If their ends join imperfectly, a white line appears through the copy.

● A worn or damaged matrix may print superfluous spots or hairlines.

● A Linotype operator may set a line with the characters ETAOIN SHRDLU (the top line of the keyboard), intending to take the line out or replace it later. Figure 11-C shows what can happen if the operator forgets.

● Sometimes slugs are slightly wider at one end than another. If an adjustment is not made when a page is put together, the rectangle will be slightly askew, like the page in Figure 11-D.

week after deciding to replace him
with two puppets . . . the station
switchboard lit up, kind of . . . 33 call-
ers voted for Teddy . . . 33 voted for
a SHRDSHRDLU
the puppets . . . Teddy, meanwhile,
has told friends a network is interested . . .

Figure 11-C.   Shrdlu

Figure 11-D.   Skewed page

TYPESCRIPT

Standard Typewritten Copy

Typewriting is a form of <u>strike-on</u> or <u>impact</u> composition.

Typewriter Capabilities

Standard typewriters type one character to each spacing unit. <u>Elite</u>
type measures 12 characters to the horizontal inch; <u>pica</u> type, 10
characters to the inch. (Note that the word "pica" is here unrelated
to the unit of printer's measure.) There are six single-spaced lines
to a vertical inch.* (Note that standard vertical measure agrees
with printer's measure; you can use a pica [12-point] gauge to
count typewritten lines.)

Specially designed typewriters can provide any of the following:

- Proportional (differential) spacing--characters of different
  width; for example, <u>m</u> wider than <u>i</u>

- Interchangeable typefaces--including fonts of mathematical
  and technical symbols

- Interchangeable type sizes--12 characters to the inch is
  called <u>12 pitch</u>; 10 characters to the inch, <u>10 pitch</u>

- Automatic or semi-automatic line justification

- Correcting tapes that lift the ink from the page when a
  character is struck over

- Some computer capabilities, such as a memory.

*Some typewriters deviate from these standards. For example, one
manufacturer offers machines that type 11 characters to the inch;
typewriters fitted with a "legal" ratchet type five lines per
vertical inch.

General Standards

Good quality in light stencils, masters, repros, or any camera-ready copy requires an electric typewriter, because it equalizes the pressure of every stroke and prints letters of uniform blackness. Pressure should be properly adjusted; when it is too great, characters punch through; for example, a period becomes a little doughnut, like this: ◦

A one-time carbon or plastic film ribbon produces sharper characters than a fabric ribbon:

fabric ribbon

carbon ribbon

Type must be clean. Filled-in letters and smudges are unacceptable. Baselines must align, and no character should crowd against another.

Special Problems

Flying Carbon

Some typewriters put little dots (bits of "flying carbon" from the ribbon) toward the top of a line, often on lines with underscoring. Watch for this particularly in bibliographies and headings. Sometimes the bottoms of characters are slightly slurred; this is likely to happen at the top or bottom of a page. Such slurring is frequently the result of an overused backing sheet. Little dots and slurred characters are unacceptable.

Corrections Made by Changing Spacing

Some typists use the backspace to <u>crowd</u>; for example, to fit five characters in the space of four:

> a hapy birthday
> a happy birthday

and to <u>spread</u>; for example, to fit five characters in the space of six:

> a happpy birthday
> a happy birthday

Corrections made by crowding and spreading are seldom acceptable. Neither are corrections made by violating image area or margins or by changing line spacing; for example, retyping a page marked with many deletions at space and a half when surrounding pages are single-spaced.

Wrong Pitch

It is possible to set a typewriter at the wrong pitch; for example:

> This is a 12-pitch typeface set at 10 pitch.
> This is a 10-pitch typeface set at 12 pitch.

Extra Space Between Words

High quality typing with ragged right margins should not have any extra space between words (although few readers will notice). Justified typing, however, cannot avoid unequal spacing between words.

Margins and Image Area

On some jobs, a typist has no leeway whatsoever in margin width; violation of the specified image area by even a hyphen is unacceptable. On other jobs, there is some flexibility.

To check the margins or the image area:

1. Make a grid of tracing paper (or any transparent or translucent sheet) ruled with a straightedge and a fine-line pen. Check each page by placing the ruled sheet over it; or

2. Use the typist's backing sheet. Place it under each page. If you can't see through the page, hold the backing sheet and the page up to the light.

Specifications for ragged right copy may include a maximum as well as a minimum righthand margin. A normal standard allows no more than six pica or eight elite characters' difference between the longest and the shortest line on a page.

Specially designed copy may require a right margin that is intentionally ragged; specifications may instruct the typist to divide words to avoid three or more consecutive lines of the same width.

Jumping Folios

For many jobs, folios (page numbers) should be typed in exactly the same position on every page. If a book or report is to be bound, this is particularly important; numbers that jump up and down and sideways as the pages are flipped disturb the reader. When one page number aligns exactly with another, it is in <u>register</u>.

You can check page number register while you check image area, using either a ruled sheet marked with the page number position or a typist's backing sheet. To be accurate, find a page number that follows the position specifications exactly, and use it as the model. Align the edges of the model and another page and hold them up to the light. If the page you are checking is more than a space off in any direction, mark it for correction. Follow the same procedure for every page. Finally, if you find many misplaced page numbers, stop checking each page and write the typist a general note.

How Corrections Are Made

The following chart provides general guidelines on acceptable correction techniques. Different jobs, however, have different requirements. Check the specifications for each job.

Corrections must be neat. Adhesive correction tape must be properly placed so that letters do not fall off its edge. For example,
this is a badly positioned tape correction. If correction fluid is
not kept thin, used lightly, or permitted to dry before retyping,
the letters will be too black, too light, or distorted, like this.
The correcting feature of a typewriter must be properly tuned or a
strike-over will not lift all the ink from the page, like this.
Cut-ins must be exactly positioned and secured with white tape on
the back of the sheet to cover every cut-line. Paste-overs must be
positioned exactly. Figure 11-E lists acceptable correction techniques for typescript.

Correction Technique	Direct Use	Camera-ready (offset)	Machine Copy
typewriter correcting key	acceptable	acceptable	acceptable
careful erasing	usually acceptable	usually unacceptable	usually acceptable
chalk paper careful scraping	usually acceptable	usually unacceptable	usually unacceptable
adhesive correction tape	unacceptable	often acceptable	often acceptable
cut-ins, cutting and pasting	unacceptable	usually acceptable	often unacceptable
white opaquing fluid	usually unacceptable	acceptable	acceptable

Figure 11-E. Acceptability of typewriter
correction techniques

On typewritten camera-ready copy, proofreaders may be expected to
make simple, inconspicuous deletions with opaquing fluid or adhesive correcting tape.* (A good rule of thumb is to use tape for
areas larger than 1 inch.) Examples of some deletions you can
make yourself follow:

Error	Wite-out Correction
terminalldoublets	terminal doublets
end of line deletions..	end of line deletions.
smudges	smudges

*Some clients object to tape; its edges sometimes print black lines
when a page is photocopied.

Error	Tape Correction*
the quick brown fox the quick brown fox jumped over	the quick brown fox jumped over

On camera-ready typing, you may be expected to use transfer sheets
to insert characters that are not on the typewriter keyboard (for
example, Greek letters or outsize braces). This is easy to do.
The characters appear on a transparent sheet. You need only fit
the character where it must go and rub over it with a burnisher
or even the point of a ballpoint pen. Some transfer type requires
rubbing the character with a translucent sheet as a third step.

The first time you use transfer type, practice on paper that will
not be harmed. Ordinary transparent tape will remove transfer type.

To make simple one- or two-character replacements, first, delete
the incorrect characters with a transfer sheet of opaque white rectangles; next, rub on the correct characters from a sheet with characters that match the type.

WORD PROCESSING

The Process

Many word processing terminals look like the offspring of a marriage
between a typewriter and a television set. The part similar to a
TV is the video display terminal (VDT), a screen that displays what
is being or has been keyboarded. In the correction process, the
operator can see on the screen what has been typed and can see make-
up changes and corrections as they are made. (See Figure 11-F.)

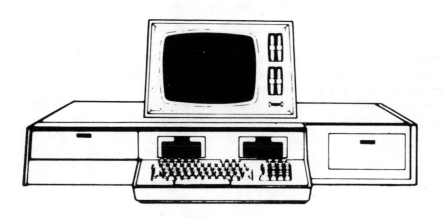

Figure 11-F.   VDT

*See footnote, p. 173.

The keyboard has more keys than a normal typewriter; these extra keys perform various text processing functions. There are many makes of this kind of equipment, each with different capabilities (and problems). This book was prepared on a Lexitron magnetic tape word processing machine. (See How To Proofread Lexitron Copy in Part III.)

In word processing, the operator's keystrokes record data on magnetic tapes or disks that will later drive a printer at high speed. Many printers are designed to permit a selection of fonts and a choice of two or three type sizes with changeable type wheels (daisy wheels). On many machines, the operator views a VDT screen that can display the matter being typed or previously typed matter.

Data recorded on a tape or disk can be sent to a remote station or to typesetting equipment by means of a telephone or other hook-ups.

Some machines will justify automatically. Word divisions usually must be decided by the operator.

Some models do not have all the capabilities of a typewriter. For example, subscript and superscript may not be possible because a machine will not half space; line spacing may be limited to single spacing and double spacing; and some characters, such as the exclamation point, may not be on the keyboard.

Because corrections, insertions, and alterations are easily made, word processing equipment is often used for form letters, billing statements, contracts, proposals, and any boilerplate (text that can be standardized for repeated use). A letter or contract, for example, can be assembled from previously recorded paragraphs; this process is called boilerplate assembly. Word processing machines are also practical for work that will go through several drafts.

How Corrections Are Made

In most systems, the typist moves a cursor (position indicator) to the error on the screen and, by striking one or two special keys and then typing, adds, deletes, or replaces characters or spaces in the text. Words, whole lines, and paragraphs can be moved quickly from one place to another on the page, from one page to another, or from one tape or disk to another.

The Proofs

Because typeface, type size, linespacing, and even margins can be reselected at the printing machine, what you see may not be what will be printed for the final copy. Drafts may be printed on a continuous roll of paper that is perforated to be folded or torn into separate sheets. The final copy, after all drafts have been proofread and corrections made and verified, may be printed on separate sheets.

All copy should be proofread with standard marks; when an error is corrected, a new page must be printed.

When an insertion requires that a word must be carried over to the next line, or when a deletion requires that a word must be carried back to the previous line, chances are that all the succeeding copy in the paragraph has been manipulated (even if not re-keyboarded), and there is the possibility of a new error. When checking corrections, you must check every changed line for errors (especially word division errors). Slugging (explained in Chapter 5) is the easiest way to tell which lines have been changed and which words have been operated on.

Special Problems

Copy from word processing (text processing, text editing) machines or automatic typewriters presents the same problems to proofreaders as standard typed copy. In addition, many problems are due to the printing mechanism rather than the keyboarded input. For example, worn-out type wheels produce apparent errors such as broken letters, commas without tails, missing apostrophes, and broken underscores; the characters do not print properly even though they are correctly entered. Because there is no way a proofreader can know if such errors are caused by a defective wheel, the only thing to do is to mark them for correction.

If the printing unit is set incorrectly, certain wrong characters may appear regularly; for example, degree symbols may appear instead of apostrophes. A wrong setting will also produce elite type printed out at pica spacing (with too much space between characters) or pica type at an elite setting (too crowded). These errors call for a general note asking for new printouts at the correct settings.

Static electricity can produce passages of gibberish on printouts, tapes, or disks.

Some machines drop the extra space after a period when moving copy. You must check after every sentence to be sure the operator has added the space.

The correction process sometimes produces unaccountable errors (especially when an inexperienced operator has been at work); for example, dropped copy on a page where no correction was marked. Corrected copy must be checked with great care; it should always be slugged and sometimes re-proofed.

The incidence of errors may be high. Because correction is simple, some organizations lower their qualifications (and pay) for word processing typists. Some operators are less careful, too, knowing how easy it will be to correct errors later.

PHOTOTYPESETTING

General Description

Phototypesetting processes of various versatility, automation, and speed produce images of text or tabular matter on a paper plate or on a <u>primary</u>--a print--on photographic paper, film, tape, clear acetate, or glass.

On many machines, an operator has quick access to a wide range of typefaces and sizes and can easily mix faces and sizes. Interword spacing is achieved automatically. Minute spacing adjustments that are difficult or impossible in other forms of typesetting are easily accomplished:

- Set width can be changed (as shown in Figure 11-G): <u>charac-ter compensation</u> reduces the set width of every character in a line to improve the appearance of display type or to squeeze text type to fit a line. <u>Kerning</u>* (minus letter-spacing) subtracts small increments of space from the set width of a character to print characters closer to each other.

- <u>Minus leading (reverse leading)</u> can crowd lines together or produce a stepping effect:

One Two Three

- <u>Letterspacing</u> (adding small increments of space between characters) can improve the appearance of display type. Some machines can be set to letterspace a word in a line automatically when necessary to fill out a justified line (this would not be done in high quality work).

Some machines can superimpose characters; for example:

89 ¢ lb

Some machines are capable of imaging an infinite variety of shapes through reproportioning lenses. A standard typeface can be con-densed, expanded, or angled; a word or line can be curved, tapered, or distorted.

Some machines can set complete pages of text, tabular material, and display lines in position.

When a machine uses film masters to produce an image, the charac-ters (matrices) are stored in a master magazine, drum, disk, film strip, or grid that contains one or more fonts. Computerized ma-chines may not use masters; digitalized information creates an image, and it is possible to store several type families on-line.

---

*Kerning is a sign of quality typesetting that proofreaders should be able to recognize. Some equipment can be programmed to set predetermined "kerning pairs."

Normal:	SPACE BETWEEN DISPLAY CHARACTERS
Reduced:	SPACE BETWEEN DISPLAY CHARACTERS
Reduced further:	SPACE BETWEEN DISPLAY CHARACTERS
Expanded (letterspaced):	SPACE BETWEEN DISPLAY CHARACTERS
Expanded further:	SPACE BETWEEN DISPLAY CHARACTERS

Normal:	Space between text characters
Reduced:	Space between text characters
Reduced further:	Space between text characters
Expanded (letterspaced):	Space between text characters
Expanded further:	Space between text characters

Normal:	fine feathers, ruffled, affect efficient flight
Kerned for ligatures:	fine feathers, ruffled, affect efficient flight

Normal:	AWAY, AWAY!
Kerned:	AWAY, AWAY!

Figure 11-G.   Changes in set width

A phototypesetter is driven directly by an operator at a keyboard or indirectly (off-line) by a perforated paper tape, magnetic tape cassette, or disk. In computerized systems, stations may be remote; keyboards and typesetting machines can be in different rooms, buildings, or cities.

Some sophisticated systems use a VDT. The screen is a cathode ray tube (CRT). As on a television set, CRT images are produced by adjoining scan lines; the density of these lines affects the image quality and the speed of the system.

Computerized Phototypesetting

Typesetting is becoming increasingly computerized. Computerized typesetting used to be considered particularly useful for matter needing retrieval (for example, price and parts lists), for complicated mathematics, and for complex tabular material. It is now used for every kind of copy to reduce typesetting costs. A good system is highly flexible and produces a high quality image.

Optical Character Recognition (OCR)

In an OCR system, the computer-driven equipment scans typewritten sheets and produces a tape or other form of input that will then drive a typesetting device or a word processor. The type the scanner will recognize may be specially designed, like those shown in Figure 11-H, or, with some newer systems, the type may be a standard typewriter or typeset face.

```
ABCDEFGHIJKLMNOPQRSTUVWXYZ
abcdefghijklmnopqrstuvwxyz
!;:',".
```

```
ABCDEFGHIJKLMNOPQRSTUVWXYZ
0123456789
.,:;=+/$*"&|'-{}%?♪¥⌐
```

Figure 11-H. OCR characters

Figure 11-I shows the steps in a phototypesetting system using OCR scanners, computerized typesetting, and VDT editing. The customer may provide the first step or more, up to the sixth step shown in the diagram. Figure 11-J is an example of coded OCR copy.

OCR copy is an intermediate step between the manuscript and the final typed or word processed copy. In the system diagrammed in Figure 11-I, OCR copy is the live copy for the first proofreading. In other systems, proofreaders may never see the OCR copy; they usually compare the manuscript directly with the final product.

When proofreading OCR copy, proofreaders need an explanation of how the particular system works and a copy of any code used. (See, How To Proofread OCR-B Copy for a Hendrix Typereader in Part III.)

Kinds of Proofs

Galleys

The term galleys, taken from letterpress, describes long sheets of primary phototype (the type itself, printed on photographic material) before it is divided into pages. The galley proofs that proofreaders see are usually machine copies of the type, 10 to 14 inches long, which are corrected with standard marks. When proofing is done directly on the original galley--the primary phototype itself--every precaution must be taken to protect the primary. (See Chapter 9 on how to proofread copy without marking on it.)

Revised Galleys

Corrections in primary phototype are usually made with cut-ins. This kind of splicing is done with a knife on a light table--a glass surface lighted from beneath. The light shines through two layers of film or paper and permits the area that will be cut out to be aligned exactly with the area that will be cut in (inserted). The knife cuts through both layers at once, the cut-out is discarded, and the cut-in is taped in position.

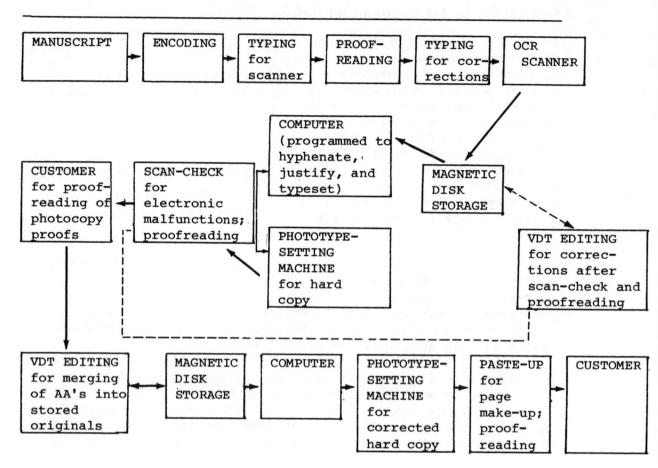

Figure 11-I.   Steps in a typical CRT phototypesetting system

Cut-ins are also used to position matter on a page and to make corrections on many kinds of camera-ready copy. (When film is involved, the technique for making cut-ins is called <u>stripping</u>.)

Page Proofs

The compositor cuts up the primary image and pastes up page forms as indicated by the dummy. Proofreaders usually see a photocopy of the paste-up. (See Chapter 13 for a more detailed discussion of page proofs.)

Printouts

Some computerized machines produce a coded printout. The operator sets type without taking time to make decisions on line length or justification, and an unjustified printout is produced simultaneously with a magnetic or punched tape. A printout may be hard to read because it is all caps or sans serif type; or because coded instructions for punctuation, spacing, indention, and capitalization are keyboarded along with the other characters. The printout is proofread and corrections are made and merged with the tape before the tape is fed to a computer.

How To Open a New Hardcover Book

  A new book needs gentle handling. If you force a book open at any section, you will break its back. Here is how to open a new book properly:

- Hold the book with its spine on a table or flat surface.

- Let down the covers, first the front, then the back.

- Hold the pages in one hand while with the other you alternately open a few leaves at the front, then a few at the back, allowing the leaves free play, and gently pressing open each section until you reach the center.

- Repeat two or three times.

(1) Dead copy

/ud72How To Open a New Hardcover Book/c/c

/ud73/mA new h¤book needs gentle handling. If you force a book

open at any section, you will break its back. Here is how to

open a new book properly:+t000/l

/ud01=b{tHold the book with its spine on a table or flat surf

face./l

=b{tLet down the covers, first the front, then the back./l

=b{tHold the pages in one hand while with the other you alterf

nately open a few leaves at the front, then a few at the back,

allowing the leaves free play, and gently pressing open each

section until you reach the center./l

=b{tRepeat two or three times./l/l

(2) Live copy ready for the scanner

Figure 11-J. OCR copy

To do a proper job, proofreaders must have a copy of the code. Different machines, and sometimes different typefaces on the same machine, use different codes. Figure 11-K is an example of a simple code for one make and model of a photocomposition machine.

Description/ Function	Mark-up/ Proofreading	Printout	Keyboarding
opening command	(	⌐	⌐
closing command	)	⌐	⌐
quad left	QL	/l	(lf) or /l
quad right	QR	/r	/r
quad center	QC	/c	/c
quad middle	QM	/m	/m
call (first group)	©	/f	/f
call (second group)	Ⓐ	/s	/s
tab left	(TL)	/<	Cont.l (el)
tab right	(TR)	/>	Cont.r
tab center	(TC)	/∧	Cont.c
tab around	(TA)	/a	/a
with x	(WX)	/:	/:
single line justify	(SLJ)	/j	/j
thin space	①	!	❚
en space	½	+	+
em space	❑	#	#
space band	#		
en dash	⅟n	–	ital ⅟n
em dash	1/m	—	rom ⅟m
slash	/ (slash)	*	*
discretionary hyphen	=	[oq]	[oq] or /-
lower rail	/L	/L	/L
upper rail	/U	/U	/U
combined command	(cc)	[cc]	[cc]
add lead	(ca)	[ca]	[ca]
point size	(cp)	[cp]	[cp]
type face	(ct)	[ct]	[ct]
line length	(cw)	[cw]	[cw]
parenthesis	⊀ ⊁	( )	( )
hold reg. (save)	(HS)	[HS]	[HS]
hold reg. (recall)	(HR)	[HR]	[HR]
supershift	ss	~	~
astrik	*	ital 1\8	ital 1\8

Figure 11-K. Symbols for coded photocomposition

Operations used in many systems are listed in the Description/Function column in Figure 11-K. Their meanings are described here:

● <u>Quad left</u>: moves characters flush left and fills out the line with space. This command must be given for the last line of a justified paragraph or the space band will justify   a   line   like   this

- <u>Quad right</u>: moves characters flush right and fills out the line with space

- <u>Quad center</u>: centers characters in a line and fills out the line at left and right with space

- <u>Quad middle</u>: moves one justified column flush left and another column flush right, and sets space between columns

- <u>Call (first group)</u>: sets a programmed series of functions; for example, a 12-point head, centered, followed by 4 points of leading, followed by a paragraph indention

- <u>Call (second group)</u>: sets a programmed series of functions different from the first group

- <u>Tab left, tab right, tab center</u>: sets groups of characters in columns as for tables; tab left sets a column flush left, tab right sets a column flush right, tab center sets a column with centered lines

- <u>Tab around</u>: sets items between columns, for example, the words "U.S.A. only" to appear only once or twice in a long list of books

- <u>With x</u>: can mean various things, for example, "with x." sets leaders, "with xr" sets a baseline rule

- <u>Thin space</u>: sets one-third of an em space (a three-to-the-em space) in most machines

- <u>En space</u>: used to align figures; for example, for the first space in the second line: 1234
                                                                567

- <u>Discretionary hyphen</u>: overrides the computer's word division

- <u>Lower rail, upper rail</u>: designates two groups of type fonts, for example, /U2 sets the second font in the upper group

- <u>Hold reg. (save)</u>: enters matter in the computer's memory for later retrieval. For example, a magazine's masthead could be entered in the memory and would not need to be reset for every issue

- <u>Hold reg. (recall)</u>: retrieves matter from the memory

- <u>Supershift</u>: accesses pi characters. <u>Pi characters</u> are characters other than letters or numbers usually not found on a standard typewriter keyboard; for example:

●÷×○©■□★%☆◆◇][¢□©®●™%₵=®−@+

Figure 11-L shows a manuscript with the corresponding printout marked by the proofreader according to the code in Figure 11-K.

Barbados	Israel	Romania
Benin	Ivory Coast	Rwanda
Bhutan	Jamaica	Sao Tome and
		Principe
Bolivia	Jordan	Senegal
Botswana	Kenya	Sierra Leone
Brazil	Korea, Republic of	Singapore
Burma	Lebanon	Somalia
Burundi	Lesotho	Sri Lanka
Cameroon	Liberia	Sudan
Cape Verde	Malagasy Republic	Surinam
Central African	Malawi	Swaziland
Republic		
Chad	Maldive Islands	Tanzania

(1)   Manuscript

```
00321 Barbados/<  Israel/<  Romania/1

00322 Benin/<  Ivory Coast/<  Rwanda/1

00323 Bhutan/<  Jamaica/<  Sao Tome and/Prin        QL/J

00324 Cipe/I                                   TL  TL  ac/Prin

00325 Bolivia/<  Jordan/<                        Senegal/I

00326 Botswana/<  Kenya/<  Sierra Leone/1

00327 Brazil/<  Korea, Republic of/<  Singapore/1

00328 Burma/<  Lebanon/<  Somalia/1

00329 Burundi/<  Lesotho/<  Sri Lanka/1

00330 Cameroon/<  Liberia/<  Sudan/1

00331 Cape Verde/<  Malagasy Republic/<  Surinam/1

00332 Central African/<  Malawi/1                TL/ run on

00400 Swaziland/1

00401 #Republic/1

00402 Chad/<  Maldive Islands/<  Tanzania/1
```

(2)   Printout

Figure 11-L.   Manuscript and reduced printout

WORD PROCESSING/TYPESETTING INTERFACE

Word processing machines can interface with phototypesetting machines directly, through a telephone line, or through a computer. The interface is programmed to act as reader and translator of the coded signal that has been typed on the word processor.

Codes

In systems with interfaces or OCR scanners, or in systems that produce printouts, several kinds of codes are used. Proofreaders must have instructions or copies of the codes, which vary from system to system and often from font to font. (See Part III for a sample instruction sheet, How To Proofread Lexitron Copy Coded for the Computer.) Several kinds of codes are used:

Macro codes, used instead of traditional typemarking and proofreading symbols, convert editor's marks and type specifications to the use of the typist. For example, a "move right" bracket translates to QL. (The Mark-up/Proofreading column in Figure 11-K shows a macro code.)

Command codes are instructions to the typesetting machine for spacing, styling, and formatting given in combinations of regular typewriter characters. A coded command may be a series of arbitrarily chosen symbols (///%%fb104965c///), or it may be a mnemonic code or a combination.

In mnemonic codes, often a one-word command is coded (after a special character) with its first letter, and a two-word command is coded with the first letter of each word. For example, the code for quad left may be :QL, or the code for "use ligatures" may be !li.

Precedence codes are based on the composing machine's "supershift" position. The following layout shows the characters on the top row of a keyboard in unshift, shift, and supershift positions for one font. To set an opening bracket in this font, a precedence code (always starting with a special character such as a slash) might read /ss7 (slash, supershift, 7 key).

	¾	fi	fl	⅓	⅔	−	−	[	]	÷	•	⅛	⅜			
	¼	!	@	#	$	%	¢	&	*	(	)	—	=			
	½	1	2	3	4	5	6	7	8	9	0	-	×			

To code for most pi characters, a mnemonic or precedence code may be used.

COMPUTER PRINTOUT EQUIPMENT

Some of the computer "printers"--the machines that print out computer data, including text--are highly sophisticated, very fast, and capable of producing excellent type quality. The fine typesetting machines of the future may develop from this category.

Line printers work so fast that they seem to print out a line at a time. Actually, they produce a set of the same characters in one line at a time; for example, all the a's at once, then all the b's, and so on.

Serial printers print out one character at a time, usually for-
ward--from left to right--but some machines go forward for one
line, then backward for the next, and continue reversing direction.

Impact printers, line and serial, produce an image by the forceful
contact of the print character and ink against the printing surface.
(A typewriter is a simple impact printer.) Impact printers include
those with their characters on a ball, a chain, a drum, or at the
ends of spokes on a "daisy wheel."

Dot matrix printers create characters from a dot pattern, something
like this: ::: The dot matrix, which permits a ready change of
font, is used in several kinds of printers. Some of these printers,
in a graphics mode, can increase or decrease the number of dots
in an area and produce a halftone. Some require special paper--
thermal, electrographic, electrostatic, or xerographic. An impact
dot matrix printer strikes specific dots against ribbon and paper,
one row of dots at a time. An ink jet printer directs jets of
ink droplets through a dot matrix against blank paper.

Digital plotters use an implement to write on a surface; for example, an ink pen to write on paper or a laser to write on photo-
sensitive material. A drum plotter draws on a writing surface
wrapped around a drum; a flat-bed plotter draws on a flat surface.

Special Problems With Cold Type Composition

The term "cold type composition" refers to a variety of processes,
including typing, word processing, phototypesetting, computer printouts, and any others that do not involve hot (molten metal) type.

You must not mark on the image area of any camera-ready copy. There
are several ways to mark--in the far margins, on a tissue overlay,
on a correction list, or on a wide, folded-over margin (marking on
the back of the paper, line for line). If marks are made on the
copy itself, they must not touch type or any image and must be in
a nonreproducing color--usually pale blue for the camera and pink
for laser copy. Marking techniques for camera-ready copy are discussed in detail in Chapter 9.

If a correction that is cut into or pasted onto a phototype primary
has been set on a different machine or with a different lens (or
if a variation is introduced in the developing process), the type
will look slightly different, almost like the wrong font. On a
proof, circle such a word or passage and write "wf? check type"
in the margin. A primary that buckles (does not lie flat) will
result in a proof with a passage of distorted type or a white
line through a page; this requires the marginal mark, "check type
for buckle." Density of the image may be a problem; if a word
or passage appears too bold or too light, write "check type for
density."

Copying machine copies may have spots from dust or other particles
that are not on the proof. When you see a black spot on a photocopied proof, look at the following pages. If the same spot appears in the same place on more than one page, do not mark it.

An OCR scanner cannot correctly read broken or faint letters. For example, it may read h as n, g or p as o, y as v, I as l, double quotes as single, and opening quotes as closing. Figure 11-M illustrates this problem.

MR. BLAKEY: Would you have any indication y/
from just street knowledge, are people beginning to g/g
set up their operations with an idea of your down
time involved?

MR. VERNIER: Not that I am aware of, no, sir. h/

MR. BLAKEY: Would you expect that to be a
normal development once they find out about it?

MR. VERNIER: Yes. If the down time were extended to a two-or three-week period, certainly we y/
could expect some countermeasures on the part of
traffickers.

MR. BLAKEY: Have you found any difference y/
now—I am asking you practically—between the g/p
New York experience where you had access to the
state process and had a short down time, and your
current Detroit experience where you have a long h/
Federal down time? Has that down time
impacted—not on your desire—but your street ef- p/y
fectiveness?

Figure 11-M.   Proof from bad OCR copy

Do not worry about the general quality of type from certain CRT typesetters. In a proof mode, to increase speed these typesetters print fewer scan lines to the inch. The characters will be denser and sharper in the final printing.

Recurrent crowded or widely spaced characters in copy from a keyboard machine may come from an escapement problem. The escapement is the ratchet device that regulates the spacing on a typewriter mechanism. Figure 11-N illustrates bad escapement and other problems and describes them in the correction list. (Note that the list is written in general terms because the problems occur too often to mark individually.)

In artwork, boxes and borders should have perfectly mitred corners. In geometric designs such as boxes, lines must be clean and of even width and blackness. The adjacent box is not acceptable.

Poorly drawn box

Wrong-reading matter occurs when film, or a portion of it, is stripped in wrong side up; for example:

ƨⱯƐ⋜l

SALESMEN'S COMPENSATION AND ACTIVITIES
JULY 1975

JOB DEFINITIONS

1. RETAIL SALESMAN: Covers retail trade in assigned territory. Performs both sales and merchandising jobs.

2. JOBBING SALESMAN: Covers jobbers, chains, and selected important accounts.

3. COMBINATION SALESMAN: Covers jobbers, chains, and retail trade in assigned territory.

4. ACCOUNT MANAGER: Covers headquarters and retail outlets of major chain and wholesale accounts. Territory follows distribution pattern.

5. INSTITUTIONAL SALESMAN: Covers hotels, restaurants, hospitals and similar accounts, both direct and indirect, in an assigned territory.

6. SUPERVISOR - TY   nd supervise   en. A selling, if

7.

```
        (1)   Copy with problems
```

```
        ●  Bad escapement:  Note close
           spacing between N and S,
           I and O; wide spacing between
           R and V, R and E, and often
           after A
           (A CTIVITIES, S ALESMAN)

        ●  Misalignment:  Note, for
           example, in top line,
           t is below baseline,
           o is above it

        ●  Dirty type:  Note, for example,
           relative blackness in item 1
           of the following:
           retail trade
```

```
    (2)   Correction list
```

```
        Figure 11-N.  Bad escapement and other problems
```

If a paste-up or cut-in drops off, it will leave a blank space, an uncorrected error, or a hole in the paper. The example in Figure 11-O shows what happened when a cut-in correction was insecurely taped to typewritten camera-ready copy.

Oral Argument[22]

     The Seventh Circuit strongly favors oral argument. As lawyers who represent clients regularly before the ▌ederal Courts, we find oral argument to be essential in most appeals.[23] The Court of Appeals for the Seventh Circuit does not eliminate oral argument without the consent of

Figure 11-O. Dropped-off cut-in

A cut-in or pasted-up word, line, or block of type must be precisely spaced and aligned, or the result is a frequent cold type problem--crooked or badly spaced copy. Figure 11-P shows a crooked paste-up.

---

deliberations of the Commission itself. That does not mean, however, that we regard all of our recommendations only as topics for further study. There seem to us good reasons for implementing several of the suggestions and no strong arguments to the contrary. Among these we would include: beefing up the capability of ARA to handle regional issues, particularly economic ones; appointing a special assistant to the assistant secretary (ARA) to assess the impacts of U.S. actions on Latin America; and establishing mechanisms for improved consultation between State and Congress. Creating an advisory panel or shifting responsibility for instructing U.S. delegates to multilateral banks would probably be more difficult to accomplish but could well have more effect on policy outcomes.

align

Figure 11-P. Crooked paste-up

Figure 3-B, an example in Chapter 3 of incorrect leading, could also serve as an example of bad paste-up. There is often no way to tell whether leading was incorrectly set or whether the paste-up was careless; you can know only if you have the camera-ready copy or if you can see the cut-lines (knife lines) around the edges of the cut-in or paste-up. Whatever the cause of the crookedness, mark such an error as a leading error.

Some machines depend entirely on the operator to make end-of-line divisions. Others are programmed for correct word division according to a dictionary.

Some machines can be set to divide words automatically by logic rather than by meaning. In such machines, an audible signal can

be set to sound when a line is in justification range. The operator can then check the automatic word division and override it the
few times the machine makes a wrong division; this process is known
as discretionary hyphening. To save typesetting time, it is often
practical to ignore the override feature, let a few words be mis-
divided, and correct the errors after proofreaders have marked them
as in Figure 11-Q.

confounded by the cha-
racteristics of their surroundings.

if the industry was una-
ble to control the agents and facilities.

—Electricity ge-
nerated from chicken manure is

Figure 11-Q. Wrong word division

QUESTIONS FOR STUDENTS

1. Define in your own words: pitch, escapement, jumping folios,
minus leading, pi characters, quad right, impact dot matrix printer.

2. What do these acronyms stand for: VDT, OCR, CRT?

3. Why would the following situations be considered poor
proofreading?

    a. You are proofreading the galley proofs of a bibliography.
    The typesetter has set every group of page references with hy-
    phens instead of en dashes. You mark each one for correction.

    b. You are proofreading six galleys. On galley 3 you find
    a footnote callout. The footnote itself is set on galley 6.
    You mark the bottom margin of galley 3 for the insertion of a
    cut-off rule and the footnote.

    c. You find 20 defective lowercase d's on one galley. You
    mark them all.

    d. You are proofreading single-spaced typescript on 8-1/2"
    X 11" pages with one-inch margins. On line 38 of page 5 you
    find a callout for a table. The three-inch-deep table appears
    on page 6. You mark it to be moved to the bottom of page 5.

    e. You are revising word processing copy. Every place you
    marked =/ for a hyphen you find that the typist has inserted
    an equal sign. You invent a new mark, ⩘ , to be sure the
    copy will be properly corrected this time.

Chapter 12

Typographic Standards

If the Ignorant look upon PRINTING without admiring It; it is, because they do not understand the same: The Learned have always judged it far otherways; and have, with Reason, thought, That, for almost the Three Ages wherein this Wonder hath been seen in Europe, the Wit of Man did never invent any Thing that was either more lucky, or more useful for Instruction.

--The History of the Art of Printing
printed by James Watson, 1713

CHAPTER OVERVIEW

This chapter describes conventional standards for dealing with typographic problems ranging from bad breaks to crooked paste-up.

INTRODUCTION

You must know which corrections are practical and suitable for the copy you are working with (as discussed in previous chapters), and you must know what constitutes an error.

Few standards are inflexible. Often the answer to a typographic question is, "It depends." Tight deadlines, low budget jobs, inadequate specifications from a customer, or other factors require lower standards than fine press printing. Newspaper work ignores many of the standards given in this chapter for leading and spacing; it is miracle enough to get so much information in print daily. For all these reasons, keep these guidelines in mind for every job:

- Know what the customer and the typesetter or typist expect.
- When you are sure of bad style, mark it for correction.
- When you are unsure, query.

BAD BREAKS

A break is a division of a word or line. Bad breaks include the following:

- <u>Illogical divisions</u>--of groups of characters, words, lines, or heads

- <u>Badly proportioned lines</u>--in a head, next to an illustration, or in other display matter

- <u>Unsightly blocks of similar characters</u> on a page

- <u>Widows</u> (discussed later).

Figure 12-A shows several kinds of bad breaks from the bottom of one column to the top of the next: a short line ends a column, single and double quotes are separated, and a closing quote begins a line.

"People that have been working and such are just very reluctant until the very last resort to go in and say, 'I need that,'

/" said Hopkins. "It's a great deal of pride that people have."

Figure 12-A.   Bad breaks

Blocks of Same Characters

Hyphens

Most style guides and typesetters allow no <u>ladders</u> of more than three successive lines ending with hyphens--except in short measure, when greater leeway is needed to avoid bad wordspacing or bad letterspacing. Figure 12-B shows (1) a block of seven hyphens--unacceptable by any standard, (2) a block of four marked for correction, and (3) the correction of (2).

Thus, under current law, what the Bell System does do under court order is the following. It provides information to government agents or police about the location of cable or telephone connections of specific lines approved for interception and, when requested, it rents a private-line connection from the intercepted line to a government office where a listening post may be located.

(1)   Block of seven hyphens

Office of the International Decade of Ocean Exploration
(This office supports U.S. federal and nonfederal participation in the U.N. IDOE program in selected major oceanographic research efforts in the four main IDOE program categories of environmental quality, environmental forecasting, seabed assessment and living resources.)

(2)   Galley with marked errors

Office of the International Decade of Ocean Exploration
(This office supports U.S. federal and nonfederal participation in the U.N. IDOE program in selected major oceanographic research efforts in the four main IDOE program categories of environmental quality, environmental forecasting, seabed assessment and living resources.)

(3)   Revise with correction

Figure 12-B.   Blocks of hyphens

Same Words

When the same word or words end successive lines, mark for correction or query. Figure 12-C is a gross example of this problem, which is marked with a query because rewriting would be needed to solve the problem; the narrow measure prohibits a typographic solution.

Reasonable rules prohibit more than two lines ending in the same word and more than one line ending with the same two words (as in Figure 12-D).

The man who handles the soccer details for the league is George Patrick Duffy, the general manager of Rhode Island Oceaneers, the 1974 champions and the backbone of the league. The Oceaneers are one of the teams that comes close to having a major league appeal. The Boston Astros and the Cincinnati Comets are the others.

Figure 12-C. Block of
            same word

"The only issue is whether conservation will be mandated by an emergency or whether it will be done in a sensible way, conserving by eliminating waste rather than eliminating jobs."

Figure 12-D. Block of same
            two words

Paragraph Breaks

The last line of a justified paragraph should have interword spacing approximately equal to the lines above and below it. Standards vary for how long the last line of a paragraph should be. One standard accepts no last line at full measure; at least an en space must end the last line. Another standard accepts last lines at full measure; however, when a last line is shorter than full measure, that standard calls for an em space or more at the end of the line. (See the section on widows in this chapter for further discussion of breaks at the last line of a paragraph.)

Word and Unity Division

Word Division

> Theories are elastic,--are expansible and compressible;
> but types of metal have set dimensions of extension,
> and, in some circumstances, absolutely refuse to budge,--
> wherefore theories must gracefully yield, and allow, it
> may be, a two-letter division even in a wide measure.
> Types are tyrannical, and will sometimes perpetrate
> solecisms under the plea of necessity.
>
> --Benjamin Drew

Word divisions are line-end word breaks. Words are normally divided at the ends of lines to justify copy, or to avoid short lines or blocked lines in unjustified copy with intentionally uneven margins (instructions may state, for example, "Divide words only to avoid three lines the same width").

The American style of word division is based on the pronunciation, not the root, of a word; for example:

>   bureauc-racy (not bureau-cracy)
>   dep-rivation (not de-privation)
>   extraor-dinary (not extra-ordinary)
>   han-dler (not hand-ler)
>   knowl-edge (not know-ledge)
>   microm-eter (not micro-meter; but centi-meter is correct)
>   noth-ing (not no-thing)
>   photog-raphy (not photo-graphy)
>   psychol-ogy (not psycho-logy)
>   res-toration (not re-storation)

Common sense can tell you when a word division is misleading. When a break leads a reader to think the word is a different one, the break should be corrected. Remember the child's riddle with intentionally misleading syllabication: What does po-lop-ony spell? Not polopony, polo pony! Such deceptive breaks (poloponies) should be avoided.

A widely followed printer's convention calls for dividing the word "service," and similar words such as "novice," after the _v_ to avoid such unfortunate lines as the second in the following:

>   My life of public ser-
>   vice has been rewarding.

Divisions that are not between syllables, such as the following, _must_ be avoided: bed-raggled, cop-ilot, cow-orker, miss-pelt, misl-ed, the-rapist. Divisions of one-syllable words, as in the following examples, are never acceptable: plan-ned, ship-ped, quench-ed, tor-que.

Divisions such as the following _should_ be avoided, even though they are made between syllables: read-just, reap-pear, serv-iceman, ser-viceman. Dividing after a separately pronounced prefix and before a base word or between other combining forms is the answer (re-adjust, re-appear, service-man).

Beware of double consonants in present participles. Always divide on the base word--that is, before _ing_ when the base word ends in doubled consonants and between doubled consonants when the second consonant would not appear in the base word alone: toll-ing, process-ing, add-ing; swim-ming, refer-ring, forbid-ding.

Dictionaries or style guides do not always agree on word division. Following are a few of the words on which they differ:

>   af-ter, aft-er   wo-man, wom-an
>   bus-i-ness, busi-ness   as-cen-dant, as-cend-ant
>   mea-sure, meas-ure   be-ha-vior, be-hav-ior

When no style guide or dictionary is specified, words may be divided according to any acceptable system of syllabication. No known system would accept any of the divisions in Figure 12-E.

where the brideg-
room is serving a term

Amelia Island, Fla., pu-
blishes a monthly newsletter

tenants have low-paying, unst-
able winter jobs.

section 30-13.3 (Generalized Development Plan Re-
gulations) requiring "owners" signature for proffers,

lack of control over resources handicaps State's effectiveness

a national system ope-
rated by the United States, with a

dozens of sweepstakes and cont-
ests held as attention-getting devices

everybody was mo
aning about how they had found

fundamental retren-
chment

now com-
es with a steel cutting blade.

pour it into home mor-
tgages.

the fri-
end has become a big wheel

local gover-
nment measures

to regulate lan-
dlords and

Figure 12-E.   Unacceptable word divisions

Homographs

Homographs--words with the same spelling but different meaning and often with different pronunciation--may be divided differently.

One group of homographs is divided on the base word when er is added to indicate a person or device performing the action of the base word; for example:

    ad-der (snake); add-er (one who adds)
    coun-ter (against); count-er (one who counts)
    foun-der (to sink); found-er (one who originates)
    gai-ner (high dive); gain-er (one who gains)
    wa-ger (bet); wag-er (one who bets)

Another group is divided differently according to pronunciation; for example:

    ar-ith-metic (adj.); a-rith-me-tic (n.)
    at-tri-bute (n.); at-trib-ute (v.)
    de-sert (something deserved; to abandon); des-ert (barren land)
    even-ing (making even); eve-ning (nightfall)
    in-va-lid (not well); in-val-id (not valid)
    leg-ate (n.); le-gate (v.)

```
min-ute (60 seconds); mi-nute (small)
nest-ling (n.); nes-tling (v.)
pe-ri-od-ic (at intervals); per-i-od-ic (chemical term)
pres-ent (n., adj.); pre-sent (v.)
pro-duce (v.); prod-uce (n.)
prog-ress (n.); pro-gress (v.)
proj-ect (n.); pro-ject (v.)
pro-tes-tant (law); Prot-es-tant (religion)
re-bel (v.); reb-el (adj., n.)
rec-ord (adj., n.); re-cord (v.)
ref-use (adj., n.); re-fuse (v.)
trav-erse (n.); tra-verse (v.)
```

A third group of homographs and near homographs follows no apparent logic; for example:

```
stran-ger (n.); strang-er (adj.)
ex-per-tise (n.); ex-pert-ize (v.)
pi-a-no (softly); pi-an-o (instrument)
```

Errors in any of the three groups would not be considered blatant; you would not mark them in a job requiring minimal correction.

Division of Unities

Certain expressions made up of nouns, symbols, abbreviations, numerals, or combinations of these form unities that must not be broken; for example, an ellipsis shown with asterisks or periods must not be broken, nor can any of the following:

19(2)	pp. 9-11	38° C.
page 12	1971 A.D.	$20.45
Chart A	8:30 p.m.	FY 1968

Some unities may be broken at a normal word division or where a word begins; for example:

Right: . . . section (a)(4)   Wrong: . . . . . . section (a)(4)

. . . . sec-
tion (a)(4)

Right: . . . . . . Table 2   Wrong: . . . . Table 2

. . . . Ta-
ble 2

Right: . . . . . Appendix A   Wrong: . . . . . Appendix A

. . . . Appen-
dix A

Right: . . . US$274 million

. . . . US$274
million
. . . . US$274 mil-
lion

Wrong: . . . . US$
274 million

Right: . . . . January 29,
1976
. . . . Janu-
ary 29, 1976

Wrong: . . . . . . January
29, 1976

Right:*. . Mr. Henry Johnson

. . . Mr. Henry John-
son

Wrong: . . . . Mr.
Henry Johnson

Right: . . Henry Jones, Jr.

. . . . Henry
Jones, Jr.

Wrong: . . . Henry Jones,
Jr.

Right:*. . . . J. F. Kennedy

. . . . . J. F. Ken-
nedy

Wrong: . . . . J. F.
Kennedy

Some long unities may be broken at a logical division; for example:

. . . pp. 2345-
2349.

Figure 12-F shows broken unities needing correction.

---

randa and Decision Memoranda) is listed in Annex
A.

(1) Widow and broken unity

[1]Poll of AAAS members, *Science*, Vol. 145, 24 July 1964, p.
368.

(2) Broken unity

Food Problem found U.S. delegates like Senator
Richard Clark among the most vocal participants.[1]
[1] Indeed, Senator Clark and his congressional col-
leagues were the most animated spokesmen for a

(3) Broken unity (footnote callout 11)

Figure 12-F.   Broken unities

---

*Some styles do not permit division of a proper name except in
narrow measure.

Standards in Division

Before starting to proofread, find out what standards apply to
the job.

Even low standards should not permit any of the following:

- Illogical syllable division

- Division of a one-syllable word, including a one-syllable
  contraction

- Division that isolates one letter, numeral, or symbol.

Figure 12-G shows examples of this last rule broken.

is three years old and home to more than 2,-
500 persons living in houses selling for $32,-

when you reach the age of eight-
y, you deserve.

. said that the signs, "u--
biquitous" throughout

the disturbance must be clearly audible a-
cross property lines or through partitions.

Figure 12-G.   Isolation of one character

Normal standards do not permit any of the following, even in short
measure:

- Any of the divisions listed under the low standards above

- Division that splits a syllable:

  <u>Right</u>: Wednes-day   <u>Wrong</u>: Wed-nes-day
         colo-nel   col-o-nel

- Division that is confusing or misleading:

  <u>Right</u>: Worcester-shire   <u>Wrong</u>: Wor-ces-ter-shire
         fa-cetious   face-tious
         scarc-ity   scar-city
         funer-al   fun-eral
         ma-terial   mate-rial

- Division that splits a short unity, as described previously

- Division leaving a carryover of <u>ed</u> or <u>es</u>.

Normal standards permit none of the following in a normal measure
but allow reasonable leeway in short lines:

- Division of short words (five or fewer letters)

- Division of numerals with five or fewer digits

- Carryovers of fewer than six digits in a numeral

- Division of compound words at any place other than the orthographic hyphen

- Division in abbreviations, acronyms, or symbol groups of fewer than six characters; carryovers of fewer than three characters

- Division of two-syllable contractions

- Division of the last word in a paragraph

- Division in more than three successive lines.

Extra high standards do not permit the following:

- Any of the divisions listed under low and normal standards

- Division of the last word on a page

- Division of proper names, unless unavoidable

- Division leaving any two-letter carryovers

- Division in more than two successive lines.

Hyphens and Dashes

Do not add hyphens to any of the following divisions:

- Long references. Break them after a closing parenthesis. Add no hyphen. The following entry may be broken at three places:

  14(A)(3)(b)(ii)

- Long abbreviations or acronyms. Break them after letters denoting a complete word. Add no hyphen. The second letter group in the following example can be broken at only one place:

  CINC SOUTHCOM

- Lines ending in a virgule. Break them after the virgule. Add no hyphen (see Figure 12-H).

- Land description symbol groups. Break them after a fraction: $W\frac{1}{2}SE\frac{1}{4}SE\frac{1}{4}$. Add no hyphen.

- Scientific, mathematical, or technical equations or formulas. Add no hyphen. In some cases, they may be broken after a hyphen that is part of the original group:

  2,4-dihydroxy-1(4-methylpentyl)benzine

gested that the present scope of the economic/-
commercial cone is too broad and that the Foreign

(1) Bad break

These general observations are but prelude to
the main theme of this essay. The environmentalist-
(run back) /conservationist theme in congressional decision-
making forms an important context for understand-

(2) Bad break

These general observations are but prelude to
the main theme of this essay. The environmentalist/
conservationist theme in congressional decision-

(3) Correction of (2) shows proper break

Figure 12-H. Dividing on a virgule

Some styles* specify that lines may not begin with hyphens or dashes
(see Figure 12-I) unless they are list items, credit lines, signa-
tures, or quotations in certain foreign languages. In the most
usual typewriter style, dashes are closed up.

Over the past few years the role of the consumer
—policy officials who rely on economic intelligence
—has gained increasing attention within the Government. So far as departmental analysis is con-

run over so 2 dashes do not begin lines

Figure 12-I. Em dashes begin lines

Ideally, typeset dashes are set with a hairspace on either side.
In practice they are often either closed up or set with as much
space as between words, and both ways often appear in the same
document.

Re-proofreading Word Division Corrections

Figure 12-J shows that a one-character correction may make little
difference in spacing. Figures 12-K and 12-L show how great the
changes can be when several characters are involved.

Note that in Figure 12-K all lines but the last have been respaced
and three new word divisions have been introduced. In Figure 12-L,
all lines have been respaced, a new line has been created, and the
revised paragraph ends in a divided word.

All words in reset lines must be re-proofread, preferably by two-
person proofreading against the draft rather than against the

*Including GPO style.

previous proof. All new word divisions must be checked. Even with word processing or computer typesetting, when re-keyboarding is not always needed, there is always the possibility of new errors.

---

prehensive level focuses concern upon the overarching purpose of making and keeping the planet habitable. However, such efforts do not provide a viable basis for the design of international regimes.

(1) Incorrect word division in galley

prehensive level focuses concern upon the overarching purpose of making and keeping the planet habitable. However, such efforts do not provide a viable basis for the design of international regimes.

(2) Correction in revised galley

Figure 12-J. One character respaced

The current OMB/OSD advocacy system is less desirable than some form of independent consideration of the marginal $5 billion (or so) in the Defense/non-Defense trade-off. Whether that independent agency is OMB acting with greater authority over the Defense budget, an expanded DPRC, or an independent executive agency in the EOP is far less important than the establishment of the function itself—a periodic NSSM 3 exercise, done on a smaller scale with a permanent staff.

(1) Incorrect word division in galley

The current OMB/OSD advocacy system is less desirable than some form of independent consideration of the marginal $5 billion (or so) in the Defense/non-Defense trade-off. Whether that independent agency is OMB acting with greater authority over the Defense budget, an expanded DPRC, or an independent executive agency in the EOP is far less important than the establishment of the function itself—a periodic NSSM 3 exercise, done on a smaller scale with a permanent staff.

(2) Correction in revised galley

Figure 12-K. Several characters respaced

General Principles for Ragged Right Copy

On ragged right pages, to avoid margin violations and bad breaks, mark for short lines rather than long. If an unbreakable word goes over the margin, mark the entire word to run over. (<u>Sloughed</u> and <u>quenched</u> are eight-letter one-syllable words. <u>Through</u>, <u>brought</u>, <u>sleight</u>, and <u>roughed</u> are among those with seven letters. The longest known one-syllable word is an invented one meaning "traveled by brougham"--<u>broughammed</u>.)

Another fault you must always mark on ragged right copy, even when a short line will result, is a <u>buck tooth</u>--an entire word that projects beyond the end of the line below it. Mark a buck tooth to run over or, if possible, to break.

Sense Breaks

Heads

Be sure that all heads longer than one line are broken "by sense." Some newspapers rule that "by sense" means a head's first line cannot <u>end</u> in an article, adjective, preposition, or conjunction. Editors of some publications may interpret "by sense" to mean that a line cannot <u>begin</u> with a preposition or a conjunction. Whatever

The lack of control over resources handicaps State's effectiveness in science and technology policy in a number of ways. Conventional FSOs, when assigned to this area, do not adequately understand problems and programs involving resources and do not quite know how to handle them in a foreign policy framework. People from the scientific and technical fields brought into the Department laterally as civil servants or FSRs understand programs, but they do not usually have a strong background in foreign policy and are thus intellectually handicapped in integrating science and technology with the needs of foreign policy. Moreover, they are bureaucratically handicapped within the Department by virtue of being looked down upon as people who do not quite "belong." Thus, even when promising policy initiatives integrating science and technology with foreign policy are proposed, they are likely to meet multiple hurdles in being accepted. Quite apart from the regard in which scientific and technical people are held in the Department, promising policy initiatives involving science and technology may not be favorably received because this is much too esoteric a subject for the more traditional diplomats occupying key positions in State. There are thus built-in disincentives for State personnel with scientific and technical backgrounds and a genuine concern for fundamentals of policy to project themselves into the policy area by leaning on their technical expertise.[18]

run over

The lack of control over resources handicaps State's effectiveness in science and technology policy in a number of ways. Conventional FSOs, when assigned to this area, do not adequately understand problems and programs involving resources and do not quite know how to handle them in a foreign policy framework. People from the scientific and technical fields brought into the Department laterally as civil servants or FSRs understand programs, but they do not usually have a strong background in foreign policy and are thus intellectually handicapped in integrating science and technology with the needs of foreign policy. Moreover, they are bureaucratically handicapped within the Department by virtue of being looked down upon as people who do not quite "belong." Thus, even when promising policy initiatives integrating science and technology with foreign policy are proposed, they are likely to meet multiple hurdles in being accepted. Quite apart from the regard in which scientific and technical people are held in the Department, promising policy initiatives involving science and technology may not be favorably received because this is much too esoteric a subject for the more traditional diplomats occupying key positions in State. There are thus built-in disincentives for State personnel with scientific and technical backgrounds and a genuine concern for fundamentals of policy to project themselves into the policy area by leaning on their technical expertise.[18]

widow

(1) Incorrect word division

(2) Correction in revised galley

Figure 12-L.   Several lines respaced

the guidelines, certain breaks are not sensible, and you must mark them for corrections.

Pay attention also to the appearance of heads, and avoid lines much shorter or longer than others.

With the sense and the appearance of a head in mind, its first line should be as close to full measure as possible. Figure 12-M demonstrates this principle with column heads. (See also the section on heads in Chapter 16.)

Normally, word breaks are not allowed in centerheads (centered heads) but are permitted in heads blocked flush left or indented.

Last Word on Page

Specifications may state that if the last line on a page would complete a sentence that does not end a paragraph, a word must be run over. This rule would apply particularly to blocked, ragged right paragraphs so that the reader does not think a paragraph begins on the next page. The rule might also apply to extra high quality work--to lead the reader from one page to the next.

IMPROVING THE QUALITY OF LIFE (REGIME A)

    Rainmaking in Southeast Asia—A Bureaucratic Nightmare

IV. UNCOVERING AND MAKING AD HOC ADJUSTMENTS FOR UNFORTUNATE INTERLOCKS OF OPERATING STYLE

Science and Technology in the Agency for International Development (AID): Present Organization vs. New Requirements of Foreign Policy

(1) Bad breaks in headings

IMPROVING THE QUALITY OF LIFE (REGIME A)

    Rainmaking in Southeast Asia— A Bureaucratic Nightmare

IV. UNCOVERING AND MAKING AD HOC ADJUSTMENTS FOR UNFORTUNATE INTERLOCKS OF OPERATING STYLE

Science and Technology in the Agency for International Development (AID): Present Organization vs. New Requirements of Foreign Policy

(2) Corrected breaks

Figure 12-M. Breaks corrected for sense and appearance

Widows

<u>Widow lines</u> (page widows) occur

- when the first line of a page or column is the last line of a paragraph (<u>page-top widow</u> or <u>top-line widow</u>), and

- when the last line of a page or column is the first line of a paragraph (sometimes called an <u>orphan</u>, a <u>page-bottom widow</u>, or a <u>bottom-line widow</u>).

<u>Paragraph widows</u> occur

- when the last line of a paragraph is the last half of a broken word (<u>broken-word paragraph widow</u>), and

- when the last line of a paragraph is a single word (<u>single-word paragraph widow</u>).

<u>Head widows</u> occur in heads or captions with long lines

- when part of a word stands alone on a line, and

- when one word stands alone on a line.

Unacceptable top-line widows are variously defined. Some printers and publishers consider the last line of an item in a list acceptable when other listed items follow. Some consider a line three-quarters as wide as full measure acceptable. By either of these standards, the top line in Figure 12-N is not a widow.

---

16   8   1024 0   0
ENDS ON MS. P. 7195

the effectiveness of U.S. assistance efforts,

6. Drawing on the financial and management assets of private enterprise through broader guarantees and investment surveys,

7. Mobilizing free world aid sources by coordinating multilateral programs, increasing amounts of aid, and lengthening commitments, and

8. Separation of economic and social development assistance from military assistance by proposing a separate authorization bill for military assistance, requesting appropriations for military assistance as part of the Defense budget, and providing coordination within State for military assistance with the economic assistance policies.

What Effects, Intended and Otherwise, Were Actually Experienced? The effects of the reorganization are

Figure 12-N.   Widow?   Not by some standards

Page widows are not acceptable in meticulous work. In commercial work, bottom-line widows are considered a lesser evil than top-line widows. Some standards accept bottom-line widows at any time and top-line widows when they are needed to maintain uniform page length and make-up (the U.S. Government Printing Office has these standards).

Usually, in pages with columns, a top-line widow is unacceptable only in the lefthand column, and a bottom-line widow only in the righthand column.

Although single-word paragraph widows were frowned on in the past, some designers today consider it desirable to break up a page with single-word paragraph widows; however, few approve broken-word paragraph widows (see Figure 12-O), especially if the runover has fewer than seven letters.

Early in fiscal year 1976, administration of the LEAA courts program was transferred from the Office of National Priority Programs to the Office of Regional Operations.

Figure 12-O.   Broken-word paragraph widow

Head widows are rarely acceptable. When every line of a head or caption is short, however, one word on a line is not an undesirable widow.

In fine press work, the best way to eliminate widow lines may be to do so editorially--by rewriting. In commercial work, the best way to eliminate widows may be to do so typographically: Space around subheadings may be increased or decreased, extra leading may be inserted between paragraphs (or even between lines), or word-spacing may be increased or decreased in a paragraph to create or lose a line. In books, widows can often be eliminated by shortening or lengthening facing pages by one line. But unless they are painstakingly done, any of the typographic solutions to widows can cause problems more unsightly than a widow.

WORDSPACING

In different typesetting methods, wordspacing may be measured differently--in points, divisions of ems, or other units. Each phototypesetting system uses a different unit system.

When the spacing unit is fixed (not variable), as on many typewriters, lines can be ragged right (flush left), ragged left (flush right), or centered (both margins ragged). If both margins are flush (justified), the result is unequal wordspacing, and a page will have many "holes" of white space.

When the units of space are variable, both margins can be set even (justified), which is the common format. Some typographers prefer a ragged right format because wordspacing can be made uniform and blocks of type shaped more interestingly.

Standards

Ideally, the space between words should appear the same in all lines of text on a page. If bad breaks are to be avoided, however, the ideal is impossible to achieve in typeset justified copy. Even in the highest quality printing, some small unevenness is inevitable. For most kinds of printing, standards require nothing more than equal wordspacing within each line.

Instructions for phototypesetting often specify wordspacing as loose, normal, tight, or very tight. Here are examples of each:

> **Loose wordspacing looks like this.**
> **Normal wordspacing looks like this.**
> **Tight wordspacing looks like this.**
> Very tight wordspacing looks like this.

> Loose wordspacing looks like this.
> Normal wordspacing looks like this.
> Tight wordspacing looks like this.
> Very tight wordspacing looks like this.

For high quality, typeset roman lowercase text, certain conventions normally apply; for example:

- Wider spacing than between words is normal between a period following a numeral in a list or title and the first letter.

- The space after a question mark or exclamation point within a sentence should be tighter than that after a punctuation mark ending a sentence.

- A thin space may be set at the side of each hyphen in a line with many hyphened words (to avoid over-wide spacing).

For high quality roman full capitals and for small caps or expanded type of 15 or more ems to the alphabet, loose or normal wordspacing is best. For high quality condensed type, black letter, or script, thin spacing is best:

Loose or normal wordspacing is best for expanded type.

Tight spacing is best for condensed type.

Tight spacing is best for black letter.

Tight spacing is best for italic.

Errors

Compressing the space between words is <u>spacing in</u> (squeezing, white space reduction), and expanding it is <u>spacing out</u> (spreading). Generally, squeezing improves appearance more than spreading.

Wordspacing that is too wide or too narrow in a line or passage may occur in narrow measure, especially in copy that must meet a short deadline. We see it every day in newspapers. With enough time, a line's appearance can be improved in several ways:

- Rewriting to space (this is expensive, a matter for querying)

- Resetting

- Letterspacing (adding space between letters), but note that letterspacing lowercase is not considered good style in fine printing.

Figure 12-P shows how a passage may be rewritten to improve wide wordspacing. Figure 12-Q shows how a passage can be reset.

---

straighten ||

In a brief discourse following their meeting, the pope also referred to "full communion between our churches" but reflected less urgency in his remarks than did the archbishop.

~~referred to~~ *spoke of /?*

to decrease # in next line by bringing up "churches"

Figure 12-P. Rewriting to fit space

The success of export promotion efforts is dependent upon the competitiveness of the home economy and its structure, as well as the general state of international demand. Further, it is difficult✓to✓show✓that✓export✓promotion✓has✓more than a marginal impact on a country's international economical situation. Given elements eluding policy makers' control and the methodological✓difficulty✓of✓evaluating✓alternatives, cost-benefit analysis of national plans for export promotion✓cannot✓be✓rigorous✓or✓definitive. Should an upsurge or decline in sales occur, it would be difficult, under these conditions, to show the impact of governmental efforts.

reset wide spacing

(1) Galley

The success of export promotion efforts is dependent upon the competitiveness of the home economy and its structure, as well as the general state of international demand. Further, it is difficult to show that export promotion has more than a marginal impact on a country's international economic situation. Given elements eluding policy makers' control and the methodological difficulty of evaluating alternatives, cost-benefit analysis of national plans for export promotion cannot be rigorous or definitive. Should an upsurge or decline in sales occur, it would be difficult, under these conditions, to show the impact of governmental efforts.

(2) Revised galley

Figure 12-Q. Wide wordspacing reset

Every space between words in one line should appear equal to every other. Unequal wordspacing is hard to find in machine-set copy, but it occurs when a manual typesetter must make the decisions on spacing between words or when cut-in corrections are made carelessly. Figure 12-R shows an example.

with a great bowl of white wine and sugar
in his right hand, and his whifflers staff
in his left: then follows the eldest steward,
and then another whiffler, as the first,
with a bowl of white-wine and sugar before the second steward, and in like manner another whiffler before the third, and

eq #

They are more closely a-
kin to our traditional ene-
mies, the Hyksos, than
they are to us. Joseph may
have been an exception.

eq #

Figure 12-R.   Unequal wordspacing

Wide wordspacing can result in rivers of white--long, uneven lines
of white space--or in lakes--holes of white space.   Rivers and
lakes are rare.   When they occur, they are marked to "break up,"
as shown in Figure 12-S.

—The Crime Control Act of 1973 (Public
Law 93-83). This Act further refined
LEAA's administrative structure, revised
block and discretionary funding requirements, expanded the role of the National
Institute of Law Enforcement and Criminal
Justice, and added security and privacy
guidelines to safeguard criminal history
information.

break up rivers

(1) River of white

The commission, an independent
agency of 12 members of Congress
and three executive branch officials
who evaluate and encourage compli-
ance with the 1975 agreement signed
by 35 nations, held hearings Wednesday and yesterday on the human
rights guarantees of individual
"freedom to p r a c t i c e and profess
. . . religion or belief" and "of equal-
ity before the law" for minorities.

break up lakes

the Freedom of Information Act, the Pri-
vacy Act, the Federal Advisory Committee
Act, the Clean Air Act, the National
Environmental Policy Act, the National
Historic Preservation Act, the Uniform
Relocation Assistance and Real Property
Acquisition Policies Act, the Intergovern-
mental Personnel Act, the Congressional
Budget and Impoundment Control Act, the

break up rivers

(2) Lakes

Figure 12-S.   Rivers and lakes

Optical Word Spacing

Optical (or visual) wordspacing varies the space between words to
make it appear equal, allowing for the irregularities in the shapes
of different characters.   Type larger than 12 points may be opti-
cally wordspaced when the method of typesetting permits and when

such a nicety is desired. This kind of wordspacing is a painstaking process and takes an artist's eye.

In optical wordspacing, a typesetter thinks in terms of the size
and shape of the letters ending one word and beginning the next.
Some characters occupy less space than others and therefore need
less interword spacing. For example, periods and commas take less
than half the type body and leave a lot of blank space. On the
other hand, capital Q takes nearly all the type body. More space
is needed between upright lines (for example between dh or HB)
than between angled lines (yw, AV). Less space is needed between
rounded lines (BO, eC); and still less between lowercase letters
without ascenders or descenders (eo, cu).

LETTERSPACING

Lowercase

Because letterspacing lowercase breaks the unity of a word, decreases readability, and alters the character and the color of a
page, it has been considered bad typography in high quality book
work; some customers will not accept it. However, in other forms
of printing, as shown in Figure 12-T, narrow measure may necessi-
tate letterspacing. It is often done in newspapers and other
periodicals when a deadline prevents rewriting or extensive resetting, and it is seen increasingly in books. Figure 12-U shows
the word "blood" letterspaced to fill out the fourth and eighth
lines; note the difference from "blood" in the third line. Some
phototypesetting machines can be set to letterspace one word to
fill out a short line. The result is always distressing to proofreaders. Figure 12-V shows entire lines letterspaced to somewhat
better advantage.

Sort of surprised
me, too. To be
offering a kit for
d e c o r a t i n g
jeans. But it's in
and I wanted you
to be sure that
t h e o n e y o u
s p e n t y o u r
m o n e y o n
w o r k e d a n d
s t a y e d o n i n
machine wash-
ings. Iron these
on, and they will
stay. Aluminum.
A s s o r t e d
shapes. Make
y o u r o w n
designs. Not
expensive.

Volunteers from the Nursing Program at
Northern Virginia Community College will be
testing patients' hearing, vision, blood pressure and b l o o d chemistry. Tests for oral
cancer, tuberculosis and glaucoma will also
be available. A complete health screening
takes only 45 minutes and is free of charge.
A series of 12 additional b l o o d chemistry
tests costs only $3.00.

Figure 12-T.   Letterspacing
to fit narrow
measure

Figure 12-U.   Letterspacing of
one word in a
line

six scheduled performances, which are: Verdi's "Il Trovatore," Puccini's "Tosca" and "La Boheme," Mozart's "The Magic Flute" — a Saturday matinee performed in English — and two new Met productions, Wagner's "Lohengrin" and "Le Prophete" by Meyerbeer.

The couples there who expressed problems in working as equals seemed to be the ones who were very caught up in conventional role-playing."

Figure 12-V. Letterspacing of one line

Properly done, letterspacing lowercase can be inconspicuous (although a trained eye can always spot it). The trick is to follow the rules discussed previously under optical wordspacing and later under optical letterspacing of capitals, a time-consuming job. In addition, some typesetting methods have too little spacing flexibility to permit a good job. Depending on the nature of the publication and the taste of the customer, a proofreader might call for letterspacing lowercase in a very short line. The following examples and quotation are taken from The Complete Guide to Editorial Freelancing by Carol L. O'Neill and Avima Ruder (Dodd, Mead and Company; New York, 1974):

> Occasionally the proofreader will call for letter-spacing as the only solution for a particular line of type. This is most likely to be necessary on a top-of-page widow or a very short line (as alongside a photograph).

> Richard   M.   Nixon
> cheered the ball team.

There is too much space between words in the first line of this example, which is set to a very short measure. The whole word "cheered" cannot be brought up to fill the first line because it is too long; "cheered" cannot be divided, so no part of it could be brought up. The best solution would be to letterspace the first line.

> Richard M. Nixon
> cheered the ball team.

In the same example, for a customer who considers a letterspaced line more of a blemish to a page than a small unjustified block of type, an alternative would be an unjustified block of type; you would mark the line "Richard M. Nixon" for wordspacing equal to the line "cheered the ball team."

For such a problem, the alternatives are (1) justified copy with wide wordspacing in one line, (2) justified copy with letter-spacing in one line, or (3) unjustified copy with proper word-spacing and no letterspacing.

The equal space mark is used both for unequal wordspacing and unwanted or badly done letterspacing, as in Figure 12-W. Bad escapement may be a cause of unequal letterspacing. Figure 12-X shows
this.

national organization concentrated in the
industrial cities of the Northeast. Unlike
labor unions, it prohibited striking, but its
membership included everyone from
patrolmen to chiefs.

Figure 12-W. Unwanted letterspacing

Other action projects funded through
discretionary funds include a project in
Illinois that uses peer groups to help
students resolve their problems and ease

Figure 12-X. Bad escapement

Typeset copy may need to be marked for a hair space between characters that run into each other or that are set too close for clarity
or good appearance; for example, *add space*:

- Between misleading letter combinations--c and l or o and l
  too close together look like d; r and n too close together
  look like m

- Between double and single quotation marks

- Between a letter and a footnote callout if no punctuation
  intervenes

- Between the superior figure in a footnote and the first
  letter

- Between quote marks and upright lines of letters (a cap A
  would be an exception)--anyplace where the tail of a quote
  touches the letter.

Extra high standards avoid the appearance of too much space between
certain letters by character compensation (as described in Phototypesetting, Chapter 11), or by using two-letter mats, specially
cast or mortised letters, or kerned pairs. These special characters might include the following:

- T, V, W, and Y before any lowercase letter; before A; before
  any punctuation mark; and after A or L

7. (• Numeral 1 before any letter,) and any letter before numeral 1

7. • b, e, o, and n before v, w, y, period, and comma.

Capitals

Even (equal) letterspacing puts the same amount of space between each capital letter. In typeset text sizes, caps and small caps may be evenly letterspaced to improve legibility and appearance.

Optical (or visual) letterspacing uses varying amounts of space between capital letters to make the spaces appear equal. More space is added between letters with little apparent space between them; less, between those with more apparent space. In larger display sizes, caps benefit from visual letterspacing.

The juxtaposition of straight lines, diagonal lines, curves, and open letters must be considered. For example, in the following word "capitals," the space between the C and the A, and that between the T and the following A appears greater than the space between other letters. With space added between the other letters (AP, PI, IT, AL, and LS), all appear equally spaced:

without letterspacing: CAPITALS

letterspaced: CAPITALS

EXAMPLES OF SPACING ERRORS

Figure 12-Y shows examples of spacing errors and their correct proofreading marks.

In summary, therefore, I see the most appropriate organization as a cabinet department, the head of which would be served by an analytic and planning staff with strength on the domestic as well as the foreign side; would directly control all U.S.] diplomatic and military personnel and all U.S. aid programs in the region; would control any clandestine operations and monitor all intelligence gathering in Latin America; would monitor activities there

(1) Short line at right

Jim Hartz is being such a loveable nuisance out at Channel 4 . . . with his family still up in New York . . . the new anchorman's hanging around

(2) Misaligned letters

Figure 12-Y. Spacing errors

NBC will air some big pilots plus a special Irwin Allen disaster film, "Fire," Clint Eastwood in "The Eiger Sanction," remakes of "Our Town" with Hal Holbrook and "The Hunchback of Notre Dame" plus specials featuring Chevy Chase and Princess Grace of Monaco.

(3) Short line at left

In an outside aviary where they've had a chance to acclimate to the changing seasons as they gradually occur, your "healthy" birds can take a surprising amount of cold weather pro-

space out

(4) Narrow wordspacing

'Environmental Extremism'   *straighten*

(5) Letters off their baseline

Steering Group for Trade Negotiations
President's Committee on East-West Trade Policy
Committee for Implementation of Textile Agreements
Adjustment Assistance Advisory Board
Export Administration Review Board
President's Interagency Committee on Export Expansion

III. ECONOMIC ASSISTANCE GROUPS

President's National Advisory Council on International Monetary and Financial Policies (NAC)—(Also has Export-Import Bank responsibilities)
Development Loan Committee (DLC)
Interagency Staff Committee on PL 480 (ISC)
Development Coordinating Committee (DCC)

(6) Failure to indent subordinate lines

Figure 12-Y. (Continued)

QUESTIONS FOR STUDENTS

1. Rank the widows in the following list in order of their acceptability, with most acceptable ranked 1:

    top-line widow
    bottom-line widow
    broken-word paragraph widow
    single-word paragraph widow

2. Write out the incorrectly divided words from Figures 12-E and 12-G. Draw vertical lines at each place these words can be correctly divided.

3.   Why would the following situations be considered poor proofreading?

   a.   You find so many word division errors in galleys that you stop marking them and write a general note, "Frequent errors in word division."

   b.   You see a typeset page proof with the entire image area crooked on the page; the top left margin is narrower than the bottom left; the top right margin is wider than the bottom right.   You mark it as a crooked paste-up.

4.   Draw vertical lines at each place these unities can be broken correctly:

Chapter 12	120°F
February 1	120° Fahrenheit
Amendment 14(a)	Justice Van Devanter
9:00 a.m.-10:19 a.m.	Ms. Henrietta Smith

Chapter 13

Final Steps in Production

<u>Printing</u>

In me all human knowledge dwells;
The oracle of oracles,
Past, present, future, I reveal,
Or in oblivious silence seal;
What I preserve can perish never--
What I forego is lost forever.

I speak all languages; by me
The deaf may hear, the blind may see,
The dumb converse, the dead of old
Communion with the living hold.
All hands are one beneath my rule,
All nations learners in my school.

Men of all ages, everywhere,
Become contemporaries there.

--James Montgomery (1776-1854)

CHAPTER OVERVIEW

This chapter discusses the final set of specs--the dummy, the standards for balance in page proofs, the terminology used in specifying margins and folios, the parts of a book (with tips on how to proofread front matter), and the kind of camera-ready copy called a mechanical. The chapter ends with a brief section on printing processes.

THE DUMMY

A <u>comprehensive layout</u> (comp) is a working model of a page, or part of a page (as in a small advertisement), usually full size, closely resembling the finished job. A comp shows all necessary design details. Usually page forms are made according to instructions given in a <u>dummy</u>--a multipage comprehensive layout for an entire book or publication.

A dummy represents the finished work with the actual number of pages, or at least the opening and closing pages of each section. It is usually full size but may be scaled to a fraction such as one-half or one-fourth of the finished product.

Dummy sheets usually have ruled areas (sometimes preprinted) that show the type page (or image area) in relation to the paper page. Dummy sheets also often show a <u>bleed</u> line (where illustrations printed beyond the paper page may be cut off and "bleed" off the page) and a <u>trim line</u> (where the page will be cut in the binding process). The sheets may also show the location of page numbers, running heads, logos, mastheads, and other page elements.

The text may be supplied separately, or the editor or designer may cut out the columns of type from the galley proofs and arrange them on the pages, inserting heads, subheads, running heads, captions, legends, illustrations, folios and text, including all

---

needed spacing. Notations are made about margin widths, particularly head (top) and back (inside left or right) margins, and about whether a page is a lefthand or righthand page.

Sometimes a dummy is bound, showing the method of folding and cutting; sometimes it is on loose pages. It may include pages of different colors to code for certain sections, insert pages, or different surfaced papers. It may have pinholes at each of the four corners to show the size of the type page.

BALANCE AND PAGE LENGTH

Standard design requires adjacent columns and facing pages in typeset copy to line up at the top and the bottom. Figure 13-A shows columns reset to balance (even up) their bottom lines. Some styles allow up to 1/2 pica difference in the length of adjoining columns or facing pages. If a variety of page lengths or column lengths is desired, the specifications must make this clear.

versus domestic goals and the relative costs and effectiveness of programs in the two spheres, as well as public versus private spending. Perhaps the most desirable mechanism would be assignment of this function to OMB and a requirement that the director of OMB chair an interagency study like the NSSM 3 study undertaken at the outset of the Nixon Administration. Alternative arrangements would include the establishment of a new White House staff reporting to a cabinet-level oversight committee for macro-resource allocation; a similar staff in a new

Defense, Robert McNamara, conducted his own internal review of the nation's military posture. (Generally) it is during the first year of a new administration that more radical alternatives to an existing military force structure are examined; the existence of a base of expertise and informed analysts (Recommendation 6) to undertake an examination of more administration options would be of enormous benefit at this time.

[8]Former NSC and OSD staff member, August 1974 interview.

(1) Unequally balanced columns in galley

tive priorities of . . . national security goals versus domestic goals and the relative costs and effectiveness of programs in the two spheres, as well as public versus private spending. Perhaps the most desirable mechanism would be assignment of this function to OMB and a requirement that the director of OMB chair an interagency study like the NSSM 3 study undertaken at the outset of the Nixon Administration. Alternative arrangements would include the establishment of a new White

agenda of . . . the Kennedy OEA as provided by the Samuelson Task force. The new Secretary of Defense, Robert McNamara, conducted his own internal review of the nation's military posture. (Generally) it is during the first year of a new administration that more radical alternatives to an existing military force structure are examined; the existence of a base of expertise and informed analysts (Recommendation 6) to undertake an examination of more administration options would be of enormous benefit at this time.

[8]Former NSC and OSD staff member, August 1974 interview.

(2) Correction in revise; columns evenly balanced

Figure 13-A. Balance of columns

Most standards allow facing pages to run one or two lines short to avoid a widow line or to fit footnotes or heads on the page. A single page may be one line short if a subhead would fall at the bottom of the page without at least two lines of text following it.

Opposite pages of typewritten text prepared for printing back-to-back should vary no more than two or three lines in depth. To avoid widows in typescript, mark for short rather than long pages.

Leading may be adjusted to balance facing pages or adjoining columns. Figure 13-B is an example; the left column has 51 lines, the right has 50. This kind of adjustment is not acceptable when modular leading (equal leading that aligns all the baselines of type on facing pages or on adjoining columns) is specified.

---

to the condition of mutual dependence. And to many leaders in the business and industrial communities the practice of occasionally selling off portions of the stockpile represented a repeated threat to the price structure on which a steady flow of investment in exploration and development of critical resources depended. Investigations by Senator Stuart Symington and others acquainted key officials with the double-edged character of stockpiling: it offered an attractive hedge against short-term scarcities of raw materials normally obtained abroad, but it tended to diminish the long-term expansion of supply because the very existence of large stockpiles made calculation of future profit margins uncertain. The extended and often painful exposure of Congress to the problems of stockpiling proved a useful education for a number of members.

Two other threads with significant national security coloration helped weave the fabric of legislative sensitivity to environmental matters during the 1950's and 60's. One emerged in the labors of the Joint Committee on Atomic Energy, whose extensive hearings and reports on the biological effects of nuclear warfare did much to form a global conception of man's relationship to the planet. Often faulted for alleged willingness to sacrifice environmental needs to a desire to promote the use of nuclear energy, the Joint Committee was undoubtedly the decisive forum for illuminating the peril which scientists began to detect in radio-active fallout from nuclear weapons tests, prospective disposal of nuclear wastes in the oceans and elsewhere, and especially the profound danger to human safety and genetic integrity that would face even the survivors of any large-scale nuclear holocaust. It overstates the case only slightly to suggest that an entire generation of congressmen, not to mention journalists, academics, and other citizens, garnered their principal education in the hazards of nuclear energy through the publications of the Joint Committee. It overstates it not at all to say that the committee contributed immensely to the dawning public realization that man had acquired the capacity to jeopardize the atmosphere, the soil, and the oceans with potentially lethal pollutants. By feeding this apprehension, even while pressing forward with affirmative programs to exploit the potential of nuclear energy, the Joint Committee paved the way for later congressional alertness to problems of the environment.

A second aspect of the Joint Committee's history also warrants some commentary. Although born out of the gravest dilemmas of national security, the Joint Committee on Atomic Energy, like the Atomic Energy Commission, consistently attempted to reconcile the nation's military needs with its political ambitions to build a peaceful international community. It represented an attempt to move beyond purely military control of the U.S. nuclear programs and to assure the ascendency of civilian direction, to ensure legislative as well as executive participation in high policy, and to open the door for international cooperation in nuclear energy whenever possible. While always ambivalent about the degree to which America's nuclear knowledge and capabilities should be shared with other countries, the Joint Committee did not fall prey to a hyper-nationalistic inclination toward nuclear monopoly. In general, it represented a cautious but positive influence on attempts to promote sensible international regimes for the varied applications of nuclear technology. In this regard it confirmed and reinforced the striking contrast between the disposition of the modern Congress to favor international approaches to common problems and the historic inclination of legislators prior to 1945 to minimize foreign engagements whenever possible.

Perhaps the most vivid lesson in the budding congressional anxiety over environmental hazards of nuclear energy was the prolonged debate over a nuclear test ban in the late 1950s and early 1960s. The dire genetic consequences of unlimited nuclear contamination provoked a great deal of legislative activity to speed action on the problem. In a pattern which recurs frequently among committees with overlapping jurisdictions, the technical explorations of the Joint Committee on Atomic Energy prompted the endeavors of other committees. The Senate Foreign Relations Committee, through its Subcommittee on Disarmament chaired by Senator Hubert Humphrey, became a principal advocate of an international treaty to limit nuclear testing. Even the persistence of Cold War behavior, including the Soviet Union's surprise abrogation of the 1959–61 test moratorium, did not deter the widespread congressional impulse to seek an accommodation on this issue. Thus, following the unexpected resumption of Soviet testing in the fall of 1961, legislative pressures for a more durable and verifiable accord remained. Senator Humphrey was

Figure 13-B. Leading adjusted to balance columns

On the last page of a chapter, footnotes should be set immediately under the last line of text, even if the result is a short page. Figure 13-C shows correct and incorrect footnote placement.

pant in the process. During the Dulles pe[...] sure, the planners played an important role, but only via the NSC Planning Board, rather than within the Department, itself.

Having said this, I believe that the original concept of policy planning in the Department of State must somehow be reconstituted with a small group of innovative thinkers close to the policy process,

[...] ould have be[...] in 1975? Or must we wait for the problem to evolve into attention-grabbing dimensions before we become seized with it and then merely flail around for the quick fixes and the policy band-aids?

And yet, as Lord Keynes said three decades ago, "There will be no harm in making mild preparations for our destiny."

[3]There are several cases that come to mind that document this proposition, but this goes beyond the scope of this essay.

[4]In my more ebullient moments, I, too, have been guilty of this.

(1) Incorrect placement of footnotes

pant in the process. During the Dulles pe[...] sure, the planners played an important role, but only via the NSC Planning Board, rather than within the Department, itself.

Having said this, I believe that the original concept of policy planning in the Department of State must somehow be reconstituted with a small group of innovative thinkers close to the policy process,

[...] ould have be[...] in 1975? Or must we wait for the problem to evolve into attention-grabbing dimensions before we become seized with it and then merely flail around for the quick fixes and the policy band-aids?

And yet, as Lord Keynes said three decades ago, "There will be no harm in making mild preparations for our destiny."

[3]There are several cases that come to mind that document this proposition, but this goes beyond the scope of this essay.

[4]In my more ebullient moments, I, too, have been guilty of this.

(2) Correct placement of footnotes

Figure 13-C. Page with footnotes ending chapter

MARGINS

Margins include the <u>top</u> (or <u>head</u>) margin, the <u>bottom</u> (<u>tail</u> or <u>foot</u>) margin, and the <u>side</u> margins. In two-page spreads, the side margins include the <u>front</u> (<u>fore edge</u>, <u>outside</u>, or <u>thumb</u>) margins and the <u>back</u> (<u>gutter</u>, <u>binding edge</u>, or <u>inside</u>) margins.

Margins represent the difference between the size of the paper page and the type page. In any photographic process, the type page is equivalent to the <u>image area</u>--the area that will be photographed. Image area is a crucial measurement; anything outside it will not print. In books, usually the back margin is smallest; top, outside, and bottom margins are progressively greater.

Galleys and first page proofs are often printed on paper larger than the final page will be. You cannot verify margin measurements on them. You can, and should, however, check the margins of typewritten pages and camera-ready copy and check the image area whenever it is specified.

FOLIOS

Folios (page numbers) are either expressed (typed or printed) or blind (counted in sequence but not expressed). Display pages and blank pages usually have blind folios.

Front matter folios are often expressed in lowercase or small cap roman numerals. Text and back matter folios are almost always expressed in arabic numerals, often as part of a running head. In back-to-back matter, odd numbers appear on righthand pages and even numbers on lefthand pages, often at the outside margins as part of the running heads. Running heads are omitted from chapter beginnings and from display pages such as full-page illustrations and tables; the folio also may be omitted in these cases. At chapter beginnings, the folio is often centered at (or sometimes inside) the bottom margin.

Page numbers should be positioned with care on typewritten camera-ready copy to avoid "jumping folios." (See Chapter 11, Special Problems.)

Be sure that folios are in their correct sequence. Some documents begin a new folio sequence with each chapter; for example, the first page of Chapter 2 might be 2.1, II-1, or (2)1.

Check the folios given in the table of contents against the text. When you see a cross reference to a folio printed with a cap O, an X, a black square, or a blank, make a note in the margin for the editor to fill it in; for example:

   This topic is discussed on page 00.   *fill in p. no.*

If you do not signal missing page references, they may remain in the final pages, as shown in this example:

> store in the Lenox Mall, presided over **an** autograph party that may hold the record as the largest one in history (see p.00). Among 30 nationally prominent authors present for the mass signing,

PARTS OF BOOKS

Books usually have three major segments: front matter (or preliminaries, or prelims), main text, and back matter (or reference matter).

Front matter pages are usually folioed with lowercase Roman numerals. These pages may include the following: <u>half title</u> (<u>bastard title</u>, <u>false title</u>)—frequently displaying a shortened form of the full title; series title; list of contributors; <u>frontispiece</u>—an illustration usually on the page facing the title page; title page; copyright notice, publisher's agencies, printing history, Library of Congress catalogue number, International Standard Book Number (ISBN); dedication or epigraph page, table of contents (often titled merely "Contents"); list of illustrations; list of tables; foreword, usually an introductory note or endorsement by someone other than the author; preface, usually by the author; acknowledgments (if not in the preface or the back matter); and introduction (if not in the text).

Sections of the main text may be preceded by <u>part title</u> pages (dividers).

Back matter may contain appendixes, notes (endnotes), a glossary or vocabulary defining words in the book, a bibliography (a list of books used for research or recommended to the reader), and one or more indexes. The last page of the book may contain a <u>colophon</u> (if the information is not in the front matter) naming the manufacturer, designer, or printer, and sometimes incorporating the names of the typefaces, paper stock, and other design information.

Proofreading Front Matter

When proofreading front matter such as a table of contents or list of illustrations or tables, proofread the live copy list against the live copy text. Editors often make changes in the text as they go along and forget to change the lists; the dead copy is often wrong. The front matter list and final text must, of course, match. Here are some ways to be sure they do:

- Insert the folios. If that has been done, check their accuracy.

- Check to be sure chapter heads, table titles, and figure captions in the text agree with front matter lists in wording, punctuation, and capitalization if both are clc.

- Check to be sure all heads or subheads at the levels specified are present and that no lower levels are listed.

- Add the index folio (the number of the first righthand page of the text after the back matter) to the table of contents if possible.

If proofs for a publication arrive in increments that must be returned as the work is done, keep the table of contents and the lists. You will need them to read against each increment.

MECHANICAL COMPOSITION

The image to be printed may appear on a mechanical--camera-ready copy that unites all the elements of a page (text and display type, line and halftone artwork). A mechanical is a page form with the image pasted up, sometimes two or mores pages at a time, on stiff white board (cardboard). Sometimes the original boards, sometimes photocopies, serve as the live copy.

On a mechanical, fine black or red lines may mark the four corners to show the trim size or image area. Fine lines may mark the position for folding, scoring, perforating, or die cutting. Cut-in "windows" of red acetate or fine marks show where halftones should be placed.

The image on a mechanical is produced in any of the ways type or illustrations are composed for camera-ready copy. The methods discussed in previous chapters and the following ways may be used:

Original artwork includes freehand lettering such as calligraphy, freehand drawing, and mechanical drawing--lettering, symbols, and rules--and graphs, diagrams, and designs, using a stencil or other mechanical drawing device. Drawings are usually done in black India ink with a pen or brush.

Photolettering (photodisplay) equipment produces lines of display type for headlines in a range of sizes and styles by means of semi-mechanical devices. On some equipment, the operator can determine the space between letters and words. The prints adapt well to enlargement, reduction, and modification.

Preprinted type includes the following:

- Clip art. Preprinted type and illustrations to be cut out and pasted up on copy come from commercially available clip books. If clip art is copyrighted, the purchase price includes reproduction rights.

- Pressure-sensitive graphics. Preprinted individual letterforms or pictorial components to be transferred to artwork by hand are commercially available. A wide selection includes many typefaces in various sizes, patterns, rules, borders, screen dots, symbols, and ornaments. Pressure-sensitive graphics come in two styles--adhesive graphics, which peel off a backing (rules and borders may come in rolls like tape) and dry transfer graphics, which transfer from a sheet by rubbing.

If mechanicals are your live copy, do not be dismayed by a blue grid pattern, white paint, paste-ups, cut-ins, blue pencil (on camera copy), or pink pencil (on laser copy); they will seldom show up in the final product. Too many pasted-up layers, however, can cause distortion, and shadows around the edges of thick layers may print. Sometimes a camera will pick up cut-lines (knife lines), especially if the cut-in is improperly backed with transparent instead of white tape, or a camera will pick up shadows from a pencil used so heavily that it plows a furrow.

Corrections are made the same way mechanicals are put together. They are cut in or pasted over errors; or drawn, typed, or rubbed on over white paint or another opaquing substance covering the errors.

PRINTING

When this book was published, there were four important categories of printing; relief, intaglio, planography, and stencil.

Relief printing is done from a surface raised above the nonprinting surface. Familiar examples include rubber stamps and block prints. The major relief printing process has been letterpress. Letterflex, an adaptation of letterpress, is becoming the major relief process. Letterpress is the oldest printing process from movable type and the only one that uses metal type directly.

In intaglio printing, the image is recessed below the nonprinting area. The ink fills the depressions, and the surface is then wiped clean. When the impression is taken, the ink is pulled from the depressions to form the image. Familiar examples include etchings, art engravings, and steel-die and copperplate engravings. The major intaglio printing process is gravure.

In planography, a plane (flat) surface is treated to produce both image and nonimage areas by heat, light, electricity, chemical re-action, a combination of these, or other means. Familiar examples include art lithographs, many forms of duplicating and machine copying (gelatin, spirit, electrophotography, blueprints, white prints, vandykes, and photostats), and photography itself (contact prints). The major planographic printing processes are photo-offset lithography and photogelatin printing (collotype).

Letterpress (including its letterflex offshoot), gravure, and off-set lithography are the three principal printing processes now used in publishing.

Stencil printing, a fourth category, includes mimeographing and silk screening (seriographs). The major stencil printing process at present is screen printing (porous printing).

Printing technology is advancing rapidly. It's up to you to find out how the documents you proofread will be printed so that you can write sensible instructions. (See Part III for recommended books about printing processes.)

QUESTIONS FOR STUDENTS

1. Define the following: bastard title, comp, dry transfer graphics, mechanical, prelims, white line.

2. What are the three main divisions of a book?

3. Describe how corrections are made on mechanicals.

4.

```
        ┌─────────────┊─────────────┐
        │      1      ┊      1      │
        │ xxxxxxxxxxx ┊ xxxxxxxxxxx │
        │ xxxxxxxxxxx ┊ xxxxxxxxxxx │
        │2 xxxxxxxxxxx 3 xxxxxxxxxxx 2│
        │ xxxxxxxxxxx ┊ xxxxxxxxxxx │
        │ xxxxxxxxxxx ┊ xxxxxxxxxxx │
        │ xxxxxxxxxxx ┊ xxxxxxxxxxx │
        │ xxxxxxxxxxx ┊ xxxxxxxxxxx │
        │      4      ┊      4      │
        └─────────────┊─────────────┘
```

Identify the following margins by the number shown in the diagram of a double-page spread:

    back____
    binding edge____
    bottom____
    foot____
    front____
    gutter____
    head____
    inside____
    outside____
    tail____
    thumb____
    top____

Chapter 14

Editorial Style

Men differ as much in style of writing as in personal appearance, and we might as well expect the same robe to fit all forms, as that one set of rules should nicely apply to the endless diversities of diction.

--Benjamin Drew

CHAPTER OVERVIEW

This chapter defines editorial style, describes differences in some of the categories of style, and presents some rules you may need to review.

INTRODUCTION

What is Editorial Style?

Editorial style rules aim to eliminate inconsistencies that would distract the reader and lower a publication's quality. Style rules provide guidance on abbreviation, capitalization, compounding, punctuation, numbers, spelling, and word division. Editorial style may also dictate word choice (memoranda, memorandums; toward, towards) and the treatment of foreign words, book titles, quotations, footnotes, and bibliographic data.

Many organizations codify their own "house" style. Some widely used style guides are published by the American Psychological Association, the Council of Biology Editors, the American Medical Association, the Modern Language Association, United Press International, the Associated Press, the New York Times, the Washington Post, the U.S. Government Printing Office, and the University of Chicago Press. Words Into Type (Prentice-Hall) is another standard reference, used in many organizations.

Examples throughout this chapter are designed to show the kinds of things proofreaders may encounter, not to prescribe a certain editorial style.

Figure 14-A, for example, shows a few differences in the editorial styles followed by the GPO Style Manual,* A Manual of Style (The University of Chicago Press),* and The Associated Press Stylebook.

---

*Summaries of the style points that often arise in GPO style and University of Chicago Press Style, are in Part III of this book.

Category	GPO Style	Chicago Style	AP Style
abbreviations - Eastern standard time - ships	e.s.t. the U.S.S. _Iowa_	EST the U.S.S. _Iowa_	EST the USS _Iowa_
capitalization	The Star-Spangled Banner Lake Erie, Lakes Erie and Ontario Washington State, the State of Washington	The Star-spangled Banner Lake Erie, Lakes Erie and Ontario Washington State, the state of Washington	The Star-Spangled Banner Lake Erie, lakes Erie and Ontario Washington state, the state of Washington
compounding	a well-worn book, the book is well worn	a well-worn book, the book is well worn	a well-worn book, the book is well-worn
punctuation - serial comma - apostrophe	a, b, and c the 1920's	a, b, and c the 1920s	a, b and c the 1920s
numbers	They had many animals: 10 dogs, 6 cats, and 60 hamsters.	They had many animals: ten dogs, six cats, and sixty hamsters.	They had many animals: 10 dogs, six cats and 60 hamsters.
spelling	marihuana subpena	marijuana subpoena	marijuana subpoena
word division	ad-verb-i-al pe-ren-ni-al	ad-ver-bi-al pe-ren-ni-al	ad-ver-bi-al per-en-ni-al

Figure 14-A. Examples of editorial style differences

Here is the same paragraph in two different editorial styles:

GPO Style: Bridge To Be Built From Town to Suburbs
    Samuel Smith, the Senator from the State of New Illiana and candidate for the office of Vice President, announced today that Federal funds are needed to build a larger sized bridge than originally gaged at the confluence of the Illiana and Westering Rivers. The bridge will link Inverness, Georgeville, and Five Corners to route workers to Inverness' booming industrial center.

Chicago Style: Bridge to Be Built from Town to Suburbs
    Samuel Smith, the senator from the state of New Illiana and candidate for the office of vice-president, announced today that federal funds are needed to build a larger-sized bridge than originally gauged at the confluence of the Illiana and Westering rivers. The bridge will link Inverness, Georgeville, and Five Corners to route workers to Inverness's booming industrial center.

This chapter does not discuss rules that are immutable and obvious (for example: A sentence ends with a period. The name of a country is capitalized). It does discuss rules that are immutable and troublesome, as well as rules that vary with different style choices. (Chapter 15 discusses spelling and Chapter 12 explains word division.) The final authority is the author or editor, but it's often up to you to catch problems. Keep these guidelines in mind at all times:

- Know what the customer or editor expects.

- When you <u>suspect</u> incorrect or inconsistent editorial style, either look up the point (and follow the next principle given here), or trust the author or editor and do nothing.

- When you are <u>sure</u> of a style error, query--and be prepared to back up your query with a reference work acceptable to the customer.

Querying

When a particular editorial style is specified, it must be followed. Your personal style preferences are irrelevant, and you as a proofreader should limit your queries about deviations from the specified style. Extensive querying of page proofs is useless; changes are too expensive. With an early draft, querying takes extra time (especially if it involves looking up style points in a manual) that clients seldom want to pay for.

Get a clear understanding of how closely the rules of the specified style are to be followed. For example, when proofreading an early draft in GPO style, querying might be limited to points of number style, compounding, and use of serial comma, with time spent referring to the style manual and the GPO word division booklet confined to inconsistencies on the same page.

If no style is specified, you must try to discern the author's or editor's style as you read, and then query inconsistencies only to the level allowed. With heavily edited or handwritten dead copy, querying is very likely to be needed.

ABBREVIATIONS AND ACRONYMS

Abbreviations and acronyms are standardized in some style manuals, dictionaries, and technologies. Current trends favor decreased use of periods and capitals, along with fewer abbreviations in general writing and more abbreviations in technical writing. <u>Tight matter</u>--matter set in a small space (for example, tables, charts, maps, bibliographies, and footnotes)--often uses many abbreviations.

Watch for inconsistency. Does the same abbreviation have the same capitalization, punctuation, and spacing throughout? Is the same word consistently spelled out or abbreviated in the text? In tight matter? For example:

- Inconsistent abbreviation: Madison, Wis.
                               Milwaukee, Wisc.

- Inconsistent spelling out: Of the fifty percent studied,
                               20% were under age.

- Inconsistent spacing: A.K. Miller, Ph.D.
                               R. B. Smith, Litt. D.

State abbreviations have two forms--the traditional (Ala., Ariz.,
Ark., and so on) and the U.S. Postal Service two-letter form (AL,
AZ, AK, and so on). The two-letter form is usually reserved for
use with a ZIP code.

Avoid marking an uncommon or ambiguous abbreviation with (AP); supply
the entire spelled-out form. The abbreviation A.M., for example,
can stand for ante meridian (before noon), master of arts, anno
mundi, and amplitude modulation.

When "no abbreviation" is specified, watch for errors; typesetters
can mistake words like "in" or "no" for abbreviations. (The typesetter of a concert program once converted "Gounod's Fourth Mass"
to "Gounod's Fourth Massachusetts" and "Ave Maria" to "Avenue
Maria.")

Acronyms are symbols or shortened names formed from the initial
letters of words. A common style calls for an unfamiliar acronym
to be introduced in parentheses the first time its spelled-out form
appears; for example, "The post of Assistant Secretary of State
for the Bureau of South East Asian Affairs (SEAA) is vacant."

Acronyms may take different forms:

- All caps (SALT talks)
- Initial caps (Alcoa)
- Lowercase (radar).

The same acronym in the same text should not vary in form.

ALPHABETIZING

To verify the alphabetical sequence of bibliographies, indexes,
directories, and other listings, you must be able to recognize
the rules the author or editor followed.

Common Methods

There are two main methods for alphabetizing: (1) word-by-word and
(2) letter-by-letter, with some variation possible within either.

In the letter-by-letter method, alphabetical order is followed up
to the first punctuation mark, disregarding spaces and hyphens between words, and disregarding capital letters and diacritical marks.

The word-by-word method is more common today because computers follow its nothing-before-something logic. A space precedes a punctuation mark, and a punctuation mark precedes a letter. Alphabetical order is followed up to the end of the first word; it is continued with the second word only if the same first word occurs more than once.

The following example shows how the same list would be alphabetized differently by these two methods.

Letter-by-Letter	Word-by-Word
Southbridge	South Fork
South-brook Meadow	South Port
Southern Pines	South River
South Fork	South Tunnel
Southport	South-brook Meadow
South Port	Southbridge
South River	Southern Pines
South Tunnel	Southport

Exceptions

Mc and Mac

Some styles call for names beginning with Mac, Mc, and M' to be alphabetized as if Mac were used; some alphabetize letter-by-letter, some word-by-word (with the second cap treated as the beginning of a new word--MacMillan is equivalent to two words). The following examples illustrate these three methods.

As If Mac	Letter-by-Letter	Word-by-Word
Macaulay, Margaret	Macaulay, Margaret	MacLean, Ian
McAuley, Louise	MacLean, Ian	MacMillan, Donald
MacLean, Ian	Macmillan, Arthur	Macaulay, Margaret
Macmillan, Arthur	MacMillan, Donald	Macmillan, Arthur
McMillan, Bruce	Macmillan, James	Macmillan, James
MacMillan, Donald	McAuley, Louise	McAuley, Louise
Macmillan, James	McMillan, Bruce	McMillan, Bruce

Another treatment of names beginning Mac, Mc, and M' lists them separately, before or after other names beginning with M.

Abbreviations

Examples of the two treatments of abbreviations, letter-by-letter, and as if spelled out, follow.

Letter-by-Letter	As If Spelled Out
N.C.	Nebr.
N. Dak.	Nev.
Nebr.	N.H.
Nev.	N.J.
N.H.	N. Mex.
N.J.	N.Y.
N. Mex.	N.C.
N.Y.	N. Dak.

In lists of names, St. or Ste. (for Saint or Sainte) is often treated as if spelled out.

Acronyms are usually treated letter-by-letter.

Numerals

Numerals may be grouped in numerical order preceding the letter <u>A</u> (as in lists for computer retrieval) or may be listed as if spelled out ("12" alphabetized as "twelve"). Years may be listed the way they are usually spoken ("1776" alphabetized as "seventeen seventy-six").

Introductory Articles

Introductory articles may be listed before a name and ignored alphabetically ("A Manual of Style" listed under <u>M</u>); they may be omitted ("A Manual of Style" listed as "Manual of Style"); or they may be placed after a name ("A Manual of Style" listed as "Manual of Style, A").

Prepositions and Conjunctions

Prepositions and conjunctions may be disregarded in the alphabetization scheme of indexes. The following example ignores "before and after" and "in":

    Comma (135-138): before and after abbreviations (136);
    in apposition (136); before dash (137); in dates (137)

Names

Geographic names may be alphabetized according to a specific or a general name ("Lake Michigan" or "Michigan, Lake").

In listings that place surnames first, foreign names do not always follow the same order as English. For example, in Chinese, the family name usually precedes the given name ("Deng Xiaoping" should be listed under "Deng"); in Spanish, a surname may be a compound ("Luis Echeverria Alvarez" should be listed as "Echeverria Alvarez, Luis").

The usual rule for compound names and those with particles is to follow the individual's personal preference or the form decreed by tradition; wide variation occurs; for example:

Compound Names	Names With Particles
Carte, D'Oyly, Richard	Gogh, van, Vincent
Doyle, Sir Arthur Conan	van Dongen, Cornelius
Lloyd George, David	Vandyke, Sir Anthony
Schumann-Heink, Ernestine	Velde, Van de, Jan
Toussaint L'Ouverture, Pierre Dominique	

Sometimes, within an alphabetical list, another sequence is used. For example, in an index, subentries may be listed in chronological or mathematical order.

ARTICLES

A useful rule calls for choosing between the indefinite articles a or an according to the sound that follows--a before a consonant sound, an before a vowel sound:

Vowel Sound	Consonant Sound
an NSC finding	a National Security Council finding
an onion	a union
an 11-year-old child	a 4-H club
an H. P. rating	a horsepower rating
an herb	a historical review
an honor	a hand

Some writers use an before an h that begins an unaccented syllable: an historical review, an herbivorous animal.

CAPITALIZATION

Proper nouns are capitalized; common nouns are lowercased. Different styles define proper nouns differently, however, and the rules for capitalization in a particular style may be fairly complex. (When no style is specified, watch for inconsistencies.)

Here are some examples of two extremes:

Down Style	Up Style
Vice President Bush	Vice President Bush
the vice president	the Vice President
George Bush, vice president	George Bush, Vice President
astronaut Glenn	Astronaut Glenn
editor-in-chief Jones	Editor-in-Chief Jones
Gone with the Wind	Gone With the Wind
federal government	Federal Government

Most styles lowercase nouns that are derived from a proper noun but that no longer depend on the original meaning; for example:

brussels sprouts	roman type
french fries	plaster of paris
herculean	venetian blind
pasteurize	

Trademarks and brand names should be capped. Dictionaries list registered trademarked names. A short list follows:

Band-aid	Laundromat	Sanforized
Coke (soft drink)	Levi's	Scotch tape
Frisbee	Lucite	Thermos (vacuum bottle)
Kleenex	Mace	Vaseline
Kodak	Peg Board	Xerox

Mc and Mac in All Caps

If specifications call for people's names in all caps, two treatments are possible for names beginning with <u>Mc</u> and <u>Mac</u> followed by a <u>C</u>: (1) the all-cap rule must be broken or (2) a blank space must be added; for example:

    McCarthy becomes (1) MC CARTHY or (2) McCARTHY
    MacConnell becomes (1) MAC CONNELL or (2) MacCONNELL

The second choice, with lowercased <u>c</u> and <u>ac</u>, is preferred, but whichever treatment is chosen should be used consistently.

Names beginning with <u>Mc</u> or <u>Mac</u> followed by letters other than <u>C</u> are capitalized with no other change; for example: MACDONALD, MCKNIGHT, MACMILLAN.

COMPOUND WORDS

There are three kinds of compound words:

- <u>Open compounds</u> (separate words); for example: cross section, pitch pipe, flow chart

- <u>Hyphenated compounds</u>; for example: thirty-one, do-it-yourself, great-grandfather

- <u>Solid compounds</u>; for example: headache, notebook, lifetime.

Someone once said that a hyphened word is two words on the way to becoming one. The tendency of the language is toward solid compounds. Sometimes the historical progression is from open through hyphened to solid; other times the hyphen stage is skipped.

Style manuals, dictionaries, and individual preferences seldom agree on compounding. When rules are made, they are often complex.

Most styles require most words with combining forms, prefixes, and suffixes to be written solid; for example: subcommittee, nonimportant, prescreen, preempt, reenter, cooperate.

Most styles* require hyphens for the following conditions:

- Duplicated prefixes (re-redirect, sub-subcommittee)

---

*Including GPO and Chicago styles.

- Capitalized words (mid-April, post-World War I)

- Already hyphenated words (semi-winter-hardy strain)

- Words that could be confused or mispronounced (re-ink, co-op, pre-judicial--as distinguished from prejudicial).

Some words are always spelled correctly when open; for example: no one, all right.

A <u>unit modifier</u> (u.m.) is an adjectival unit of two or more words preceding a noun and often hyphened; for example: <u>fire-tested</u> material; <u>job-related</u> skills. Do not confuse a unit modifier with a predicate adjective, which may use the same words but is seldom hyphened; for example: The material has been <u>fire tested</u>; his skills are <u>job related</u>.

Most styles* require unit modifiers to be open (not hyphened) in the following cases:

- When the first element is an adverb that ends in <u>ly</u> (wholly owned subsidiary)

- When the first two elements are adverbs (very well worth reading; not too distant future).

Do not confuse unhyphened verbs with the same words used as compound nouns and adjectives (unit modifiers and predicate adjectives). The following list gives a few examples:

Verb	Noun, Adjective
cease fire	cease-fire
cut back	cutback
drive in	drive-in
hold up	holdup
write off	write-off

Some correct usages you may see follow:

- Long- and short-term loans (the first is a suspensive hyphen)
- Non-civil-service jobs (prefix plus unit modifier).

NUMBERS

Number style specifies when a number is spelled out and when figures (numerals) are used. There is considerable variation in the rules for general text. GPO style, for example, uses numerals for numbers with more than one digit; Chicago style, however, uses numerals for numbers with more than two digits. Usage can depend on whether a number is used with a unit of measurement, a symbol,

---

*Including GPO and Chicago styles.

or an abbreviation and on whether there is another number in the same sentence or the same paragraph.

No major style permits a numeral, even a year, to begin a text sentence.

Watch for consistency in the use of commas with four-digit numbers (1000 or 1,000) and in the use of apostrophes with plurals (the 1920's, the 1920s). Watch for consistent use of commas with day and year (June 3, 1935, and...; June 3, 1935 and...).

Some styles require the use of <u>cardinal numbers</u> (simple counting numbers--1,2,3) to be consistent with that for <u>ordinal numbers</u> (numbers specifying sequential order--first, second, third). For example, if a style calls for cardinal numbers over nine to be spelled out, the rule should also apply to ordinals over <u>ninth</u>: Group 10; the 10th group.

Abbreviations for ordinals should be consistent: 2nd, 3rd; 2d, 3d.

See Part III for a list of Roman numerals.

PUNCTUATION

As all rules suitable to guide human conduct lie folded up in the golden rule, so all rules for pointing sentences are embraced in this: Punctuate so as to bring out the author's meaning. And by their consonance with this great rule all special rules must be judged. Yet in this, as in all other matters, men disagree in their judgments; and we must be content in our diversities.

--Benjamin Drew

Italic and Boldface Punctuation

Italic and boldface insertions require punctuation marks in italic and boldface; for example:

<u>Italic</u>   <u>Boldface</u>

Spell it *right!*   **Proofreader's Manual:** Chapter I

Exceptions are proper noun possessives in italic; in these, the apostrophe <u>s</u> is properly set or typed in roman; for example:

Webster's spelling

Apostrophes

Because many people have trouble with apostrophes, the rules for using these marks are given in some detail.

A possessive indicates a close connection between words, usually that one "belongs to" the other; for example: George's book (the book belonging to George), a week's visit (a visit lasting a week), a dollar's worth (worth amounting to a dollar).

Possessive Nouns

- Add apostrophe and s ('s) to the following:

  - singular nouns not ending in s (a prince's fortune, a woman's prerogative, a tree's growth)

  - plural nouns not ending in s,* (the children's school, women's changing role).

- Add apostrophe alone (') to plural nouns ending in s,* (two days' work, the Joneses' house, the hostesses' workshifts).

- Treat singular nouns ending in s or with an s sound according to the chosen style (Burns' poems, Burns's poems; appearance' sake, appearance's sake).

Possessive Pronouns

Possessive pronouns (theirs, his, hers, ours, yours, or its) should never have apostrophes. Be sure to distinguish between its (possessive) and it's (contraction of it is).

Joint or Individual Possession

When two or more groups jointly belong to the noun, use an apostrophe only with the last in the series; for example: soldiers and sailors' home (same home), Smith and Nelson's store (same store).

When two or more groups individually or alternatively belong to the noun, use an apostrophe after each member of the series; for example: editor's or proofreader's opinion (different opinions); the Army's and the Navy's work (different work); men's, women's, and children's clothing (different clothing).

Compound Nouns

Put the apostrophe and s with the word closest to the compound noun; for example: attorney general's decision, ambassador at large's appointment, John Smith, Jr.'s account.

Indefinite or Impersonal Terms

Use an apostrophe with indefinite or impersonal pronouns; for example: each other's books, somebody else's proposal.

---

*Simplified rule for plurals: If the last letter is s, add the apostrophe. If the last letter is not s, add apostrophe and s.

Proper Names

Follow the official form for proper names, with or without the apostrophe; for example: St. Elizabeths Hospital, Freedmen's Hospital.

"Frozen" Possessives

Some possessives are "frozen"; that is, the apostrophe is omitted. These include the following:

- Names of countries and organized bodies ending in s; for example: United States laws, House of Representatives session, United Nations meeting

- Words more descriptive than possessive (words not indicating ownership); for example: teachers college; the Editorial Experts, Inc., Proofreaders Manual

- Acronyms (it is better style to avoid both apostrophe and s with acronyms); for example: CRS policies, HUD reorganization, GPO style.

Double Possessives

"This opinion of the Congressman" is not the same as "this opinion of the Congressman's." The first is what someone else thinks about the Congressman; the second is what the Congressman thinks. In "a friend of our parents" or "a friend of our parents'" no such distinction exists; either way is acceptable.

Contractions

Use an apostrophe to indicate the omission of letters or numerals; for example: don't, can't, class of '97. Be sure the apostrophe marks the exact place where characters are omitted. In contractions with more than one omission, the apostrophe should replace the greater number of omissions (m'gr, not m'g'r). Note that formal writing seldom features contractions except in direct quotation or in a well-known phrase.

Possessive Abbreviations

For abbreviations with periods, some styles retain only the possessive apostrophe and drop the period: Co's is preferred to Co.'s.

Other Uses

Styles differ on whether an apostrophe should be used in plurals of numbers and abbreviations (1920's, 1920s; YMCA's, YMCAs). For clarity, an apostrophe should be used before an inflectional ending (RSVP'ing, OK'ed) and for plurals of letters or of words as words (the why's and wherefore's, a's and b's).

Colons

A colon has four main uses:

- After a salutation; for example:
   My Dear Sir:

- In some styles of bibliographic citation, between place of publication and name of publisher and to separate book titles from subtitles; for example:
   Washington, D.C.: U.S. Government Printing Office
   Scholarships: Graduate
   Witherspoon, Alexander, Common Errors in English:
      And How To Avoid Them

- In sentences, after a phrase introducing an independent clause (a complete sentence),* or after an introduction to a run-on list, a quotation or an explanation; for example:
   The answer is: Yes, I believe you.
   There are two factors: first, preparation; second, mobilization.

- After introductory lines in lists or tables, when sub-entries follow; for example:
   Case:
      Nominative
      Objective
      Possessive

Commas

The serial comma--a comma before and, or, or any conjunction in a series of three or more words--is required by most modern grammarians and by several style manuals;** for example: red, white, and blue; x, y, or z; men, women, but not children; Monday, Tuesday, through Wednesday.

Some styles--especially newspaper styles--omit the final comma in a simple series, and some writers omit the final comma in any series. Whether the serial comma is used or omitted, the style should be consistent throughout.

As a very general rule, unless you cannot make sense out of what you are reading, do not query the use of commas other than serial commas; their use is highly individual.

---

*But sometimes a comma may be used; for example: The question is, Shall the bill pass?

**Including GPO and Chicago.

Dashes and Hyphens

The following examples show a typeset en dash (in the first line), a hyphen (in the second line), and an em dash (in the third line):

Turn to section 20-C.
Did you say twenty-three?
No, not three, C—as in Charles.

Hyphens and dashes may end lines but in careful typing or type-setting should not begin lines of text.

Hyphens

In typeset copy, a hyphen is usually shorter and fatter than an en dash. In typewritten copy, a hyphen is the same as an en dash.

The hyphen has the following uses:

- To connect the elements of certain compound words (orthographic hyphen): sky-blue walls, happy-go-lucky
  Caution: Different editorial styles compound words differently.

- To divide words at the end of a line (dividing hyphen):...syl-lable
  Caution: Different editorial styles may divide words differently.

- To represent deleted or illegible letters:* d--n, George H. R------

- To connect the units of certain chemical terms: plutonium-210, Cr-Ni-Mo

- To separate letters of a spelled-out word: s-p-e-l-l-e-d

- To represent the en dash in all typewritten copy and some typeset copy.

En Dashes

A typeset en dash (short dash) is usually longer and thinner than a hyphen. Some typeset copy does not call for en dashes for three reasons:

1. Cost. Use of en dashes increases typemarking and proof-reading time.

2. Ignorance. Some typesetters, especially those in small shops, do not know what an en dash is and do not recognize the mark for it.

---

*Some styles use a 2-em dash for this.

3. <u>Unavailability</u>. Not all fonts of type in all systems
   provide en dashes.

There is no en dash on a typewriter; mark for hyphens, not for
en dashes, when copy is to be typed.

The en dash is a nicety with the following uses:

- To separate groups of figures and letters to make them
  easier to read. Usually an en dash marks the start of a
  subcategory or further breakdown:

figure 6–A*	ABC–TV network
phone 301–942–8360	AFL–CIO merger
DC–14	WETA–PBS–TV
Public Law 85–3–b	

- To replace the words "to" or "through" in expressions
  like these:

  1939–42,** $15–$20, pp. 2–19

- To indicate a date in the future: John X. Public, 1920–

- To separate parts of a compound adjective when one part is
  two words or hyphened:

Typeset:	large-scale–small-scale table
	New York–London flight
Typewritten:	large-scale - small-scale table
	New York - London flight

<u>Caution</u>: Different editorial styles decree somewhat different
uses for the en dash. Some do not recognize the last rule given.
For typewritten copy, note that the en dashes shown in the last
two examples have space on either side; this spacing is an exception to the closed-up spacing required for the other uses of
hyphens and dashes.

Em Dashes

A typeset em dash (long dash) is 1 em long (twice the length of
an en dash). Ideally, em dashes are typeset with only a hairspace
separating them from the words on both sides. However, a typeset
document may have dashes that are closed up entirely and others
that have space around them to allow for a line to be justified.
If you see both forms in a typeset document, even in the same

---

*Some styles require an em dash here.

**When a period of time is preceded by the word "from" (from Janu-
  ary to June), many styles, including GPO and Chicago, require
  the word "to" instead of the hyphen or en dash.

line, let them stand (unless you are aiming for very high quality and can afford the expense of resetting perhaps an entire paragraph).

There is no em dash on a typewriter. The convention is to type an em dash with two hyphens closed up to the words on either side of the dash, like this: word--word. It is possible, but inconvenient, for a typist to fill in the space between hyphens by backspacing and half spacing (—). Some people use only one hyphen with space on both sides, like this: word - word. Be sure all the em dashes in a typed document follow the same form.

The uses of the em dash include the following:

- To show that a further explanation or summary is coming: Pencil, pica pole, and dictionary—these are the proofreader's tools.

- To mark a major interruption or change of thought in a sentence:
  The editor—shall we call him fool or rascal?— approved an inaccurate statement. The proofreader missed it, too—but you know the rest of that sad story.

- After a phrase, to introduce a list in which each item will complete a sentence:
  As did Caesar, he—
      came
      saw
      conquered.

- To indicate an unfinished word or sentence in a speech:
  It reads, "Fourscore and seven—."
  Q. Did you see— A. No.

- After a question mark instead of a colon:
  How do you explain this?— Two pages are missing.
  (But few styles now approve an em dash after a comma, colon, or semicolon.)

- Before a credit line or signature (—Longfellow)

- After a run-on head:
  Typeface Classification.—Statement of Characteristics
  (Some styles use other punctuation here.)

- After a number in a caption (Table 6.—Income Levels).
  (Some styles use other punctuation here.)

- In some typographic styles, instead of a hyphen in a line of capitals.

Extra-long Dashes

2-Em Dashes. The typeset 2-em dash is twice as long as a 1-em dash. The typewritten equivalent is made with four consecutive hyphens. The 2-em dash is used to indicate missing letters: (d———n, George H. R———). (Some styles use a hyphen for each omitted letter.)

3-Em Dashes. The typeset 3-em dash is three times as long as the 1-em dash. The typewritten equivalent is made with six consecutive hyphens or with underscoring. The 3-em dash is used as follows:

- To indicate an entire word omitted; space is left on each side of a 3-em dash in this case (To ——— with it!)

- To indicate repetition in a bibliography or list:

  Shakespeare, William; The Tempest
  ———; Romeo and Juliet
  (An underscore, usually 15 spaces long, is often used in typing.)

Exclamation Points

An exclamation point replaces a comma, a period, or a question mark; for example:

"Great!" he shouted.   Who called, "All aboard!"

Parentheses

Numerals or letters enumerating the items in a run-on list may be placed inside full or half parentheses; for example: The colors are (1) green, (2) violet, and (3) orange. The colors are a) green, b) violet, and c) orange. Look for consistency within each manuscript.

Braces

Braces (curly brackets) may be individual characters: ⏜ ⏜ or may come in sections (piece braces): ⎣ ⏝ ⎯ ⎦ . The two varieties look different and should not both be used for the same enclosure. Watch for careful alignment of piece braces.

Brackets

Square brackets may be used instead of parentheses, as copy indicates, in the following:

- Bills, contracts, and transcripts of testimony or hearings to enclose omissions and editorial explanations and corrections; for example:

```
The conference [lasted] 2 hours.
This matter is classified.  [deleted]
Mr. Smith [presiding].
The statue [sic] was on the statute books.
They fooled only themselves.  [laughter]
```

- Quotations, to indicate a word was inserted or replaced by the editor; for example:

```
All men [and women] are equal.
O what fun it [was] to ride in a one-horse open sleigh.
```

Just as single quotation marks are used inside double, so brackets are used inside parentheses; for example:

```
(The result is described in section 2 [see paragraph 3.17].)
```

But when brackets are the first level, parentheses go inside; for example:

```
All men [and women (and for that matter children)] are equal.
```

Periods

A run-on head is usually followed by a period; numerals and letters preceding words in heads usually take periods; and some abbreviations take periods.

Periods may be omitted after the following:

- Lines on title pages or divider pages

- Heads on lines by themselves

- Continued lines

- Boxheads of tables

- Scientific, technical, and other symbols

- Abbreviations for units of measure (ft, cm, lb; but always in. to distinguish it from the preposition).

Multiple periods are incorrect; for example:

```
The sale was made by the Jones Co..
```

Question Marks

A question mark may occur at the end or in the middle of a sentence; for example:

```
Can he do it? or you? or anyone?
```

Semicolons

Semicolons are used to separate two independent clauses when they are not joined by <u>and</u>, <u>but</u>, <u>or</u>, <u>nor</u>, <u>for</u>, or <u>yet</u>; for example:

> The records are missing; they cannot be found anywhere.

(A long dash or two complete sentences are alternatives.) When none of the conjunctions listed in the preceding rule is used, and when the word <u>however</u>, <u>therefore</u>, <u>nevertheless</u>, or <u>notwithstanding</u> ends the first of two independent clauses or begins the second, a semicolon is needed to indicate which clause the word belongs to; for example:

> Semicolon needed: This is undesirable, however, it has just a few arguments in its favor.

> First possibility: This is undesirable, however; it has just a few arguments in its favor.

> Second possibility: This is undesirable; however, it has just a few arguments in its favor.

Semicolons should be used instead of commas in a series with individual elements already containing commas; for example:

> The units will be located in Richmond, Va.; Baltimore, Md.; and Washington, D.C.

> Applications were received from George Simpson, professor of economics, Carlton College; Hamilton Smith, editor of the Lacston Journal; and Jennifer F. Connor, director, Knowlton Jones, Inc.

ITALICS AND UNDERSCORING

Underscoring in typed copy and italic in typeset copy are equivalent. A typesetter interprets characters underscored in manuscript to mean "set in italic." And most of the standards for underscoring characters in typing are the same as those for using italic in typesetting.

Different rules apply in different styles. Some require but others forbid italicizing or underscoring the names of newspapers, magazines, or other periodicals; and Latin or other foreign words or abbreviations. Sometimes foreign words familiar to the intended readers are not scored or italicized, but unfamiliar ones are. If you have no editorial guidance on this point, see whether the more familiar foreign words and abbreviations (ibid., et al., a priori, and so on) are consistently in roman, or query.

The style for legal cases varies:

John Roe <u>v</u>. The City of Richmond

<u>John Roe</u> v. <u>The City of Richmond</u>

Most styles require that the underscore should otherwise be uninterrupted:

Right: <u>post hoc ergo propter hoc</u>.

Wrong: <u>post</u> <u>hoc</u> <u>ergo</u> <u>propter</u> <u>hoc</u>.

In typing, a punctuation mark at the end of underscored words is not usually underscored (see the preceding "Right" example).

In typesetting, italic punctuation marks should be used after italic type (see the section in this chapter on Italic and Boldface Punctuation).   Roman characters are used for the plural and posses-sive endings of words in italic; for example:

There were four *Daily News*es left.
Many *Hamlet*s have been produced.
Webster's spelling

QUESTIONS FOR STUDENTS

1.   Define the following in your own words: tight matter, acronym, open compound, unit modifier, serial comma.

2.   Which system of alphabetizing is used in the index of this book?

3.   Dashes and hyphens: Fill in each blank with the name of the punctuation mark described (hyphen, en dash, or em dash).

a. The _____ divides a word between syllables at the end of a line. Example: .... syl-lable.

b. The _____ joins the elements of certain compound words. Examples: sky-blue walls, happy-go-lucky.

c. The _____ signals a sudden change in thought in a sentence. Example: When the stockpile was sold--indeed, dumped as surplus--sales were hard hit.

d. The _____ shows that a further explanation is com-ing. Example: Oil, steel, and wheat--these are the sinews of industrialization.

e. In typeset material, the _____ replaces the con-junctions "to" or "through" in expressions involving numeri-cal sequence. Example: pp. 4-8, chapters I-V, exhibits 3-5.

f. The _____ separates figures (numerals) and letters, often indicating the start of a subcategory or a further break- down. Examples: Public Law 85-2, Appendix 2-B, WTOP-TV.

4. Consulting the style summaries in Part III, underline GPO style and draw a circle around Chicago style for the following:

Back in the (1970's/1970s) your (follow-up/followup/
follow up) was too late for the (decisionmaking/
decision-making/decision making) (dialogue/dialog).
This year we look for your (re-evaluation/reevaluation)
of the suggested (federal/Federal) program in the next
(3 days/three days).

sounds like
fish

ghuti fish
cough
business
nation

GHUTI

gh as in cough F→

u as in business

ti as in nation

Chapter 15

Spelling

It's a damned poor mind that can think of only one way to spell a word.
                                        --Attributed to Andrew Jackson

CHAPTER OVERVIEW

This chapter discusses the problems of spelling, some precautions for proofreaders, and alternative spellings. It also includes some spelling aids and a list of frequently misspelled words.

INTRODUCTION

(See also Compound Words in Chapter 14 and the subsection on word division under Bad Breaks in Chapter 12.)

The English language has at least 400,000 words and the most irregular spelling of any language. As an extreme example, G. B. Shaw pointed out that if you pronounce gh as in cough, u as in business, and ti as in nation, then put them together, you will say the word "fish." G-h-u-t-i, however, does not spell fish. Rules prevent this kind of spelling, although they are complex and have many exceptions.

When you read proof, do not accept misspellings; query them or correct them if you are given the authority. The problem is in defining a misspelling. Is judgement incorrect, merely old fashioned, or the only acceptable spelling because the combination "dgm" is an abomination? As in many cases, the answer is, "It depends." Judgement is wrong when specifications for editorial style require judgment (as in GPO style or any style based on the first choice in current Merriam-Webster dictionaries). Judgement is right when the author or editor uses it consistently and its use does not contradict a specified style.

The problem of correct spelling is compounded for proofreaders by the two kinds of homonyms--homographs (words spelled alike but divided differently when the sound or the meaning is different: re-fuse, ref-use); and homophones (words sounding alike but often spelled differently when the meaning is different: aught, ought; correspondents, correspondence).

Junctures* (groups of words sounded alike in ordinary speech) also make trouble: Julius served an iced drink to the sick Smiths; Julia served a nice drink to the six Smiths.

---

*Another name for juncture is mondegreen, from an old ballad in which "laid him on the green" became "Lady Mondegreen."

The different preferences of different authorities can cause problems. Furthermore, spelling changes; when enough people misspell
a word enough times, the misspelling finds its way into dictionaries
and style guides and eventually becomes acceptable.

SOME PRECAUTIONS

Unfamiliar Words

There are many words that look like typos to someone unfamiliar
with them. Be careful not to "correct" a perfectly good word.
For example, all of the following can be correct: adsorb, corrasion,
diplomate, discrete, perspicuous, principial, holistic, specious,
are (a metric unit of land measure, not acre).

Surnames

You are responsible for making certain that a surname is spelled the
same in the live copy as in the dead copy and for querying when the
same name is spelled inconsistently. You are not usually responsible for looking up the correct spelling of surnames (in bibliographies, for example), although you should catch misspellings of
the names of well-known contemporaries and of famous historical
personalities:

   Leonard Bernstine)
e   Charles Lindbµrgh

If you see the same name several times, generally with the same
spelling, do not mark the exceptions for correction assuming that
the most frequent spelling is right.

Keep in mind that the misspelling of a person's name is a kind of
insult and that the correct spelling may be unique. In the last
census, an enumerator reported that three members of one family
each disliked the others' spelling of their surname, and each
used a different spelling.

Foreign Words and Diacritical Marks

It is not normally your responsibility to do more than check the
final copy against the draft when foreign words and diacritical
marks are involved. If you should recognize an error, however, so
much the better:

ê /à/ê   tête-à-tête
ó   adiós

As a rule, unless you know the language, do not change or query
foreign spellings in references and bibliographies--and do not permit the typesetter to make changes.

Be careful of correcting British spelling. (See the list following
the subsection on American and British spellings under Spelling
Aids later in this chapter.) Many American professional journals
keep the British spelling in articles by non-American authors.

ALTERNATIVE SPELLINGS

Alternative spellings include those preferred by printing offices,
such as the U.S. Government Printing Office, over spellings in
standard dictionaries. Whatever the writer's choice, a word should
be spelled consistently throughout a document. Alternatives include
the following categories:

dge

Most authorities* drop the e before ment in words whose root ends
in dge: abridgment, acknowledgment, judgment. Consistent use of
the e, however, does not constitute misspelling.

Doubled Consonants

Some authorities* do not double the consonant before a vowel in an
ending added to a multisyllable root when the new word is stressed
on the first syllable.

This includes root words ending in gram, l, p, s, and t:

gram: diagram--diagramed, diagraming (but, with changed
       stress, diagrammatic); program--programed, programing,
       programer, programmatic

l: cancel--canceled, canceling, canceler (but with
       changed stress, cancellation); counsel--counseled,
       counseling, counselor; marvel--marvelous; wool--
       woolen. Other words in this class include council,
       label, impanel, model, marshal, parallel, rival,
       travel, and total

p: kidnap--kidnaped, kidnaper, kidnaping; worship--
       worshiped, worshiper, worshiping

s: bias--biased, biasing; focus--focused, focusing
t: benefit--benefited, benefiting; limit--limited,
       limiting; orbit--orbited, orbiting

Exceptions: Compound words, when the last component word would
ordinarily double the consonant: handicap--handicapped, handi-
capping. Horsewhip, overstep, weatherstrip, eavesdrop, and many
others also fall into this category.

---

*Including GPO style.

gue

Some authorities* drop the <u>ue</u> ending from the following words:
catalog, decalog, demagog, dialog, epilog, prolog, travelog.

How Do You Spell It in English?

Putting words into written English from other languages can involve <u>transliteration</u>--converting from one alphabet to another--
and <u>phonetic spelling</u>--trying to reproduce in English spelling
the sound of a foreign word.

Different systems of transliteration or phonetic spelling result
in different English spellings. King Bhumipol and King Phumipon
(Thai) are the same person; Hanukkah and Channukah (Hebrew),
the same holiday; Chekhov and Tchekhov (Russian), the same person; and Peking and Beijing (Chinese), the same city.

One spelling is not necessarily more correct than another. Watch
for inconsistency of spelling. With proper names, do not assume
that your English dictionary, atlas, or biographical reference is
the supreme authority; the author may be using a different system.
When in doubt, query.

Latin Diphthongs

Some authorities* drop Latin diphthongs in some words: encyclopedia (encyclopaedia), esophagus (oesophagus), esthetic (aesthetic),
pharmacopeia (pharmacopoeia), phenix (phoenix), subpena (subpoena).

Other Alternative Spellings

The following list gives some other alternatives often used:

adviser**	advisor
aline**	align
buncombe**	bunkum
bur**	burr
cantaloup**	cantaloupe
confidant (n.)	confidante
gage**	gauge
goodby**	goodbye
infold**	enfold
marihuana**	marijuana
monies	moneys**
sirup**	syrup
theater**	theatre
whisky**, ***	whiskey
wooly	woolly**

---

*Including GPO style.

**GPO style.

***British usage distinguishes Scotch whisky from all other
   whiskeys.

Choice of Word

Some authorities prescribe a particular word; for example:

> flammable* (rather than inflammable)
> insure* (rather than ensure)
> memorandums* (rather than memoranda)
> ward (rather than wards) as in toward, eastward, sideward,
>   backward, landward, homeward, and so on, but note that any
>   authority distinguishes between beside (at the side of)
>   and besides (in addition to).

SPELLING AIDS

Plural Forms

Anglicized Plurals

Many words from Latin or other foreign languages have been angli-cized by some authorities:* appendixes, curriculums, memorandums, indexes (but a mathematical expression may have indices). Some Latin words, however, remain the same:* addenda, agenda, criteria, symposia.

Words Ending in ful

Add s to words ending in ful: five bucketfuls of cement (one bucket filled five times). Add s to the previous word when the word full is used: five buckets full of cement (five separate buckets).

Compounds

Add s to the most important word in a compound: attorneys at law, comptrollers general, grants-in-aid, assistant attorneys general, deputy chiefs of staff.

When all key words in a compound are equally important, add s to all or make all plural: Bulletins Nos. 27 and 28 (but Bulletin No. 27 or 28), coats of arms, secretaries-treasurers, women employees.

When a noun is hyphenated with another part of speech, add s to the noun: goings-on, listeners-in, passers-by.

When neither word in a hyphenated compound is a noun, add s at the end: also-rans, go-betweens, higher-ups, cut-ins.

Words Ending in o

Nouns ending in o following a vowel always add s to form a plural; nouns ending in o following a consonant generally add es, but there

---

*All examples follow GPO style.

are many exceptions, including Eskimos, pianos, provisos, solos, tobaccos, tyros, virtuosos, zeros. Either volcanos or volcanoes is acceptable, but the word should be spelled consistently.

American and British Spelling

This list shows British spellings in parentheses:

> apologize, capitalize (apologise, capitalise)
> center (centre)
> color, honor, labor (colour, honour, labour)
> connection, inflection (connexion, inflexion)
> defense, offense, practice, (defence, offence, or practise)
> dispatch (despatch)
> enroll, fulfill (enrol, fulfil)
> jewelry (jewellery)
> mold, molder (mould, moulder)
> plow (plough)
> program (programme)
> skeptic, skeptical (sceptic, sceptical)
> specialty (speciality)
> sulfate; sulfur (sulphate, sulphur)

Words With Prefixes or Combining Forms

Rule

A prefix or combining form before a root word usually keeps its spelling, as does the root word.

Examples

<u>Prefixes</u>
de--deemphasis*, de-emphasis**
dis--disappear, disagree, dissolve
il--illegal
im--immature
ir--irregular
over--overrun
pre--preempt
re--recommend, reenter
mis--misspell, mistrust
un--unnecessary

<u>Combining Forms</u>
Style guides and dictionaries differ about which words combine to make solid (one word, unhyphened) compounds. These spellings, following GPO style, keep all the letters of the combined words: barroom, bathhouse, bookkeeper, cupboard, cutthroat, earring, fishhook, golddigger, headdress, heartthrob, jackknife, lamppost, newsstand, roommate, roughhewn, withhold.

---

*GPO style.

**Merriam-Webster dictionary.

These compounds lose a letter from their original words: pastime, threshold, wherever.

Words With a Root Ending in Two Consonants

Rule

A root word ending in two identical consonants usually keeps both consonants before an added ending.

Examples

ebb--ebbed, ebbing
odd--oddly
stiff--stiffen, stiffening,
  stiffness
install--installation
bless--blessed
less--lesser
expell--expellent
ill--illness (but illy;
  see exceptions)
shell--shell-like ⎫
hull-hull-less ⎭

will--willful, willfulness
enroll--enrollment
dull--dullness (but dully;
  see exceptions)
full--fullness (but fully;
  see exceptions)
canvass--canvassing
cross--crossing, crossroad
fuss--fussing, fussy
fuzz--fuzzy
Add a hyphen when an ending adds a third identical character; see exceptions for <u>ly</u> endings

<u>Exceptions</u>
pontiff--pontific, pontifical
words with <u>ly</u> added to make an adverb of the root that ends
  in double <u>l</u>:
  ill--illy
  dull--dully
  full--fully
  hill--hilly
  smell--smelly

Words That Drop Silent e Before a Vowel Ending

The rule to drop silent <u>e</u> before a vowel is fairly reliable: guide--guiding, guidance; manage--manager, managing; mature--maturity; force--forcible. Most authorities* prefer (but some writers do not) size--sizable; live--livable; sale--salable; move--movable.

<u>Exceptions</u>
mileage
words that keep soft <u>c</u> before <u>able</u>: notice--noticeable;
  peace--peaceable; trace--traceable
words that keep soft <u>g</u> before <u>ous</u>: advantage--advantageous;
  courage--courageous

---

*GPO style and others.

words that keep soft g before able: change--changeable;
   manage--manageable
words that need e to keep their identity: hoe--hoeing;
   shoe--shoeing; dyeing, singeing, tingeing (to distinguish
   from dying, singing, tinging).

Words Ending in ant and ent

There is no easy rule to help you with this class of words. Be
alert to the problem. Some examples follow:

adamant	consistent	dissident	incumbent	resistant
adherent	contingent	divergent	itinerant	significant
antecedent	correspondent	dominant	precedent	superintendent
competent	defendant	equivalent	protuberant	
complacent	diffident	existent	resilient	

The words in the preceding list are adjectives that change t to ce
(and sometimes also cy) in their noun forms: competent, competence,
competency; existent, existence. Some words in this class are only
nouns: contestant, proponent. Some words are both nouns and adjectives: combatant, component, defendant.

Note: In some styles, including GPO style, a few words have different endings as nouns and as adjectives:

Noun	Adjective
pendant	pendent
propellant	propellent
repellant	repellent

Words Ending in able and ible

Here is one reliable rule: If the corresponding noun ends in ation,
the right ending is able (dispensation--dispensable, indispensable;
termination--terminable, interminable). For hundreds of able and
ible words, there is no rule, however.

The GPO manual lists over 250 words ending in ible and tells you all
the rest end in able. Be alert to the problem. Some ible words:

admissible	defensible	possible, impossible
compatible	divisible	perceptible, imperceptible
comprehensible	forcible	permissible, impermissible
		sensible, insensible

Words Ending in ise, ize, and yze

Most words in this class end in ize; almost any noun or adjective
can become a verb by adding ize. Fewer than 40 words end in ise.
Words ending in ise include arise, comprise, compromise, exercise,
franchise, revise, and rise.

A few words with roots ending in l take yze: analyze, electrolyze.

Distinguish between the following:

```
advise (verb); advice (noun)   prise (force); prize (value)
devise (verb); device (noun)   apprise (inform); apprize (appraise)
```

Words Beginning in for and fore

Many words beginning with fore imply "before": foresee,
foretell, forefather
```
forego (to go before); forgo (to abstain from, to renounce)
forebear (ancestor); forbear (do without, hold back)
foreword (words before the main part); forward (to move on;
   no e even when "before" is implied)
```

Words Ending in n and ness

When the base word ends in n and ness is added, the result is
two n's:

drunkenness	meanness	openness
keenness	suddenness	plainness

Words Ending in ic

After ic, a k is added before ed, er, ing, and y:

```
picnic--picnicked, picnicker, picnicking
frolic--frolicked, frolicker, frolicking, frolicky
traffic--trafficked, trafficker, trafficking
```

Words Ending in ceed, cede, and sede

The only words ending in ceed are exceed, proceed, and succeed
(memory device: to succeed, proceed to exceed your competitors).
Supersede is in a class by itself; no other word ends in sede.
All other words end in cede; for example, accede, precede, secede.

Words Ending in l and ly

When the base word ends in l and ly is added, the result is two
l's: coolly, incidentally, principally, occasionally, totally.

Words Containing rrh

Several medical terms contain the combination rrh, including
cirrhosis, diarrhea, hemorrhage, and hemorrhoids.

Words With Silent e Before a Consonant

Before a consonant, root words ending in silent e generally keep
the e when another ending is added:

awesome	ropelike	stately
hopeful	docilely	judgeship (but
inducement	futilely	judgment is
issueless	solely	usually preferred)

<u>Exceptions</u>
Some words drop the <u>e</u> when silent <u>e</u> follows another vowel
(besides <u>e</u>): argue--argument; due--duly; true--truly.
Fledgling, wholly, scaly are exceptions to the rule. Words that
sound the <u>e</u> in the root word do not follow this rule: ample--
amply; bristle--bristly; gentle--gently; simple--simply.

Legal Terms Ending in or

The following words are spelled differently in legal and nonlegal
work:

<u>Nonlegal</u>	<u>Legal</u>
abetter	abettor
accepter	acceptor
bargainer	bargainor
covenanter	covenantor
deviser	devisor
intervener	intervenor
relater	relator
settler	settlor

I Before E Except After C

The full rule goes like this:
   <u>I</u> before <u>e</u>
   Except after <u>c</u>
   Or when sounded like <u>a</u>
   As in <u>neighbor</u> and <u>weigh</u>.

Some exceptions to the rule are included in this sentence: The
weird foreign heir seizes neither leisure, sleight of hand, nor
seismic pleasure at their height.

FREQUENTLY MISSPELLED EXPRESSIONS

Here are the traditionally correct spellings for a few often-heard
expressions:

bated breath	nerve-racking
derring-do	pore over a document
free rein	straitjacket
hale into court	

FREQUENTLY MISSPELLED WORDS

If you know how to spell the words in the following list, or even if you only know which words are listed and look them up when necessary, you will have solved most spelling problems. To help you master the words on the list, it includes some definitions and tricks for choosing the right spelling.

In some cases, this list includes <u>preferred</u> spellings; alternatives may appear in certain dictionaries. Be sure of your ground--and your customer's wishes--before you correct a misspelling. Query if you have the slightest doubt.

<u>A</u>
accept (take); except (leave out)
acceptance
accommodate
accumulate
achieve
acquiesce
admissible
affect (always a verb--<u>a</u>lter, sw<u>a</u>y); effect (as a verb--<u>e</u>stablish;
  as a noun--<u>e</u>nd <u>r</u>esult)
allotment, allotted
all ready (prepared); already (previously)
all right (always two words; remember its antonym--<u>all</u> <u>wrong</u>)
all together (all at the same time and place); altogether
  (completely)
allusion (indirect reference); elusion (evasion); illusion
  (deception)
all ways (every way); always (forever, every time)
annual
anoint (use <u>an</u> <u>o</u>intment)
anteroom and other words beginning in <u>ante</u> and <u>anti</u>
  <u>ante</u> means "before": antedate; <u>anti</u> means "against":
  antifreeze
antiquated
argument
arrangement
assistant
attendance (at ten, dance)
awhile (adv.); while (n.):
  She will be gone awhile; she will be gone for a while

<u>B</u>
balloon (two <u>l</u>'s as in <u>ball</u>)
battalion (two <u>t</u>'s, one <u>l</u>, as in <u>battle</u>)
beginning
believe
borne (carried, in many senses: airborne. Also to have given
  birth to: She has borne three children.); born (other meanings
  having to do with birth: One of her children was born deaf.)

C

capitol (building where state or federal government functions
   are carried out); capital (all other uses, including a city
   where a capitol is)
carat and karat (unit of weight or fineness); caret (wedge-shaped
   mark for insertion); carrot (vegetable)
Caribbean
casual (informal, unimportant); causal (pertaining to cause)
champagne (wine); champaign (open country); Champaign, Ill.
changeable
cirrhosis, cirrhoses (pl.)
climactic (climax); climatic (climate)
coercion (Only two common words have this ending; the other is
   suspicion.)
committed, committing, commitment
committee
complement (complete); compliment (praise)
complexion, complected
computer
concomitant
Connecticut (first I connect, then I cut)
connoisseur
conscience, conscientious
consensus (a consensus makes sense)
corollary (two l's, as in follows or parallels)
council (group of people); counsel (advise); consul (officer in a
   consulate)
crystal, crystallize

D

data (the plural of datum, always takes a plural verb: The data
   are insufficient.)
decide
deductible (with an i, as in IRS)
defendant
definite
dependent (take your dependents to the dentist)
descendant (descendants come from ancestors)
desert (something deserved; barren land); dessert (sweet and sugary)
desiccate
desirable
development
diarrhea
dictionary
dilettante
disastrous
dissension (preferred spelling)
divide
drunkenness

E

ecstasy
embarrass
emigrate (go away from); immigrate (go into)
engineering
envelop (v.); envelope (n.)

espresso (coffee)
exaggerate
exceed
exhilarate
existence
explanation

F
February (Br! It's cold)
Filipinos (people from the Philippines)
forcible
friend (a fri_end_ to the _end_)

G
genealogy
glamour (preferred)
gorilla (ape); guerrilla or guerilla (warfare)
grammar (bad gram_mar_ will _mar_ your progress)
gray (with _a_ as in America; grey is English--with _e_ as in England)
greyhound
grisly (preferred in the sense of horrible); grizzly (somewhat
  gray; bear)

H
harass
height
hemorrhage
hemorrhoid
hypocrisy

I
inadvertent
incidentally
independent (when the U.S. became indepen_dent_, it made a _dent_ in
  the British Empire)
indispensable (remember dispens_a_tion)
inoculate (one _n_, one _c_, as in _inject_)
insistent
iridescent
irresistible
its (possessive); it's (it is)

J
jodhpurs
judgment (usually preferred)

L
liaison (two _i_'s)
library
limousine
liquefy

M
manageable
Massachusetts (state); Massachusets (members of Indian tribe)
memento (from memory; preferred)

millennium
minuscule (contains <u>minus</u>; originally the name for lowercase,
   as opposed to majuscule for caps. Some permissive authorities
   allow min<u>i</u>scule.)

<u>N</u>
necessary
Newbery award
nickel
nuclear

<u>O</u>
objets d'art (no <u>c</u>)
obstacle
occasion, occasionally
occurred, occurring, occurrence
ordinance (law); ordnance (military supplies)
oscillate

<u>P</u>
parallel (<u>all</u> <u>el</u> tracks are par<u>all</u>el)
passed (always a verb: He passed by); past (never a verb: past
  history; drive past the house)
percent (not usually per cent)
permissible
perquisite (privilege); prerequisite (requirement)
perseverance
perspective (view in true relationship); prospective (expected, in
   prospect)
piece (a p<u>ie</u>ce of p<u>ie</u>)
Pittsburgh, Pa., but Pittsburg, Calif., Kans., Okla., and Tex.
possession
prairie
preferred, preferring, preference
prerogative
presumptuous
principal and principle
   As an adjective, the word means "main" and always ends in <u>al</u>--
   with <u>a</u> as in <u>a</u>djective): the principal means, the principal
   parts.
   As a noun, remember what a grammar school principal taught:
   "When you mean money or myself, think of <u>pal</u>;
   otherwise think of the ending <u>le</u> as in ru<u>le</u>.": the school
   principal, an investment's principal and interest; moral
   principles, the principle of self-sufficiency.
principally (comes from principal and means mainly)
principled (means characterized by principle: a high-
   principled idea)
privilege (a privi<u>leg</u>e gives you a <u>leg</u> up)
probably
proceed
pronunciation
publicly (the only word that ends <u>icly</u>)

Q
quantity, quantitative
questionable, questionnaire
quite

R
rarefy (preferred)
realtor
receive
recommend, recommendation (the word "commend" is inside)
recur, recurred, recurring, recurrence
relevant
remuneration (not renumeration. Comes from the same root as money,
   not number)
repetition
resistant, resistance
restaurateur (no n)
rhythm (divide the six letters into two groups; each group has
 an h in the middle.)
ridiculous

S
sacrilegious (comes from sacrilege, not from religious)
seize
separate (par as in "break into parts")
siege
similar
slur
soliloquy, soliloquies, soliloquys (both correct)
sometime (formerly); some time (as in some time ago); sometimes
  (at times)
specifically
spirituous
Stanford University but Stamford, Conn.
stationary (stand still); stationery (write on it)
statue (sculpture); stature (height); statute (law)
stupefy
succeed
supersede (The only word that ends in -sede. From Latin super-
  sedere meaning to sit above)
surprise (preferred)

T
than (conj., prep.); then (adv., adj.)
their (possessive); they're (they are)
to (prep.); two (number); too (also)
totally
toxin (i as in anti-toxin)
tyrant, tyranny, tyrannous

V
vaccine, vaccination (two c's; the serum is measured in cc's)
vacuum (one c as in vacant)
venal (mercenary); venial (forgivable)

vilify
villain (the villain is <u>in</u> his <u>villa</u>)

<u>W</u>
weird (don't scream, Dracula; <u>we</u> <u>ird</u> you)
wholly (entirely); holey (with holes); holy (sacred)
who's (who is); whose (possessive)
written

For a review of spelling, turn to Exercise 28 in the
Workbook.

QUESTIONS FOR STUDENTS

Correct the misspelled names with proofreader's marks.

John Quincey Adams

Hans Christian Anderson

Jane Austen

Thomas Becket

Beelzebub

Sir James Barrie

Anne Boleyn

John Wilkes Booth

Elizabeth Barrett Browning

Thomas Carlyle

Lewis Carroll

Thomas De Quincey

George Eliot

Indira Ghandi

John Gielgud

The Brothers Grimm

Hammurabi

Georg Frederick Handel

Nathaniel Hawthorne

Joseph Haydn

Sherlock Holmes

Aldous Huxley

Henrik Ibsen

Kellogg's Corn Flakes

John Lyly

Felix Mendelssohn

Michelangelo

Wolfgang Amadeus Mozart

Nebuchadnezzar

J. C. Penney

Pontius Pilot

Edgar Allan Poe

Ptolemy

Percy Bysshe Shelley

Harriet Beecher Stowe

Stradivarius

Good King Wenceslaus

Chapter 16

Notes, Notation, Heads, and Quotation

The typographic error
  is a slippery thing and sly--
You can hunt till you are dizzy,
  but it somehow will get by.
Till the forms are off the presses,
  it is strange how still it keeps;
It shrinks down in a corner
  and it never stirs or peeps.
The typographic error,
  is too small for human eyes,

Till the ink is on the paper,
  when it grows to mountain size.
The boss, he stares with horror,
  then grabs his hair and groans;
The copy reader drops his head
  upon his hands and moans.
The remainder of the issue
  may be clean as clean can be--
But that typographic error is
  the olny thing you see.

                                    --Source unknown

CHAPTER OVERVIEW

To help you catch inconsistencies in display matter, this chapter
discusses standards and style variations in notes, notation, heads,
and quotation.

NOTES

Notes are used for explanation, cross reference, bibliographic
reference, and certain special purposes. There are several kinds:

- Footnotes appear at the bottoms of pages, usually in
  type two points smaller than the text.

- Endnotes appear at the ends of chapters or at the end
  of a document, usually under the head "Notes."

- Side notes are placed in the margin, usually at the outer
  edge of the page.

- Cut-in notes appear with white space around them (like
  the cut-in head shown under Heads later in this chapter),
  or they sometimes appear in a box. Cut-in notes are commonly set in type at least three points smaller than the
  text. They are impractical in typewritten copy and expensive in typeset copy.

- Center notes, used occasionally for cross references in
  such books as pocketsize Bibles, are set in a wide gutter
  between two columns.

- Shoulder notes are placed in the upper and outer corners
  of pages. They are used to indicate sections or chapters
  in law work, to provide cross references, and to specify
  dates in historical works.

Footnotes and Endnotes

Callouts

Footnote or endnote <u>callouts</u> (or indicators or reference marks) are the numerals, letters, or symbols indicating that a pertinent note will be found at the bottom of the page or at the end of a chapter or book. For callouts, superscript (superior) numbers are commonly used in text; letters may be used in tables.

Compositors use a seven-symbol sequence in tabular, scientific, and mathematical matter where superior numerals might be confused with exponents: * (asterisk), † (dagger), ‡ (double dagger), ‖ (parallels), § (section sign), ¶ (paragraph sign), ☞ (index sign); in a continuation, the symbols in the series are doubled: **, †† , and so on; in a further continuation, they are tripled. When final copy is typewritten, a symbol sequence may need to be invented for the specific job, using characters available to the typist. These might include the octothorp (#), the cents sign (¢), and any other symbol that will not confuse the reader.

Typographic Style

In typeset copy, footnotes and superior callouts for footnotes and endnotes are usually one or two points smaller than the text. In typewritten copy, callouts may take any of several styles; for example:

- Superscript^1
- Parentheses (1); superior parentheses$^{(1)}$
- Shelf <u>1</u>/; superior shelf$^{\underline{1}/}$
- On-line symbol#; superior symbol$^{\#}$.

Most footnote or endnote callouts follow all punctuation marks except a dash. A callout is placed inside a closing parenthesis or bracket only when the note applies to the matter within the enclosure (except, of course, when the style follows the second example above).

Footnotes and endnotes may or may not use the same style as their callouts. For example, callouts may be superior numbers but their corresponding footnotes may be numbered on-line; or the numbers may be the same type size as the notes, rather than smaller.

<u>Reference footnotes</u> are either bibliographic citations or cross references. <u>Content footnotes</u> are either incidental comments or acknowledgments.

Styles for bibliographic data vary in sequence of information, punctuation, capitalization, use of italics or underlines, and abbreviations. (See Part III for a list of editorial abbreviations, including some of those often found in footnotes.)

Editorial style can be complex. A style guide may specify rules for bibliographies different from rules for bibliographic footnotes. (See Chapter 5, How To Proofread References, for an example.)

As an example of the complexity of a single aspect of bibliographic style, here are the rules one widely used style guide* specifies for the treatment of titles in a typewritten manuscript:

- Underline the title of a book, pamphlet, bulletin, magazine, newspaper, or journal.

- Set in quotation marks the title of a chapter, short story, essay, article in a periodical or unpublished thesis or dissertation.

- Underline the title of a long poem; set in quotes the title of a short poem. Underline the title of a long musical composition; set in quotes the title of a short musical composition.

- Underline the title of a play or motion picture. Set in quotes the title of a radio or TV program.

- Do not underline or set in quotes the name of a series, edition, manuscript collection or archive, or book of sacred scripture.

Sequence

Footnote and endnote numbers or symbols may follow through a document or may start anew with each chapter. Footnote sequence may even begin anew on every page; in such cases, numbers, letters, or symbols must change according to the pagination of the live copy rather than follow the dead copy.

In Galleys

In galleys, footnotes are usually typeset separately and appear on separate proofs; they are rarely set immediately after their callouts. To prepare galleys for paging, a proofreader is expected to mark the galleys wherever a footnote callout appears. Usually this marking is done with a color different from that used for queries and other marks. First, mark in text with a reverse caret, then mark at the far edge of the margin; for example:

That scheme was built in part of one used in a previous project analyzing the studies of the Intelligence and Research Bureau. ⋁ All documents were coded by two different coders.

---

*A Manual for Writers of Term Papers, Theses, and Dissertations, Kate L. Turabian, The University of Chicago Press, 1973.

In Manuscript

A typewritten manuscript prepared for typesetting might not have footnotes at the bottoms of pages. Instead, the notes might be typed just after the line of text containing the callout or on separate pages placed immediately after the page with the callout.

In Page Proofs and Final Copy

In page proofs and typewritten final copy, at least two lines of a footnote must appear on the same page or the same column as the footnote's callout. When a footnote is continued on the next page or column, it should be either broken in the middle of a sentence or labeled "continued" at the break and perhaps again at the beginning of the continuation.

Separation From Text

Footnotes may be separated from text with a white line (an empty line) or with a cut-off rule (an underscore in typed matter). Sometimes a cut-off rule is used only above footnote continuations.

Proofreading Procedure

Proofread footnotes or endnotes immediately after their callouts to see if they seem to be in the right place. Reread (not against the draft) footnotes printed in small type as a separate step to re-check for typos and misspelling; for uniformity of typographic style, including spacing, indention, size of cut-off rule; and for other errors a proofreader should correct or query. Also as a separate step, re-check the numerical sequence of callouts and their footnotes or endnotes; proofreaders often overlook numbering errors.

Additions and Omissions

Authorities disagree on what to do when footnote numbers are wrong. When new numbers are added, there are two schools of thought: "Such evidence of negligence as a footnote numbered 4a is unprofessional," says the University of Chicago Press's A Manual of Style. "If a footnote is added in proof, use the preceding number with a superior letter added, as 15^a," says the GPO Style Manual. Opposing points of view also pertain to omitted numbers: if, for example, both the callout and footnote number 11 are missing, one viewpoint calls for all footnotes to be renumbered; another leaves the omission alone. Which rule is followed may depend on when the error is caught; in page proofs or typed camera-ready copy, changes may be deemed too expensive.

In Quotations

When a set-off quotation or extract includes its original footnotes, the original callouts are used and the footnotes are placed at the bottom of the quotation.

In Tables   (See Chapter 18.)

NOTATION

The use of numerals, letters, signs, symbols, marks, or spacing to divide a paper, to indicate the sequence of parts, or to indicate levels of subordination is called a <u>system of notation</u>.

A head schedule, list format, or paragraph style is a system of notation, as is the in-text use of underlining or of different type (italic, boldface, small caps, full caps).

Simple partitioning is sometimes indicated with symbols; for example:

- Asterisk: *

- Asterism: ***

- Octothorp: #

- Paragraph sign: ¶

- Section sign: §

Simple sequence may be indicated with Roman or Arabic numerals, with the Roman alphabet, or, in some scientific documents, with the Greek alphabet.

More complex systems of notation may indicate both sequence and subordination. A head schedule, as discussed under Heads later in this chapter, is a system of notation.

Proofreader's Responsibility

A proofreader must determine the system of notation in use and then verify that the following, when applicable to the notation, appear according to the copy and the specifications, consistently and correctly:

- Alphabetical or numerical sequence (are any notations omitted or repeated?)

- Level of subordination (for example, judged by their meaning, are any headings at the wrong level?)

- Indention, spacing

- Punctuation, capitalization

- Typeface, type size, special treatment.

Outline Form

There are several standard outline forms. One, known as the Harvard system of notation, is as follows:

```
I.  Cap Roman numeral
    A.  Cap letter
        1.  Arabic numeral
            (a) Lowercase letter in parentheses
                (1) Arabic numeral in parentheses
                    a'. Lowercase letter plus prime sign
                        1'. Arabic numeral plus prime sign
                            a". Lowercase letter plus
                                double prime
                                1". Arabic numeral plus
                                    double prime.
```

In any outline form, a number or letter should indicate that there
is more than one item at that level: If there is a I, there must be
a II; an A needs a B; a 1 needs a 2. When only one item occurs at
any level, some writers use a dash for the notation.

Paragraph Numbering

Certain kinds of books are organized for ready reference with a
system that numbers each paragraph or small segment. Any of
several systems may be used. The system used by the GPO Style
Manual and the University of Chicago Press's A Manual of Style
does not number subheads but numbers paragraphs as follows:

```
1.      Chapter head:  Arabic numeral plus decimal point
1.1     First paragraph (or subdivision, seldom longer than
        a paragraph)
1.2     Second paragraph
1.10    Tenth paragraph
1.20    Twentieth paragraph
```

Bullets and Dashes

Some authors indicate levels of subordination in lists or sub-
paragraphs with symbols. A standard system uses bullets (center
dots in typeset copy, lowercase o's or periods in typewritten
copy) and dashes, as follows:

- Large bullet (o may be filled in with a pen in type-
  written copy, as here)
  - Hyphen or en dash
  . Small bullet
    -- Double dash or em dash
      .. Two small bullets

Many variations of this bullet-dash sequence are used. Triangles,
squares, capital O's, or other shapes may be used for notation.

Lists

Text lists (horizontal lists) run on the same line with or after
a sentence; for example: The colors are (1) red, (2) white, and
(3) blue. Vertical lists (and some text lists) follow a read-in

line ending either in a colon or a dash. A <u>colon line</u> describes
or introduces the entries following it. A <u>dash line</u> is an inte-
gral part of the following entries. Read-in lines are used in
stubs or tables as well as in text.

In a short numbered list, many variations are possible. The following examples illustrate variations in spacing and punctuation
around and after the numeral, punctuation after each item and after
the last, capitalization of the first item, caps or lowercase for
each item, and use of the word <u>and</u>.

List A	List B	List C	List D	List E	List F
1. red	(1) Red,	1) red	1 Red,	(1.) Red	1, red;
2. white	(2) white, and	2) white	2 white,	(2.) White	2, white;
3. blue	(3) blue.	3) blue.	3 blue.	(3.) Blue	3, blue.

Style should be consistent within a document, but you should be
aware that apparent inconsistencies may not be true errors. For
example, periods may be used after every item in longer lists only
if at least one item is a complete sentence or only if at least
one item contains more than three words. The problem often is to
find the logic behind the style.

Some apparent inconsistencies are intentional. For example, all
lists in the same document may not be the same kind of list and
need not be introduced in the same way; both colon lines and dash
lines may be used. (Some editors dislike colons and use periods.)
Some styles do not permit a phrase such as "for example" to stand
alone as the read-in line; such a phrase must conclude a sentence.
But some authors prefer "For example:" to stand alone when the
example illustrates more than one of the previous sentences.

A frequent editorial error in lists is lack of parallel construction. This should be queried; for example:

    Strike-on composition can be done with--

- Word processing equipment

- Standard typewriters

- Proportional spaced typewriters

- <u>By</u> typewriters with interchangeable fonts, and

- <u>Using</u> interchangeable type sizes.

By S/?   *(for parallel structure)*

Typewriters using /?

HEADS

The term "heads" includes subheads, captions, legends, titles, and subtitles. Heads are subject to many variations in style. Proofreaders must check for uniformity of style in heads of the same level or in those that serve the same function. Look particularly for typos and other errors in heads; they are often missed in heads and can be extremely embarrassing (and obvious) after publication.

Style Variations

Spacing

There are many ways to vary head style, including the following: Heads may be given a separate page (as with a title page or part title page), a separate line, or run on (with the text following the head on the same line). They may be indented, centered (center head), set flush left (flush head) or flush right, or staggered on the page. They may be

Cut-in
Head
placed in the margin (side head) or cut in (this paragraph shows what a cut-in head looks like). The amount of space above or below a head is another variant. When a head is boxed (box head--an example follows), white space should usually be equal on all sides.

```
┌─────────────┐
│  BOX HEAD   │
└─────────────┘
```

Typeface and Type Size

In typeset copy, of course, heads of different levels are often set in different faces and sizes. This can also be done with certain typewriters.

Caps and Punctuation

Heads may be all caps, set with only important words initial capped, only one initial cap, or all lowercase. Terminal periods or colons are usually omitted.

Special Treatment

Boxing, underlining, or any number of special designs may be specified.

Turnover Lines

Turnover lines are subject to the same variations as paragraphs, as described in Chapter 10 under Spacing.

Standards

The following standards are normal. On some points, higher or lower standards may be followed. When in doubt, query.

For a column or type page to correspond with an adjoining column or facing page, and to avoid widow lines, it is usually proper for spacing (leading) above and below heads to be adjusted. However, the amount of white space around a head should not be conspicuously different from that around the same level head on the same page or a facing page. If columns are <u>aired</u> or <u>feathered</u> (with white space added), make sure top and bottom lines of type in both lefthand and righthand columns align.

A chapter head may or may not be set in the same typeface and size as the chapter number. The head usually begins a new righthand page with a <u>sink</u> (a deeper top margin than other pages).

A common practice calls for two- or three-line center heads to be set or typed in inverted pyramid style and longer heads in flush-and-hang style; for example:

This Sample Shows How a Head Marked To Be Centered Should Be
      Treated When Unusually Long (More Than Three Lines), That Is,
      Like a Paragraph Beginning Flush Left and Continuing in
      Lines Hanging (Indented and Blocked) From the First Line

Cut-in heads and box heads should be set to take the same amount of space throughout a document. Good style requires that cut-in heads be placed two lines below the beginning of a paragraph and that at least two lines of text fall below the cut-in head. When this does not occur, rewriting may be necessary; you must query.

<u>Running heads</u> (heads repeated at the tops of pages) or <u>running feet</u> (at the bottoms of pages) on the lefthand page usually give a book's title (or in learned journals, a shortened version of the article's title). On the righthand page, running heads or feet usually give the chapter or section title. Folios usually go at the outer margin of running heads or feet.

The running head is usually omitted from the first page of a chapter, from a display page such as a title or part title page, and from a page filled with an illustration or a table. When a running head is omitted, the folio may be kept or positioned elsewhere on the page.

Tables and illustrations may have heads at the top or bottom; generally, table titles appear at the top and figure titles appear at the bottom.

When an article jumps to a new page, it needs a <u>jump head</u> on the continuation (the <u>jump</u>). No jump head is needed, however, when the article <u>turns</u>--continues--from the bottom of the last column on a page to the top of the first column on the next page. A jump head may repeat the words of the main head, give only the key words, or be entirely different.

Terms

A separate preliminary head, such as the title of a standing
column or a head giving additional information above the main head,
is called a kicker, teaser, eyebrow, or catchline; for example:

Review of New Books

"Typos I Have Known" Hits Bestseller List

When the kicker is larger than the main head, it is called a
hammer.

A three-quarter box around a head is a hood or a cap, as in these
examples:

PROOFREADERS, UNITE!

UNITED PROOFREADERS DECRY UNEQUAL WORDSPACING

When multiple heads are grouped together, each is a bank or deck.

A head that stretches across a page or across several columns is
called a banner, streamer, or crossline. A blanket head tops all
columns occupied by an article or department, including
illustrations.

A read-in head leaves a thought unfinished until the next head or
the text is read; for example:

PROOFREADERS RIGHT ERRORS IN TYPE, BUT--
Are Proofreaders Just Typerighters?

A standing head is one that is used in every issue of a periodical.

(See Chapter 18 for a discussion of several other kinds of head
found in tables.)

Head Schedules

A head schedule (hed sked) is a plan for setting or typing the
different levels or grades of headlines. Some head schedules use
a code; some simply describe the heads; for example:

Description	Frequently Used Code	Another Code
major head	A head	Level 1
major subhead	B head	Level 2
minor head	C head	Level 3
minor subhead	D head	Level 4
running head	E head	Level 5

The typemarker may simply mark a head with its code; the typesetter or typist must then refer to the schedule and type or set the head accordingly. The proofreader must verify that the schedule was followed correctly.

Head schedules should provide all necessary information, including the following:

- Typeface, weight, form (see Chapter 10 for definitions)

- Type size

- Details of spacing and indention

  - Does this head begin a new page? If so--

    . must it be a righthand page, or can it be either left or right?
    . how much sink is needed?

  - Placement: Flush right, flush left, centered, asymmetrical, or indented (if so, how much)? Side head (in the margin) or cut-in head (if so, how wide and how much space separates it from text above, below, and at the side)?

  - Separate line or run-on?

  - How much space (leading) above and below?

  - Turnover lines: Flush right, flush left, centered, indented, or hung (if so, how much); how much space above and below?

- Capitalization: All caps, clc, initial cap only, or lc only?

- Special treatment: Underlining, boxing, use of typographic ornaments, graphics, color, reverse type, or special design?

- Punctuation: No terminal punctuation, or is period or colon used?

A head schedule for typewritten copy may identify the levels of subheads by increasing indention, decreasing capitalization, and using underlines, run-on heads, or a combination of these.

Figure 16-A shows a sample of a head schedule for typewritten copy.

FIRST LEVEL: CHAPTER OR SECTION HEAD STARTS NEW PAGE ON LINE 10;
ALL CAPS; EVERY LINE CENTERED, UNDERSCORED, AND SINGLE SPACED;
NO PUNCTUATION AT END; SKIP ONE LINE AFTER HEAD

SECOND LEVEL: ALL CAPS; EVERY LINE BLOCKED AT MARGIN, UNDERSCORED,
AND SINGLE SPACED; NO PUNCTUATION AT END; SKIP ONE LINE BEFORE AND
AFTER HEAD

Third Level: Caps and Lowercase (Initial Cap Important Words);
Every Line Blocked at Margin, Underscored, and Single Spaced; No
Punctuation at End; Skip One Line Before and After Head

    Fourth Level: Caps and Lowercase (Initial Cap Important
    Words); Indent 5 Spaces; Every Line Blocked, Underscored,
    and Single Spaced; No Punctuation at End; Skip One Line
    Before and After Head

        Fifth level: initial cap first word only; underscore
every line; indent 10 spaces; return to margin after first line;
space the same as the paragraph following (single space only if
text is single spaced); end with a period. Text runs on from head
on same line, like this. Do not skip a line before head unless a
higher level head comes immediately before.

        Sixth level: indent 15 spaces; otherwise same as
fifth level.

    Figure 16-A.   Sample head schedule for typewritten copy

QUOTATION

Opening quotation marks, both double and single, may be upright
(❜) or--more commonly--inverted (❛). The style should be consistent throughout.

American convention calls for double quotes first and single quotes
for quotations within quotations. The British reverse the order.

Headlines may use single quotes instead of double to avoid crowding.

A printer's convention puts periods and commas inside closing quotation marks--perhaps because they would look lonely outside (although logic might seem to dictate that they belong outside).
Placement of other punctuation marks in relation to quotes varies
from style to style. A reasonable rule puts marks other than periods and commas inside closing quotes only if they belong to the
matter quoted:

    Three answers are possible: "Yes"; "No"; and "Perhaps."

Remember the rule for extended quotes, which calls for an opening quote at the beginning of each paragraph and a closing quote only after the last paragraph. Except for this convention, quotation marks come in pairs; watch for omissions and inversions.

Set-off quotations and excerpts are usually significantly longer than those run on with the text. They may be set in smaller type, more closely leaded, indented right and left, indented only at the left, blocked, or set with paragraph indention. When quotations are set off, opening and closing quotation marks are not necessary, but some writers use the marks anyway.

An indented quotation without quotation marks may contain a quotation enclosed in single quotes; the logic behind this practice calls the indention a substitution for double quotes.

Quotations should be exact. As a general rule, query lightly. In extracts, testimony, or documents intended to be literally exact, faults of grammar or spelling are presumed to be evidence of painstaking accuracy. The writer or speaker is responsible for the errors. Note that the editorial style of the text (capitalization, compounding, number style) may be "violated" by a quotation. If so, ignore inconsistencies.

The rules vary for the number of points of ellipsis to indicate omitted matter. A reasonable rule calls for three periods in the middle of a sentence and four when a sentence ends and a cap follows (the extra point representing the period):

> We, the people . . . establish this Constitution. . . . All
> legislative powers . . . shall be vested in Congress.

Styles vary for spacing points of ellipsis. You may see other spacing besides that in the previous example:

> people. . . establish   people. . .establish
> Constitution . . . . All   Constitution. . . .All
> Constitution. ... All   Constitution....All
> people ... establish   people...establish

Other symbols, such as asterisks and dashes, may be used, although spaced periods are generally considered better style.

If you see copy that has more than two sets of quotation marks (single within double in more than one series), proper spacing is essential. The following is an extreme example:

> " In the New Testament we have the following words:
> ' Jesus answered them, " Is it not written in your
> law, ' I said, " Ye are gods " ' ? " ' "

QUESTIONS FOR STUDENTS

1. What is the difference between a footnote and an endnote?

2. In your own words, define the following: jump head, banner head, read-in head, standing head.

3. Figure out the head schedule used in this book and write it out as shown in Figure 18-A or A-2 (the typeface is Optima).

4. What is the difference between the American and the British convention for the use of single and double quotation marks?

5. As best you can deduce them, write the specifications used in this book for the following:

    bullet lists
    numbered lists
    footnotes

Chapter 17

Symbols, Mathematics, and Foreign Languages

Patty Piper proofed a perfectly printed page of paper.
If Patty Piper proofed a perfectly printed page of paper,
Where is the perfectly printed page of paper
      that Patty Piper proofed?

CHAPTER OVERVIEW

This chapter touches briefly on some characters proofreaders sometimes encounter in addition to the common alphanumeric characters.

SYMBOLS

To a proofreader, symbols include any character that is not a letter
of the English alphabet or a punctuation mark. The printer's term
for signs, symbols, and small ornaments is <u>dingbats</u>.

Proofreading the signs and symbols in formulas, equations, or symbol groups is a matter of making certain that the live copy matches
the dead copy character for character, space for space, and group
for group, and querying when in doubt.

If you do this kind of proofreading often, learn more about the
subject matter. Many symbol groups are equivalent to words (verbs,
nouns, and conjunctions), to phrases, and to sentences. How they
are spaced and where they break at the end of a line can be more
important than how a letter group (a word) in normal text is set
off from others or divided.

When double proofreading, both partners should know the proper
names for symbols. The section on foreign languages in this chapter
lists the Greek alphabet. Style manuals, dictionaries, and almanacs
contain more extensive lists on many subjects, usually under "Signs
and Symbols."

Use sensible shortcuts when reading aloud the names of characters.
"Less equal" is a sensible shortened name for the symbol $\leq$, "less
than or equal to." Do not, however, invent imprecise names, such
as "curlicue"; the opportunity for misunderstanding is too great.

Be sure to distinguish the following from each other (all Greek
letters here are lowercase):

> letter el (l), numeral one (1)
> zero (0), letters O, o, and Greek omicron (o)
> cap X, times sign ($\times$), and Greek chi (χ)
> letter w and Greek omega (ω)
> letter t and Greek tau (τ)
> letters P, p, and Greek rho (ρ)
> letter v, Greek upsilon (υ), and Greek nu (ν)
> letter u and Greek mu (μ)
> letters K, k, and Greek kappa (κ)
> letter n and Greek eta (η)
> letters E, e, "element of" symbol ($\in$) and Greek epsilon (ϵ)
> letter a, partial differential (∂) and Greek alpha (α and α)
> letter B and Greek beta (β)

Use the names in the following list when you must write the name of
a letter of the alphabet to distinguish it from a similar symbol;
for example:

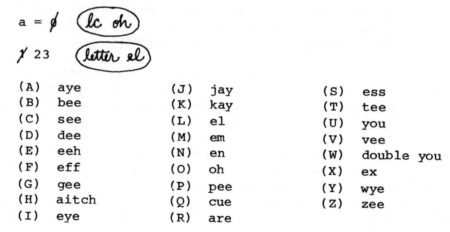

(A)	aye	(J)	jay	(S)	ess
(B)	bee	(K)	kay	(T)	tee
(C)	see	(L)	el	(U)	you
(D)	dee	(M)	em	(V)	vee
(E)	eeh	(N)	en	(W)	double you
(F)	eff	(O)	oh	(X)	ex
(G)	gee	(P)	pee	(Y)	wye
(H)	aitch	(Q)	cue	(Z)	zee
(I)	eye	(R)	are		

Ampersand

The ampersand (&) or "short and" is avoided in good style except in
tight matter and in the names of corporations and organized bodies
that use it in their letterheads. Omit the serial comma before an ampersand (Smith, Jones & White, not Smith, Jones, & White). Watch
bibliographies for the consistent use of ampersands and abbreviations. Part III lists the usage for several publishers.

A List Of Symbols

A list of symbols in frequent use follows.

Diacritical Marks		Other Symbols (continued)	
grave accent	`	second	"
acute accent	´	**Mathematical Symbols**	
circumflex	^	plus	+
dieresis or umlaut	¨	minus	−
tilde	~	plus or minus	±
cedilla	ç	plus or equal	$\pm$
macron	—	multiplied by	× or •
Reference Symbols		equals	=
section	§	is not equal to	≠
paragraph	¶	equals approximately	$\cong$
dagger	†	divided by	÷
Other Symbols		is equivalent to	$\sim$
bullet, center dot	•	is less than	<
double underscore	=	is not less than	$\nless$
left arrow	←	is less than or equal to	$\leq, \underset{-}{<}$
right arrow	→	is greater than	>
up arrow	↑	is not greater than	$\ngtr$
down arrow	↓	is greater than or equal to	$\geq, \underset{-}{>}$
checkmark	√	is perspective to	≃
pound sterling	£	is not identical with	$\not\equiv$
yen	¥	yields	⟶
degree	°	yields reversibly	⇌
minute	′	therefore	∴
because	∵	summation, cap sigma	Σ
script "el"	ℓ	two-line cap sigma	$\sum$
differential operator	∇	integral	∫
increment	Δ	two-line integral	∫

Mathematical Symbols (continued)

proportionality	$\propto$	product, cap pi	Π
infinity	∞	factorial	$!$
differential	∂	parentheses	$(\ )$
variation, lc sigma	σ	two-line parentheses	$\left(\ \right)$
radical, root	$\sqrt{\ }$		
		brackets	$[\ ]$
vertical bar, single bond, absolute value	$\vert$	two-line brackets	$\left[\ \right]$
parallels, double bond	$\Vert$	braces	$\{\ \}$
solidus, virgule, diagonal, slash	$/$	two-line braces	$\left\{\ \right\}$

For practice in proofreading symbol groups, turn to
Exercise 29 in the Workbook.

MATHEMATICS

Indices

Subscript and superscript are indices. In the following expressions,
a is a first order index, as is d.   Second order indices are b and c,
e and f.

$$x{}_a^{\,b}{}_c \qquad\qquad x{}_{\,d}{}^{e}_{f}$$

These proofreading symbols are used for second order indices:

$\vee\!\!\!\vee$ superior to superscript, e.g., b (above): $x\,_a\,_b$

$\vee\!\!\!\vee$ inferior to superscript, e.g., c (above): $x\,_a\,/c$

$\wedge\!\!\!\wedge$ inferior to subscript, e.g., f (above): $x/d\,/f$

$\wedge\!\!\!\vee$ superior to subscript, e.g., e (above): $x/d\,_e$

Remember that the position-indicating caret is not an arrow. A
character above the caret's point belongs above the line; a character below the point belongs below the line.

Editor's Marks

The American Mathematical Society* (AMS) recommends that editors use the following marks in text:

/   break in text acceptable

//   break in display or text acceptable

⟋⟍   break in display acceptable only if necessary

⟋⟍⟋⟍   do not break under any circumstances

∧   insert space (3-to-the-em or normal interword space)

⟩   insert lead

The AMS also recommends the following marking system:

red underline (one line for lc, two lines for caps): Greek letter

green underline (one line for lc, two lines for caps): German letter

blue circle (ring): script cap

orange underline (one line for lc, three lines for caps): roman

blue or black underline (one line for lc, four lines for caps): italic

Blackboard boldface is the way mathematicians show boldface letters on a blackboard in manuscript by writing them with double backs: 𝔸 𝔹 .   Editors should translate this to the wavy underline when copymarking; if this has not been done and lightface has been set, proofreaders must mark for boldface.

Enclosures

Enclosures (fences, closures, aggregation symbols) almost always come in pairs:

angle brackets (elbows) < >

bars ‖

braces { }

---

*Mathematics Into Type, Ellen Swanson, American Mathematical Society, P.O. Box 6248, Providence, RI 02904.

brackets (bracks)   [   ]

double bars   ‖

parentheses   (   )

Enclosure symbols should be as large as the terms they enclose.

Fractions

Short fractions may correctly be set stacked or slashed:

stacked: $d = \dfrac{2(s - an)}{n(n - 1)}$

slashed: d = 2(s - an)/n(n - 1)

Longer fractions should be stacked; how long a slashed fraction is acceptable depends on the editor's judgment.

In hot metal, characters can be piece fractions--separate characters that fit together, or em-set fractions (case fractions)--frequently used fractions cast as single characters:

a font of piece fractions: 1234567890 1234597860
                              1234567890

em-set fractions: |⅙ ⅛ ⅜ ⅝ ⅞ ¼ ¾ ⅓ ⅔ ½| ½ ¼

In phototypesetting, fractions may be set with a special fraction slash allowing each digit's set width to be retained.

When both kinds of fractions--piece and em-set--are used on a page, you should query the inconsistency in style.

Spacing Operational Signs

There are two conventions for spacing operational signs (such as =, +, -, ÷, ×, ±, >, <, ≥, ≤). One closes up; for example: 2x2=4. The other opens up; for example: 2 x 2 = 4. The spacing should be consistent in a document.

If the open system is used, no space should be inserted when signs are subscript or superscript, (for example: $a - b^{x-y-z}$) or when signs belong to a single term rather than indicate an operation, for example: TP = ±0.71 PP.

Equations

Equations on the finished copy sometimes look very different on the draft. If division is necessary, a general rule states that the line break should occur before an operational sign (such as +, -, ÷, and so forth), but that the equal sign should clear on the left of other signs; for example:

$$(1xX)^n = 1+nC_1X+nC_2x^2+nC_3x^3 \ . \ . \ .$$
$$+nC_nx^n$$

Where to break an equation, however, is a complex matter. If you are not competent in mathematics, leave the decision to an editor.

Numbered equations and those that take more than one line are usually <u>displayed</u> (set on separate lines from the text).

Vertical Spacing of Numbers

In a list or column of numerals with different quantities of digits to be typed or set in type at the same indention on the same page, one-digit numbers should be <u>cleared</u> (begun after an extra space) to align at the right with two-digit numbers (cleared for 10), and two-digit numbers should be cleared to align at the right with three-digit numbers (cleared for 100), and so on:

1	I
22	II
450	III

This rule applies to whole numbers in lists and in the columns of tables, to numbers preceding footnotes and heads, and to page numbers in the righthand column of a table of contents or list of illustrations. Not included in righthand alignment are parentheses, one-character fractions, or superior numbers:

3	$4\frac{1}{2}$	10^2
(20)	17	400

Exceptions

- Numbers are normally aligned at the left in the stub (lefthand column) of tables (see Chapter 18), including tables of contents.

- Decimal points are aligned with each other, and whole numbers listed with decimal numbers are aligned where the decimal point would be:

$$3.1216$$
$$45.09$$
$$103$$

- Numbers with hyphens, colons, or slashes are aligned on the symbol:

1-27	6/80	6:56
22-6	14/9	49:4

- Columns of numbers in totally different categories are aligned at the left or centered (see Table of Equivalents in Part III for another example):

Aligned at Left	Centered
3.1416	3.1416
6-4	6-4
42,000	42,000
1 ton (metric)	1 ton (metric)

- Plus or minus signs should be placed directly before numerals in columns:

  ```
   -1.0
  +10.5
   -.3
  ```

For practice in proofreading mathematics, turn to Exercise 31 in the Workbook.

FOREIGN LANGUAGES

We list here only a few tips for reading occasional foreign language matter, such as titles in bibliographies in French, German, and Spanish, or Greek letters in mathematical matter. If you proofread a text that is sprinkled with foreign words or names, you may need to ask for special instructions on how to deal with them, rather than querying them all or trusting luck. (See also How Do You Spell It in English under Alternative Spellings in Chapter 15.)

French

Diacritical Marks

grave accent: on à, è, or ù

acute accent: on é

circumflex: on any vowel, â, ê, î, ô, û

cedilla: on ç

trema: on ë, ï, or ü

Punctuation

Quotation marks may be set as in English or with angles (elbows):

  《 Bon! 》

German

German has used the Roman alphabet since the 1940's. The old
Fraktur alphabet, used in mathematics, looks like this:

𝔄 𝔅 𝔆 𝔇 𝔈 𝔉 𝔊 𝔥 𝔍 𝔍 𝔎 𝔏 𝔐 𝔑 𝔒 𝔓 𝔔 𝔕 𝔖 𝔗 𝔘 𝔙 𝔚 𝔛 𝔜 𝔷

𝔞 𝔟 𝔠 𝔡 𝔢 𝔣 𝔤 𝔥 𝔦 𝔧 𝔨 𝔩 𝔪 𝔫 𝔬 𝔭 𝔮 𝔯 𝔰 𝔱 𝔲 𝔳 𝔴 𝔵 𝔶 𝔷

Diacritical Marks

The umlaut appears on ä, ö, and ü.

For capital letters, the umlaut is sometimes represented by a lowercase <u>e</u> after the cap: <u>Ö̈L</u> is the same as <u>Oel</u>.

Ligature

  ß represents ss.

Capitalization

All nouns and some adjectives and pronouns are capped.

Greek (See also Symbols in this chapter.)

Greek lowercase letters have ascenders and descenders. The following alphabet shows this. Note especially that chi (third character
from the end) falls well below the baseline, unlike roman <u>x</u>.

αβγδεζηθικλμνξοπρστυφχψω

The letters of the Greek alphabet, listed below, are often used in
mathematics. If you must proofread Greek words rather than individual letters, accent marks and punctuation marks apply; you must
seek more information than is given here. Watch carefully that
script or italic English characters have not been set instead of
Greek characters that look similar (note especially lowercase
epsilon, nu, tau, and omega).

Learn the proper names for the letters of the Greek alphabet.

Greek Letters

Name	Capital	Lowercase
alpha	A	α
beta	B	β
gamma	Γ	γ
delta	Δ	δ
epsilon	E	ϵ
zeta	Z	ζ
eta	H	η
theta	Θ	θ
iota	I	ι
kappa	K	κ
lambda	Λ	λ
mu	M	μ
nu	N	ν
xi (zye or ksee)	Ξ	ξ
omicron	O	o
pi	Π	π
rho	P	ρ
sigma	Σ	σ
tau	T	τ
upsilon	Υ	υ
phi (fie or fee)	Φ	ϕ
chi (kye or guttural ch as in German--chee)	X	χ
psi (sigh or psee)	Ψ	ψ
omega	Ω	ω

Hebrew

The Hebrew aleph, used full size or superscript in mathematics, is often set upside down. This is how it should look: **א**

Spanish

The characters <u>n</u>, <u>ch</u>, <u>ll</u>, and <u>rr</u> are regarded as separate letters of the alphabet.

Diacritical Marks

tilde: on ñ

acute accent: on vowels, <u>á</u>, <u>é</u>, <u>í</u>, <u>ó</u>, <u>ú</u>

trema: on ü

Punctuation

Em dashes are used in dialogue in place of quotation marks:

—¿Qué tal?
—Bien, gracias.

Question marks are inverted at the exact beginning of a question: Pregunto ¿habla usted español? Exclamation marks are inverted at the beginning of an exclamation: ¡Viva Mexico!

For practice in proofreading foreign language text, turn to Exercise 30 in the Workbook.

QUESTIONS FOR STUDENTS

1. From what language does the Fraktur alphabet come? What is it now used for?

2. Name three kinds of enclosure.

3. Describe or show in writing the difference between

--the symbol for therefore and the symbol for because
--the English exclamation point and the Spanish exclamation point
--a stacked fraction and a slashed fraction, and
--a grave accent and an acute accent.

4. Turn to A List of Symbols in this chapter. Cover the words in the lefthand column. Identify the symbols the covered words name. Do the same with the righthand column.

5. Turn to the list of Greek Letters in this chapter. Cover the lefthand column (the names of the letters). Name the letters.

Chapter 18

Figures and Tables

CHAPTER OVERVIEW

This chapter discusses the general standards for figures and tables, discusses the different kinds and structural parts of tables, explains how to proofread tables, and shows the main kinds of graphs and charts.

GENERAL STANDARDS*

Each figure or table should normally be inserted as soon as possible after its first callout. One standard places figures and tables, if possible, after the line giving their callout; another standard places them, if possible, after the paragraph giving the callout. Do not mark for matter to be moved nearer to its callout unless you are certain there is enough space. "As soon as possible after its callout" will mean the next page when it is impossible to fit a long figure on the same page.

A small, unnumbered figure or table should immediately follow the callout, dash, or colon introducing it (the read-in line); for example:

---

*Much of the information in this chapter came from Manual of Tabular Presentation, U.S. Bureau of the Census, U.S. Government Printing Office, 1949.

Our study has identified about 2,155 *executive level jobs* (super-grade or FSO–2 and above) in the foreign affairs area as follows:

	Washington	*Overseas*	*Total*
State	562	479	1, 041
Other Foreign Affairs agencies	445	401	846
Other departments and agencies	236	32	268
Total	1, 243	912	2, 155

All but about 100 of the above are career officials.

In an extreme case, when a figure or table introduced by a read-in line must be moved, the text will probably need rewording and a query is in order.

If galley proofs do not already indicate where illustrations or tables are to be inserted, proofreaders must note the locations in the margin; for example:

As shown by the data in table 4, the 40-hour straight time work week has become a thing of the past to virtually all members of printing trades unions.

The growth of total net flows of financial resources to developing nations is shown in Figure 3.2.

"Pick up" (PU) is an instruction to the printer to insert art; for example:

A 24-point Times Roman ampersand looks like this: ∧
Note the difference from Baskerville.

Illustrations and tables follow the same general rules for spacing. As a minimum standard, the white space should appear equal on all sides of illustrations or tables that run into the text on the same page or on facing pages. A one-line title should normally be centered beneath such matter and, in judging the white space, should be considered part of the matter.

Full-page illustrations or tables should not exceed the type-page size (remember that in some jobs the running head, running foot, or the page-bottom folio is not part of the type-page size).

When an illustration or table begins a page and is followed by text, its top printed line--the first line of the head, top rule, or whatever it may be--should align with the top line of the text on the facing page.

Meticulous editors are careful with the words <u>above</u>, <u>below</u>, <u>preceding</u>, and <u>following</u> in callouts; an illustration or table may not fit in the expected place. When you encounter an incorrect "locational" callout (in page proofs or final typewritten copy), you must query, perhaps suggesting a change in wording.

TABLES

A table is an orderly, concise arrangement of related information in rows and columns. There are three general categories of tabular presentation: (1) leader work, (2) text tabulations, and (3) formal tables.

<u>Leader work</u> is matter presented in a simple list with items in at least one column <u>leadered out</u>--connected to the adjoining column by leaders (rows of spaced periods or broken dashes). The two columns may or may not have heads, as shown in Figure 18-A.

Typeset periods as leaders are usually en spaced. Leaders and words may close up to each other, but leaders and figures need space between them. Period leaders may be aligned as in Figure 18-A (1) or staggered as in (2).

REFERENCE MATTER

Section	Page
Appendix	recto
Notes	recto
Glossary	recto
Bibliography . . .	verso or recto
Index	recto

(1) Leader work with column heads

To convert millimeters to inches X   .03937
centimeters to inches. . . . X   .3937
meters to inches . . . . X 39.37

(2) Leader work without column heads

Figure 18-A. Leader work

<u>Text tabulations</u> are simple tables without numbers or titles, sometimes ruled and boxed. They usually are integral parts of the text, introduced by a colon line or dash line, as in Figure 18-B.

<u>Formal tables</u> have titles and numbers. These tables are almost always ruled horizontally (and less often vertically).

The following table compares the 1972 selected general statistics of the Printing, Publishing and Allied Industries with the 19 other industry groups of U.S. manufacturing:

	Rank among manufacturing	Percent of all manufacturing
Establishments	1	13
Total Employment	8	6
Payroll	7	6
Production Workers	9	5
Person-hours	9	4
Worker Wages	8	5
Value Added by Manufacture	8	6
Value of Receipts	8	4
Capital Expenditures, New	13	4
New Plant	8	5
New Equipment	12	4

Figure 18-B. Text tabulation

Anatomy of a Table

The principal parts of a table are the <u>title</u> (or <u>caption</u>); the <u>stub</u>, which is the lefthand column; the <u>body</u> (or <u>field</u>), which is everything to the right of the stub; and the <u>box heads</u> (so called because in a fully ruled table they are enclosed in boxes). Figure 18-C shows these parts of a table.

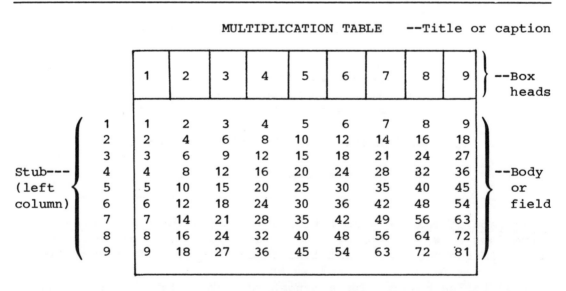

Figure 18-C. Principal parts of a table

Figure 18-D shows parts of a table in detail.

Figure 18-D. Parts of a table

The heading of a table includes the table number, title, and headnote.

The stub includes the stubhead (stub box head) and one or more blocks (also called groups) of related matter that may include heads and subentries differentiated by capitalization, type size, typeface, or indention.

The box heads include the stubhead, column heads, and spanner heads (spanners, also called straddle heads or straddles) spread across and above two or more column heads or two or more subordinate spanner heads. Spanner heads are delineated with spanner rules (or straddle rules).

A panel is a distinctive segment of the box heads consisting of a related group with its spanner, subordinate spanners, and column heads.

Box heads as well as tables can be decked. One level of a panel, such as a spanner head or the row of column heads under a spanner, is a deck.

The body of a table consists of individual cells. A cell, which is the basic unit of a table, occurs at the intersection of a stub item and a column head. A cell entry may be figures, words, a zero, leaders, a footnote callout, or any symbol with a standard meaning or an explanation in the headnote or in a note under the footrule. A cell may be blank.

A line is a horizontal row or part of a row. A data line is a full line, including stub and body. A leader line is a partial row of leaders. A ditto line is a partial line reading as follows: . . . do. . . . (ditto marks--double quotes--are not used in GPO style). A turnover line is the continuation of one line to another within the stub or column, usually indented. In hot metal, a dash line is an unbroken rule (which may be set with continuous dashes) set to partial measure, and a parallel dash line is a double dash line such as may be used for grand totals. A quad line is an empty line, as is a white line.

A stub may be set with leaders after each item extending to the first column. A space break may be specified in a table, placing an empty line at intervals (for example, after every five or ten lines to ease the reader's eye). Braces may funnel several data lines into one. A box head, cell, or stub item may include a unit indicator; for example: ($ millions), 1962, lbs.

Rules

The standard tabular rule is a hairline rule (in vertical position, it is often called a column rule), which is 1/2 point or less in depth. A medium rule, used to set off independent segments or panels, is usually a 1- to 1-1/2-point rule. A broad rule, used for special emphasis, is often a 2-point rule. Figure 18-E shows different rule sizes.

A single rule is a one-line rule; a parallel rule or double rule has two parallel lines. A Scotch rule (Oxford rule) is a double rule with one hairline and one broad line, as shown.

        parallel rule   ═══════════════

        Scotch rule   ═══════════════

Many tables are set without vertical rules; columns should be spaced so rules are not needed.

Figure 18-E.   Some rule sizes

A <u>headrule</u> (under the heading, over the box heads) may be single or parallel. A <u>footrule</u> (at the bottom of a table above the notes), a <u>cut-off rule</u> (any horizontal rule between the headrule and the footrule extending across the table), <u>spanner rules</u>, and <u>total rules</u> (above figures that give the total for a column) are single rules with two exceptions: parallel rules are often used for grand totals and to set off unrelated parts, as in tables split into two columns.

Spacing Specifications

Words and Numerals

In general, words are aligned at the left and figures at the right unless there are fractions or decimals. Rules for aligning columns of numerals are given in Vertical Spacing of Numbers in Chapter 17.

Dollar Signs

Style varies. Here are two possibilities when the head does not specify dollars:

- Dollar signs in stubs:

<u>Variation A*</u>	<u>Variation B</u>
$1 to $24	$ 1-24
$25 to $49	25-49
$50 to $100	50-100

- Dollar signs in columns:

<u>Variation A*</u>		<u>Variation B</u>	
$0.12	0	$ 0.12	$ 0
13.43	$300	13.43	300
111.11	10	111.11	10
124.66	310	$124.66	$310

*GPO style.

Note that in the three examples of Variation A, the dollar sign is closed up to the first actual figure and is not repeated in the total.

Dates

A traditional standard specifies that combinations of letters and figures be ranged left, the same as words. In practice, the spacing of month and day (or month and year) may be ranged left, justified within the stub or column, or aligned on the first numeral:

Ranged Left	Justified	Aligned on Figure
June 30	June 30	June 30
Aug 4	Aug 4	Aug 4
Oct 29	Oct 29	Oct 29

Blank Cells

Some styles (such as GPO) require insertion of an em dash in a blank cell (when neither the word "none" nor a zero is given). Some entries that may be used for cells without data follow:

--	(em dash represents "no data")
NA	not applicable
D	data withheld
S	data does not meet standards
B	base too small for reliable statistical standards
Z	less than half of the unit of measurement

Horizontal Alignment

Reasonable rules for horizontal alignment might be as follows:

1. When the lefthand column has more lines than any other column, align the bottom lines, as shown in all three columns:

Costs of financing research, development, and implementation	$9,450 12,000	$4,245

2. When the lefthand column has fewer lines than any other column, align the top lines, as shown in the stub and column 1. Column 3 follows rule (1).

Costs	$3,782 504	$476,890

Braces

Braces should reach to the top and bottom of the matter they enclose. Here are examples of their use:

Annexed to city in 1979 by vote of citizens...
$\left\{\begin{array}{l}\text{Brightwood}\\\text{Broad River}\\\text{Southport}\\\text{Timberland}\\\text{West Newton}\end{array}\right.$

Daisy   her fair English maids...........
$\left\{\begin{array}{l}\text{Harriet Smith}\\\text{Jane Thompson}\end{array}\right.$
Gertrude

Braces may be correctly placed inside or outside vertical lines;
usage should be consistent within a table:

(1) Braces inside vertical lines

(2) Braces outside vertical lines

Ditto Marks

Ditto marks--the same as opening quotation marks--or the abbreviation "do." are sometimes used to avoid repetition of the same cell
down a column. One standard specifies that ditto signs may be
used only if there are at least three and only if the signs represent words, not figures or compounds containing figures.

Heads

Heads may line up on their bottom lines or may be centered in
their vertical space; either treatment should be consistent
throughout a document. The two are shown in Figures 18-F and
18-G.

	502 NIC Households		
Gross Income	Number of Rural Families	Number Serviced by Loans	Number as Percent of All Rural Families

Figure 18-F. Heads aligned on bottom line

Gross Income	Number of Rural Families	Number Serviced by Loans	Number as Percent of All Rural Families

502 NIC Households

Figure 18-G.   Vertically centered heads

Footnotes

Footnotes in tables and illustrations are numbered (or lettered) consecutively across the page from left to right, not from top to bottom. They are ordinarily numbered or lettered independently from footnotes in the text. More than one callout with the same number or letter may appear.

On "continued" pages of tables, footnote callouts should be repeated in the stub or the box heads. All footnotes may be placed at the end of a table with continued pages; when this is done, a line such as "See footnotes at end of table" should appear on all previous pages having footnote callouts.

When a table with footnotes falls at the bottom of a page with footnotes to the text, the table footnotes should be placed before the text footnotes.

When a table at the bottom of a page ends with its footrule (no footnotes or source line), the cut-off rule normally found above text footnotes need not be used.

Classification of Tables

A standard table, called a narrow table, portrait table, or upright table, is upright on the page, reading across the narrow measure of the page, as shown in part (1) of Figure 18-H. A broad (broadside, landscape, or broadcast) table reads across the broad measure of a page and should be positioned with its top at the left in relation to standard pages as shown in part (2) of Figure 18-H.

One-page Split Tables

A table with a width of half measure or less may be split so that its parts appear side by side on a page with the continuation to the right of the beginning. This is called a doubled-up table (with three parts, a tripled-up table) or a fractional measure table. The right side repeats the box heads but the stub is different, as shown in part (3) of Figure 18-H.

A table wider than page measure but shallow enough to be split to
fit on one page may be set as a decked table (also called a stacked
table or a narrow-divide table), with its continuation underneath
(in a lower deck from) its beginning. Usually the sections are
separated by a horizontal double rule. The continuation usually
repeats the stub but the box heads are different, as shown in
part (4) of Figure 18-H.

(1) Narrow table

(2) Broadside table

(3) Doubled-up table

(4) Decked table

Figure 18-H. One-page tables

A decked table may have cut-in heads instead of repeated box heads, as shown in Figure 18-I.

		Number	
Person			
	Singular	Plural	
	Ser		-- cut-in head
1st	soy	somos	}
2nd	eres	sois	} 1st deck
3rd	es	son	}
	Estar		-- cut-in head
1st	estoy	estamos	}
2nd	estas	estais	} 2nd deck
3rd	esta	estan	}

to be in Spanish
Present Indicative

Figure 18-I.   Decked table with cut-in heads

When a table is too wide but not too deep for one page, it may be set broadside, be reduced, set in smaller type, set on a fold-out page, or given multipage treatment as a parallel table or a continued table, described in the following paragraphs.

Two-page Spread Tables

A parallel table (or parallel spread table) is read across two facing pages. The stub appears only on the lefthand page. Usually a centered title begins on one page and continues onto the adjoining page. The box heads are continuous (not repeated). Part (1) of Figure 18-J shows this kind of table. Footnotes usually are divided between the pages.

A table too deep but not too wide for one page may be set broadside on facing pages (broadside spread) with no repetition of title or box heads and with a continuous stub. Part (2) of Figure 18-J shows a diagram of this kind of table.

Continued Tables

A continued table (jump table) may be used for the continuation of either a table's width (horizontal continuation) or its depth (vertical continuation). In either case, the title on the first page may be followed with the word "continued"; on subsequent pages, "continued" usually follows the table number, and the title may be omitted or shortened.

```
                          .
                Table I.. Parallel Spread
          A  B  C  D  E  F .  G  H  I  J  K  L  M
        1                  .
        2                  .
        3                  .
        4                  .
        5                  .
        6                  .
        7                  .
        8                  .
        9                  .
       10                  .
       11                  .
       12                  .
                          .
                          .
```

(1) Parallel spread table

```
 Table II.  Broadside Spread
                                    .
   A  B  C  D  E  F  G  H  I  J      .
   _  _  _  _  _  _  _  _  _  _      .
   1  2  3  4  5  6  7  8  .  9 10 11 12 13 14 15 16 17
```

(2) Broadside spread table

Figure 18-J. Two-page spread tables

A horizontal (or narrow) jump table repeats the stub on continued pages, but its box heads are different, as shown in part (1) of Figure 18-K.

A vertical (or broadside) jump table repeats its box heads, but its stub entries are different, as shown in part (2) of Figure 18-K.

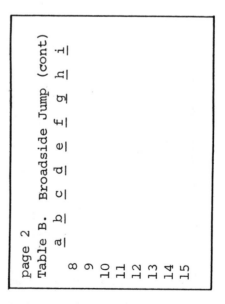

```
page 1                                   page 2
Table A.   Jump Table          Table A.   Continued
           (continued)                    f  g  h  i  j  k
         a  b  c  d  e
         1                                1
         2                                2
         3                                3
         4                                4
         5                                5
         6                                6
         7                                7
         8                                8
         9                                9
        10                               10
```

(1) Horizontal jump table

```
page 1                                   page 2
Table B.  Broadside Jump       Table B.  Broadside Jump (cont)
         a| b| c| d| e| f| g| h| i|               a| b| c| d| e| f| g| h| i|
         1                                8
         2                                9
         3                               10
         4                               11
         5                               12
         6                               13
         7                               14
                                         15
```

(2) Vertical jump table

Figure 18-K.   Jump tables

Proofreading Tables

Speed

You will save much time if you know the terminology given earlier in this chapter. For example, if you and your partner are famil-iar with the parts of a table, you could read the box heads below as follows, "Nish, top deck population spans two, second deck men spans two, women spans two, third deck employed unemployed em-ployed unemployed."

Population			
Men		Women	
Employed	Unemployed	Employed	Unemployed

Even with shortcuts, it usually takes at least twice as long to proofread a table as to proofread an equivalent area of body type. One reason for the slower rate is that numbers take longer to read than words. Many more syllables are needed to read aloud 12 charac-ters forming a number (for example, $123,456,789) than to read aloud 12 characters forming a word (for example, proofreading).

A second reason is that tables are often set in 6-point type. The small size slows proofreading because the characters are harder for the eye to differentiate and because there are often typesetting errors. The proofreading time per galley increases because more characters fit on a galley.

A third reason is that the draft may be hard to decipher:

- When tables are taken from previously published documents, the draft is often a photocopy, sometimes a copy of a copy of a copy, with indistinct characters. Even with a magnify-ing glass, typesetters and proofreaders may be unable to distinguish numerals, particularly 3, 8, 6, 9, and 0.

- Bad handwriting is a severe problem with numerals; there are no clues to deciphering illegible characters (whereas in text the meaning provides clues).

Finally, spacing problems are frequent. It takes time to figure out what's wrong and to decide how to mark errors clearly and concisely.

Problems

In addition to all the things you must watch for in text, the following must be checked with special care on tables:

1. Spacing and alignment (see Figure 18-L).

Error	Galley		Revised Galley	
	Factual	*Predict.*	*Factual*	*Predict.*
(1) Column not centered under head	2.7%	95.9	2.7%	95.9
	2.7%	4.1	2.7%	4.1
	5.4%	0.0	5.4%	0.0
	89.2%	0.0	89.2%	0.0

Error	Galley		Revised Galley	
	(% of Respondents)		*(% of Respondents)*	
	Yes	*No*	*Yes*	*No*
(2) Head not centered over column	34.0	66.0	34.0	66.0
	48.2	51.8	48.2	51.8

Error	Galley	Revised Galley
	EE *(% of Documents)*	*EE* *(% of Documents)*
	2.86	2.86
	49.2	49.2
	50.8	50.8
	18.6	18.6
	81.4	81.4
	18.6	18.6
	81.4	81.4
	0.0	0.0
(3) Decimal points misaligned	100.0	100.0

Error	Galley		Revised Galley	
(4) Heads mis-aligned with each other	*WE* *(% of Documents)*	*EE* *(% of Documents)*	*WE* *(% of Documents)*	*EE* *(% of Documents)*

Figure 18-L. Some spacing errors

2. Proper use of rules. Even when vertical rules are shown in a draft, their absence in final copy is acceptable (in fact, desirable) if spacing separates columns clearly. Mark for insertion of straddle rules and total rules when they are needed for clarity. See Figure 18-M for examples of some problems with rules.

3. Arithmetic in figures in rows and columns (see Figure 18-N).

TABLE 2.—EXISTING REGIMES

Internationally recognized interdependence "area"	Regime Types Functions carried out by:				
	Problem Recognition and Research (1)	Standardization, Measurement, Observation (2)	Property Delimitation (3)	Collective Welfare Choices (4)	Other Regimes Being Discussed

(1) Galley needs rules aligned and insertion of straddle

TABLE 2.—EXISTING REGIMES

Internationally recognized interdependence "area"	Regime Types Functions carried out by:				
	Problem Recognition and Research (1)	Standardization, Measurement, Observation (2)	Property Delimitation (3)	Collective Welfare Choices (4)	Other Regimes Being Discussed

(2) Revised galley improved

Figure 18-M. Rule problems

	Factual	Predict.		Unclassified (% of Documents)		Classified (% of Documents)	
				Yes	No	Yes	No
0–25%	2.7%	95.9					
26–50%	2.7%	4.0	Time Mentioned				
51–75%	5.4%	0.0	Past	28.4	71.6	22.3	77.7
76–100%	89.2%	0.0	Future				
			Specific Mention	25.7	74.6	31.7	68.3
			Non-Specific Mention	27.0	73.0	30.9	69.1

Predict. col total only 99.9% OK/?

25.7 74.6 / 100.3 OK/?

Figure 18-N. Errors in arithmetic

4. <u>Consistency</u> in editorial style: use of caps, punctuation (especially terminal periods), abbreviations, and so forth. Check for consistency in use of dashes, letters, zeroes, and blank cells.

5. <u>Footnotes</u>. Be sure there is a note for every callout and a callout for every note (many tables repeat the same callouts). Be sure callouts are in sequence (see also Footnotes and Endnotes in Chapter 16).

6. <u>Jump lines</u>. Query if a continued line is missing.

7. <u>Parallel structure</u> of all analogous items.

8. <u>Revises</u>. Watch for misplaced items. Figures above, below, and at the sides of corrections must be checked. Figure 18-O shows how one digit was moved to another column when a correction involved alignment and adding total rules.

add total rules & align lefthand figs

19	94		19	94
12	46		12	46
17	56		17	56
48	196		48 1	96
18.7	17.6		18.7	17.6

(1) Galley   (2) Revised galley

Figure 18-O. Digits moved to wrong column

How To Mark a Table

1. Write out instructions when necessary, as shown in Figure 18-P.

2. Avoid guidelines as much as possible. Figure 18-Q shows a table with unacceptable marks; Figure 18-R shows the same table marked without guidelines.

3. Put "feet" on in-text marks to move matter up, down, right, or left, to show exactly what is to be moved, as shown in Figure 18-S.

4. Keep markings as neat and helpful as possible. Figure 18-T is an example of a well marked table.

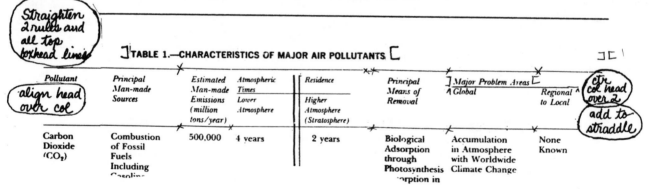

TABLE 1.—CHARACTERISTICS OF MAJOR AIR POLLUTANTS

Pollutant	Principal Man-made Sources	Estimated Man-made Emissions (million tons/year)	Atmospheric Times Lower Atmosphere	Residence Higher Atmosphere (Stratosphere)	Principal Means of Removal	Major Problem Areas Global	Regional to Local
Carbon Dioxide (CO₂)	Combustion of Fossil Fuels Including Gasoline	500,000	4 years	2 years	Biological Adsorption through Photosynthesis ...orption in	Accumulation in Atmosphere with Worldwide Climate Change	None Known

Straighten 2 rules and all top forehead lines

align head over col

ctr col head over 2 add to straddle

Figure 18-P. Written-out instructions

Table 34. Percent of Eligible Families Served by Sections 502 and 504 Loans, Loans Made Fiscal Year 1972[1]

(1)	(2)	(3)	(4)	(5)	(6)	(7)	(8)	(9)
		502 IC Households		502 NIC Households		504 Household		
Gross Income	Number of Rural Families	Number Served by Loans	As Percent of all Rural Families	Number Served by Loans	As Percent of all Rural Families	Number Served by Loans	As Percent of all Rural Families	Percent of all Rural Families (Cols. 4+5+8+)
$0– 999	450,000	3,575	0.18%	260	0.01%	95	0.02%	0.30%
1,000–1,999	726,000					1,216	0.17	
2,000–2,999	838,000	7,187	0.82	504	0.06	960	0.11	.93
3,000–3,999	873,000	12,857	1.47	1,194	0.14	467	0.05	1.64
4,000–4,999	873,000	13,608	1.39	2,804	0.29	233	0.03	1.63
5,000–5,999	981,000	11,701	1.17	6,341	0.63	83	0.01	1.81
6,000–6,999	999,000	7,508	0.72	11,800	1.13	35	Under .005	1.85
7,000–7,999	1,044,000	1,727	0.16	15,165	1.45	17	Under .005	1.61
8,000–8,999	1,048,000	131	0.01	6,506	0.70	6	Under .005	0.71
9,000–9,999	930,000	0	—		—	0	0.00	—
10,000 or more	^^					0	—	
Total	—	58,294	—	46,881	—	3,112	—	—

Figure 18-Q.   Unacceptable proofreader's marks

Table 34. Percent of Eligible Families Served by Sections 502 and 504 Loans, Loans Made Fiscal Year 1972[1]

(1)	(2)	(3)	(4)	(5)	(6)	(7)	(8)	(9)
Gross Income	Number of Rural Families	502 IC Households Number Served by Loans	502 IC Households As Percent of all Rural Families	502 NIC Households Number Served by Loans	502 NIC Households As Percent of all Rural Families	504 Household Number Served by Loans	504 Household As Percent of all Rural Families	502 and 504 Percent of all Rural Families (Cols. 4+6+8)
$0–999	450,000	3,575	0.18%	260	0.01%	95	0.02%	0.30%
1,000–1,999	726,000			504	0.06	1,216	0.17	.93
2,000–2,999	838,000	7,187	0.82	1,194	0.14	960	0.11	1.64
3,000–3,999	873,000	12,857	1.47	2,804	0.29	467	0.05	1.68
4,000–4,999	873,000	13,608	1.39	6,341	0.63	233	0.03	1.81
5,000–5,999	981,000	11,701	1.17	11,800	1.13	83	0.01	1.85
6,000–6,999	999,000	7,508	0.72	15,165	1.45	35	Under .005	1.61
7,000–7,999	1,044,000	1,727	0.16	6,506	0.70	17	Under .005	0.71
8,000–8,999	1,048,000	131	0.01	230	—	6	Under .005	—
9,000–9,999	930,000	0	—			0	0.00	
10,000 or more	—					0	—	
Total	—	58,294	—	46,881	—	3,112	—	—

Figure 18-R. Well made proofreader's marks

Effect on
Climate and
Consequent
Effects on
Agricultural
Productivity

Health Effect
Plant and
Property
Damage,
Ecological
Damage

Figure 18-S. "Feet" on marks

---

③ Turnovers marked 10x to indent

FIGURE 3.—U.S. POLICY INSTRUMENTS AFFECTING THE GLOBAL FOOD SYSTEM

① move first col left
② add straddle

	Policy Points				
Policy Domains	Internal Measures	Border Controls	International Organization Measures	Border Agreements	Penetration of other societies
Production:	Production controls, i.e. subsidies, acreage limitations, price supports, Agricultural research	Protection by quotas, tariffs	FAO research/ projects Consultative Group World Bank	Negotiations on foreign ag. support systems	Technical assistance Fertilizer importance subsidies, mainly AID
Distribution:	Consumer subsidies (food stamps)	Export controls subsidies, PL480 credits, Sales review	World Food Council Int. Wheat Council Agribusiness Multinationals GATT IMF UNCTAD OECD	Bilateral trade negotiations Market consultations, Informal guarantees[1] of supplies	PL480 Title II OPIC
Consumption:	Nutrition research, inspection and grading	quarantines	WHO and UNESCO research assistance programs	Inspection prior to export[3]	Famine relief operations PL480 self help requirements Agribusiness promotion[2] World Food Program

4 lines / lc

]/[#]/

Ed: comma after i.e. and e.g. per GPO style?

lc /] 2 lines

] 3 lines

Ed: FN3 callout precedes 2 - OK?

[1]Private investment guarantees and encouragement of agribusiness technology transfer, e.g. institutional feeding programs that reduce waste, lower costs to poor

[2]Kentucky Fried Chicken in Japan, i.e. affecting consumer tastes

[3]EEC informal visits to China to meet requirements US FDA inspectors in Japanese canneries

Figure 18-T. Well marked table

---

5. It is wise to mark all tables in galley proofs twice. First,
   make preliminary marks lightly in pencil. Second, when you
   have finished proofreading, erase the first marks as you
   make the final marks in red pen (or whatever implement is
   specified). Marking twice is recommended because problems
   frequently are not identifiable until an entire section of

a table is proofread and marked. Two of these problems are illustrated as follows:

- When a problem of vertical or horizontal alignment involves more than one line of type, instead of marking each line individually, it is better to mark the entire block of type with one symbol; for example:

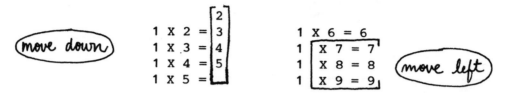

- When two or more tables are set with an identical stub or with identical box heads, a row or column of cells may be set on the wrong table. Instead of marking each cell individually, it is better to mark the entire section as shown in Figure 18-U. Note that this problem is marked here without guidelines and that the instruction is perfectly clear.

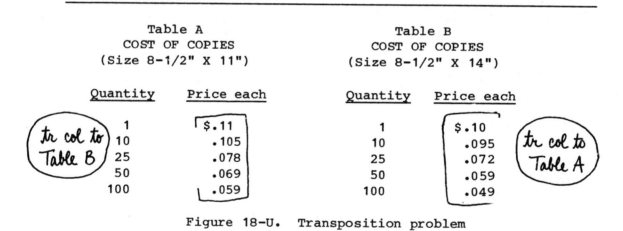

Figure 18-U. Transposition problem

Tips for Tables

Always read a table immediately after its callout to be sure its substance matches its description.

Use a straightedge to follow along the lines--an envelope if nothing else is handy.

Team proofreading is far easier than single proofreading.

Deep columns of table often lend themselves to shortcuts when columns are read down rather than across.

The person reading aloud must identify blank cells and empty lines. "Blank" is a good signal.

For practice in proofreading a table, turn to Exercise 32 in the Workbook.

GRAPHS AND CHARTS

You should know the general categories of graphs and charts, shown in Figure 18-V on page 312, to identify them when double proofing or to verify them when they are shown in one stage of copy but only described or specified in another.

QUESTIONS FOR STUDENTS

1. Classify the tables in Figures 18-P, 18-R, and 18-T.

2. In a current newspaper or magazine, find examples of four graphs and charts and identify them by category.

3. What is the difference between text tabulations and formal tables?

4. List the kinds of problems proofreaders should find in tables. Assume that the live copy for the five tables shown in Figure 18-W on page 313 matches the dead copy. What problems should be marked for correction? What should be queried?

5. In Figure 18-X on page 314, identify the following: box heads, spanner head, spanner rule, stub, body, cell, block, data line, cut-off rule, headrule, panel, stub head, column head, decks, cut-in head, title, heading, head note, unit indicator.

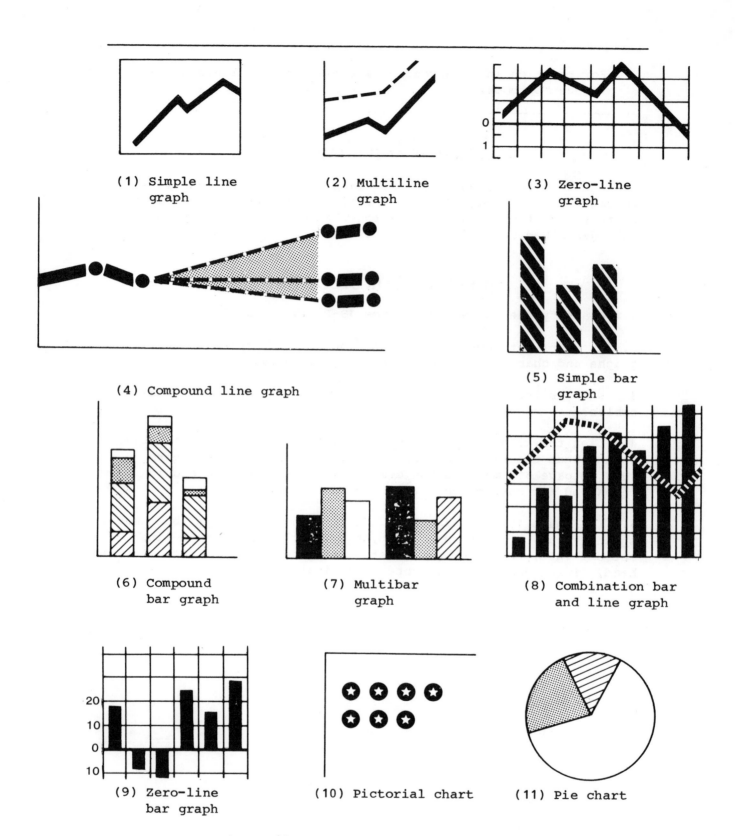

Figure 18-V.   Types of graphs and charts

Percentage	Factual	Predictive	(% of Documents) Prescriptive	Evaluative-Interpretive
0-25%	3.8	86.4	92.0	63.8
26-50%	4.6	11.8	5.6	16.9
51-75%	10.8	.9	1.9	10.8
76-100%	80.8	.9	.5	8.5

(1)

Type of Classification	% of Documents
Unclassified	34.7%
Limited Official Use	37.1%
Confidential	23.5
Secret	4.7
Routine	80.3
Priority	12.2
Immediate	7.5

(2)

	Little/None	Moderate	A Great Deal
Factual	00.0%	37.2%	62.8%
Interpretive	20.9%	48.8%	30.2%
Predictive	62.8%	32.6%	4.7%
Prescriptive	86.0%	9.3%	4.7%

(3)

TABLE 8.—PERSONAL CHARACTERISTICS OF 1969 PROMOTEES TO 0-7

	Army	Navy	Air Force
Military Academy graduates	62%	55%	29%
College graduates	100%	98%	74%
Senior service school graduates	100%	80%a	67%a
Average age	47 years	49 years	47 years
Age range	43-52 years	46-54 years	42-55 years
Average years of military service	43-52 years	46-54 years	42-55 years
Years of military service-range	21-27 years	22-29 years	20-29 years
Average number of assignments	23	23	19
Average months per assignment	13	14	14
Years in operational/command assignments	9	11	7
Years in staff assignments	9	12	13
Years in school assignments	7	4	3

SOURCE: U.S. Department of Defense, Blue Ribbon Defense Panel, *Report to the President and the Secretary of Defense,* Washington, D.C., 1970, Appendix D, Enclosure 1.
aUpper bounds; may count some officers twice.

(4)

		Producers	Users
		(% of Documents)	
39	**FACTUAL CONTENT**		
40	Little or None	00.0	3.8
41	Moderate Amount	37.2 } 100.0%	12.0 } 96.2%
	Great Amount	62.8	84.2
42	**EVALUATIVE/INTERPRETIVE**		
43	Little or None	20.9	48.9
44	Moderate Amount	48.8 } 79.0%	31.0 } 51.1%
	Great Amount	30.2	20.1
45	**PREDICTIVE**		
46	Little or None	62.8	69.6
47	Moderate Amount	32.6 } 37.3%	22.8 } 30.4%
	Great Amount	4.7	7.6
48	**PRESCRIPTIVE**		
49	Little or None	86.0	87.5
	Moderate Amount	9.3 } 14.0%	9.8 } 12.5%
	Great Amount	4.7	2.7

(5)

Figure 18-W. Tables to mark

Price List for Envelopes
(24 lb. stock)

Size		Price	
No.	Measurement	$ per 500	$ per 1,000
6-1/4	3-1/2 x 6	6.79	11.32
6-3/4	3-5/8 x 6-1/2	7.43	12.38
7-3/4	3-7/8 x 7-1/2	9.68	16.13
9	3-7/8 x 8-7/8	9.97	17.15
10	4-1/8 x 9-1/2	10.70	17.85

Open End

1	2-1/4 x 3-1/2	4.78	7.98
3	2-1/2 x 4-1/4	5.50	9.17
5-1/2	3-1/8 x 5-1/2	6.67	11.13
68	5-1/2 x 7-1/2	10.36	17.29
77	6-1/2 x 9-1/2	13.48	22.49
78	6 x 9	12.66	21.10

Clasp

55	6 x 9	17.00	28.34
93	9-1/2 x 12-1/2	27.55	45.92

Figure 18-X. Table for identification of parts

Chapter 19

Specifications for Proofreaders: A Checklist

> While it is desirable to have accurate workmanship, the reader should not forget that it is his first duty to correct, and not to edit. He must not spend unnecessary time in consulting reference books to make up the deficiencies of a careless writer. Nor should he annoy the author with any emendations that savor of pedantic nicety.
> --Theodore Low De Vinne

CHAPTER OVERVIEW

Because requirements and standards differ among jobs--even jobs for the same organization--Editorial Experts, Inc., devised a checklist that is supplied with each job to spell out the job's requirements. A blank copy appears in this chapter, along with an explanation of some of the checklist items.*

INTRODUCTION

Even though you always want to do the best possible job, factors beyond your control--including deadline, budget, and client needs--will affect what you can do on a specific job. Some publishers want--and pay for--editing help at the proofreading stage. For others, every word in a document may have some special significance: Nothing may be changed, not even obviously bad grammar or incomplete sentences. For some jobs, speed is paramount and only major typographical errors are to be marked. These are things you must accept. The guideline is to improve a manuscript only as much as wanted.

The Proofreader's Checklist described in this chapter will enable you to determine and follow the requirements of each job.

CHECKLIST CATEGORIES

The Proofreader's Checklist lists possible typographic and editorial errors. Some of the items on the checklist are divided into A, B, and C categories or levels. Errors in typographic style are more easily categorized than are errors in editorial style. The checklist itself explains typographic categories. For editorial categories, explanations and examples follow. However, even within these guidelines, you must use your judgment. (Note: Although errors are marked for correction here, if your specifications call for querying, you must query.)

---

*Additional copies can be obtained from Editorial Experts, Inc., 5905 Pratt Street, Alexandria, VA 22310 (phone 703-971-7350).

EDITORIAL EXPERTS, INC. Proofreader's Checklist   © Editorial Experts, Inc. 1979

Job _____ Date Received _____ Deadline _____

Editorial Style Guide _____

Project Manager _____ Phone _____

Special Instructions _____

Implements and Marking Instructions: _____

PE's[1] _____

Queries _____

AA's[2]   CE's[3]

Do nothing	Mark for cxn	Query	
1			Unauthorized deviations from draft or dead copy, or from specs
2			Typos, letter omissions, transpositions, doublets, repeaters, outs
3			Misspellings
4			Word division errors, bad breaks, blocks of 4 or more line-end hyphens
5			Mechanical faults (misaligned or turned characters, bad escapement, broken or dirty characters, rivers or lakes, smudges, dots, uneven ink color, etc.)
			A. glaring (conspicuous to untrained eye)
			B. moderate (instantly conspicuous to trained eye)
			C. all
6			Spacing errors* (indention, justification, line spacing or leading, type page and column width and depth, escapement, word spacing, letter spacing, horizontal or vertical alignment), placement of displayed matter or blocks of type, jumping folios
			A. glaring (conspicuous to untrained eye)
			B. moderate (instantly conspicuous to trained eye)
			C. all
7			Page widows (if 2-column copy, note whether checked items apply to left or right columns, or both)
			any top line
			top line of less than 3/4 measure (but not last item on list)
			bottom line
8			Paragraph widows
			divided word
			single word
9			Type style errors* (typeface, type size, caps, Clc, italics or underscores, in text, heads, running heads, page slugs, folios, etc.)
10			Poor graphics
11			Grammatical errors
			A. blatant only
			B. moderate faults; use discretion
			C. all; nitpick
12			Punctuation: errors and inconsistencies
			A. blatant only
			B. moderate faults; use discretion
			C. all; nitpick

*deviations from specs; bad appearance or inconsistencies in analogous items when no specs.

[1]PE: Printer's Error--deviation from dead copy, specs, or normal standards.

[2]AA: Author's Alteration--change from dead copy or specs made after live copy is prepared.

[3]CE: Copy Error--blatant, indefensible mistake in dead copy duplicated in live; correction is a form of AA.

(over)

Columns: Do nothing | Mark for cxn | Query

13 Editorial style discrepancies* (compounding, capitalization, number style, cross references, abbreviations, symbols, units of measure, spelling of proper names, use of italics or underlines, etc.)
- A. blatant (as two usages in one or two lines)
- B. conspicuous (as two usages on same page)
- C. all

14 Poor exposition
- A. material that makes no sense, obvious omissions and discrepancies, apparently incorrect or incomplete sentences
- B. somewhat confusing sections
- C. turgid, awkward, or repetitious sections; peculiarities of language

15 Errors in alphabetical or numerical sequence (folios, footnotes, figures, tables, lists, bibliographies, etc.)

16 Referenced matter (footnotes, figures, tables, etc.), doesn't follow first callout, doesn't correspond with in-text description

17 Missing pages, illustrations, graphics, etc.

18 Inappropriate or incorrect headings, running heads, titles, captions, etc.

19 Incorrect arithmetic (as addition of figures in tables)

20 Equations and formulas; incorrect break, wrong symbols, etc.

21 Tables:
- incorrect style or format* (spacing, punctuation, abbreviations, capitalization, notation for unavailable data, etc.)
- lack of clarity (bad split, need for straddle rules, etc.)
- typographical faults (broken or crooked rules, misalignments, transpositions, etc.)

22 Front matter listings, lack of correspondence with chapter/section headings (check one):
- A. mark for correction where possible (query otherwise) as follows: follow front matter _____; follow text _____; choose best _____.
- B. query all_____; C. do nothing _____.

23 Front matter folio listings, as in T of C (check one):
- A. if incorrect, mark correction; if blank, fill in when possible (otherwise query) _____
- B. query all_____; C. do nothing _____.

24 Blanks in text (items to be inserted, such as page number references) Check one:
- A. fill in where possible (query otherwise) _____;
- B. query all _____; C. do nothing _____.

25 Typewritten copy: correction techniques (check if acceptable): chalk paper _____; correcting key _____; correction tape _____; paste-over _____; pen or pencil _____; splice; cut-in _____; opaquing fluid _____; other acceptable _____.

26 Other:

*deviations from specs; bad appearance or inconsistencies in analogous items when no specs.

Grammatical Errors (Checklist Item 11)

<u>Category A</u>--blatant only. These are errors any person with an average education (good in English) could detect.

> When a student goes to college, they find books   *s / ca / s ll*
> very expensive and ~~you~~ can hardly afford them.   *s*

> Everyone has ~~their~~ books.   *his or her*

> The study will effect all our lives.   *a*

Most blatant grammatical errors involve lack of agreement between subject and verb.

> A comparative analysis of mean scores indicate,   *c s*
> which EEOC groups have the better jobs.
>   (Analysis, not scores, is the subject)

> It is this type of question that the data in
> this section ~~tries~~ to answer.   *y*
>   (Data is plural--always)

> The size and complexity of the USPS Bulk Mail
> Centers (BMCs) makes their management a   *s*
> challenging task.
>   ("Size and complexity" requires a plural verb)

> Professor Jones is one of the distinguished
> scholars who has studied the problem.   *ve*
>   (Scholars is the subject for have--not Jones.
>   Of the distinguished scholars who have studied
>   the problem, Professor Jones is one)

> None of the examples ~~are~~ valid.   *is*
>   (None represents "not one" and requires a
>   singular verb)

> About 1.8 million hectares ~~was~~ distributed by 1960.   *were*

<u>Category B</u>--moderate faults; use discretion. This includes category A and adds those errors so frequently made that they are on the borderline of becoming acceptable English, plus errors requiring a second reading to be certain they are there.

> The program will be carried no farther than necessary.   *u*

> There were ~~less~~ women than men in the sample.   *fewer*

> Table 1 presents a different picture ~~than~~ Table 2.   *from*

> Information is given to whoever inquires.   *m*

> I do not have ~~as~~ many as you.   *so*

Category C--all, nitpick. This includes categories A and B and adds errors of small consequence.

It depends‸ whether we have completed the survey by then.   *upon*

The second method is equally ~~as~~ good.   *ʃ*

The function of the Supervisory Board can be compared ~~with~~ that of a University's Board of Trustees.   *to*

There is uncertainty over what kind of ~~an~~ audio-visual system will be needed.   *ʃ*

With these results, the reliability of the test was proven.   *d*

Punctuation Errors (Checklist Item 12)

Category A--blatant only. This category includes highly conspicu-ous errors, those that could confuse the reader and those that any educated person could detect immediately.

Virtue is it|s own reward.   *ʃ*

A hen is only an eggs⌣ way of making another egg.   *(tr)*

That man is richest who|s pleasures are cheapest.   *ʃ/:e*

Some circumstantial evidence is very strong| As when you find a trout in the milk.   *⌃|(lc)*

Minds/ that have nothing to confer| find little to perceive.   *ʃ ||*

What is truth? said jesting Pilate; and would not stay for an answer.--Of Truth, Franci‸ Bacon   *c ᴎ*

Category B--moderate faults; use discretion. This includes cate-gory A and adds errors that impair clarity, slow down the reader, or reflect lapses in editing.

There are several alternatives, namely‸ I, II, and III.   *⌃*

The report/ that the committee submitted/ was well documented.   *ʃ ||*

They are/ John, Mary, and Susan.   *ʃ*

Many errors in category B involve unit modifiers--compound adjectives:

Government␣leased as well as government␣owned housing   =//
is available.

Group 6 is more/highly motivated.   ſ

A 5/percent increase is expected.   ſ

The following inconsistencies in punctuation are also included in
category B:

1. Inconsistency in serial commas (for example, "John, Mary,
   and Susan" in one paragraph, and "John, Mary and Susan"
   in another);

2. Inconsistency in list format (for example, if one list of
   phrases has the first word in "Clc" style and a comma
   at the end of the phrase, similar lists, with items
   of equal length and the same kind of introduction,
   should also follow that style).

Category C--all; nitpick. This includes categories A and B and
adds errors of small consequence to clarity.

How they wept/   (set)!

The study includes three municipal areas| Seattle, Chicago,   :/
and New Haven.

Will you please complete the following statements/   ⊙

Editorial Style Discrepancies (Checklist Item 13)

A perfectly edited manuscript contains no inconsistencies in capitalization (eastern seaboard, Eastern seaboard, Eastern Seaboard);
compounding (tax payer, tax-payer, taxpayer); abbreviations (A.M.,
AM, a.m.); the treatment of numbers (1, one; 1000, 1,000); punctuation; list format; or any other details of editorial style. Unfor-
tunately, there are few pefectly edited manuscripts, even those
done by professional editors; and proofreaders often read manuscripts that apppear not to be edited at all. It is not, however,
a proofreader's responsibility to substitute for a copyeditor, even
in jobs of category C.

Category A--blatant only. Mark or query only inconsistencies that
are near each other in the same sentence or short paragraph, in
major heads, or within two or three lines of each other. Ignore
inconsistencies separated from each other by four lines or more.

Category B--conspicuous. Mark or query inconsistencies on the same
page or in the same small unit. This means that you try only to
make each page or section consistent within itself; you ignore
inconsistencies separated by a page or more.

Category C--all. Mark or query all inconsistencies you find read-ily. When a style guide is specified or a word list provided, there is seldom a question of what is correct style. However, if the style guide is unfamiliar to you, you must ask your supervisor how much time to spend looking up rules. When no style guide is specified nor word list given, mark or query all inconsistencies you note <u>without taking the time to go back</u> in search of earlier usages.

Poor Exposition (Checklist Item 14)

Proofreaders should normally be least concerned and spend the least time on this problem; the responsibility here is very much the au-thor's or editor's. Note that the following examples have queries rather than correction marks; proofreaders should not try to rewrite.

<u>Category A</u>--disaster level. Mark material that makes no sense along with obvious omissions and discrepancies, and apparently incorrect or incomplete sentences.

As the keys are punched as the other keys are struck.   *meaning/?*

No etching is done where the gravure lines are located which they are protected by the acid resist.   *meaning/?*

Lincoln was elected in <u>1880</u>.   *1860/?*

The questions after each lesson have been formulated to help you find out for yourself just how much you have absorbed from it, of the kind you should know the answers to.   *meaning/?*

<u>Category B</u>--somewhat confusing sections. This includes category A and adds contradictory sentences, dangling participles, unin-tended meanings, nouns and pronouns with more than one antecedent, and anything that needs to be read twice to find the sense.

The study reviews the literature; it is massive.   *antecedent/?* *study? literature?*

Knowledgeable and experienced, the problem will not be difficult for our specialists.   *clarify/? sounds like problem is knowledgeable*

We bought the house for <u>200%</u> less than we sold it for.   *ok/? 100% less is zero*

<u>Category C</u>--turgid, awkward, or repetitious sections, peculiarities of language. This includes categories A and B and adds sentences in which the meaning is clear but not brilliantly so.

In the point system of measurement, the inch is equal to roughly 72 points, or 6 picas, since there are 12 points to the pica; actually, 72 points equal .99648 of an inch, but for all practical purposes we can consider them equal to a full inch.   *rewrite for clarity or break into 2 sentences/?*

Place tab ✓1 in slot ✓2 and tab ✓2 in slot ✓1.   *number tabs and slots to match /?*

Japan is in many ways <u>supremely</u> different from what it was before World War II.   *right word /?*

A stripper must be skilled in the us✓age of a graphic arts knife.   *use /?*

For a general review of proofreading, turn to Exercise 33 in the Workbook.

Part III
Appendixes
Resources and References

Recommended Tools and Supplies

EQUIPMENT

Pens and Pencils

For camera-ready copy, typed or typeset, you need a pencil (or pen if specified) of nonphotographing blue to mark corrections. With normal pressure, a soft pencil will write a good, visible blue (without leaving a furrow that will photograph), but its lead may be thick and blunt quickly. A harder pencil stays sharp and makes a neat, fine line; however, if you use it with the requisite light touch, its marks are hard to see.*

For galleys or page proofs, use a color that will reproduce, because the copy with your proofreader's marks may be photocopied. Specifications may require several separate colors and implements; for example: red ballpoint pen for corrections and black pencil for queries; black pencil for corrections and red pencil for queries; red pencil for PE's, blue for callouts, and dark green for AA's. Do not use nonphoto blue or pale green for queries or corrections; they are too hard to read. Felt-tip pens are not usually acceptable. If pencils are allowed, choose one that makes readily erasable marks; they are available at office supply or graphic supply stores.**

For query slips or lists, unless you are told to type or use another technique, use a red or dark-colored pen or pencil. Do not use pale blue or pale green.

Other Office Supplies

For many jobs you need the following supplies:

- Notepads for query and correction slips (Post-it® pads are especially handy)

- Typing paper, carbon paper, and second sheets (to use when a query or correction list is specified)

- Typewriter (for query lists or any note or query longer than three or four lines).

---

*A good pencil is Eagle or Berol Verithin Non-photo Blue, 761-1/2. A good pen is Commercial's nonreproducing light blue Illustrator.

**Good colored pencils are Col-Erase: 1277 carmine red, 1291 indigo blue, and 1278 green.

In addition, you may need the following:

- Tracing paper and drafting tape, Add-A-Margin® sheets, signals (see Special Techniques in Chapter 9)

- Paperclips, pencil sharpener, eraser

- Straightedge to test alignments and to follow difficult copy line by line (some proofers like colored paper for this)

- Adhesive correction tape and other graphic arts materials to make simple corrections (such as those described in Chapter 11)

- Magnifying glass (for reading handwritten or 6-point copy)

- Administrative forms--time sheets, bill forms.

Rules and Gauges*

Because different typefaces of the same size vary in x-height and extender height, you cannot measure type size with a line gauge. You can, however, measure the depth of lines from baseline to baseline to determine the type size plus the leading.

At the end of the Proofreading Workbook are printed rules and gauges to be mounted on light cardboard for temporary or occasional use. Metal or plastic versions are available at many office and graphic arts supply stores. For typeset copy, you will probably want a precision line gauge (a pica pole), preferably the kind that measures picas, points, inches, and centimeters. Some rules come with marked intervals of 6 through 12 points; some have smaller intervals. A line-up gauge--a heavy transparent sheet ruled in pica squares, used to check alignment--is useful. A type magnifier with a built-in comparator, such as the Instant Type Size Finder, helps determine type size.**

Personal Supplies

You may also find the following items helpful:

- An editor's eyeshade (like a tennis visor) to help prevent eyestrain from overhead glare.

- A calendar or chart to record jobs and to keep track of deadlines.

---

*Mail-order suppliers include Midwest Publishers Supply Company, 4640 North Olcott Avenue, Chicago, IL 60656; APA Graphics Store, 1306 Washington Avenue, St. Louis, MO 63103; and The Kelsey Company, Meriden, CT 06450.
**Instant Type Size Finder is manufactured by Service Engravers, 7 West 22nd Street, New York, NY 10010.

BOOKS

Style Guides

Associated Press Stylebook and Libel Manual, edited by Eileen
Powell and Howard Angione; The Associated Press Stylebook,
AP Newsfeatures, New York, N.Y., 1980.

Council of Biology Editors Style Manual, published by the
Council of Biology Editors, Inc.; distributed by the American
Institute of Biological Sciences, 1401 Wilson Boulevard,
Arlington, VA 22209, 1978.

A Manual of Style, The University of Chicago Press, Chicago,
IL, current edition.

The New York Times Manual of Style & Usage, revised and
edited by Lewis Jordan; Times Books, New York, NY, 1976.

Publication Manual of the American Psychological Association,
American Psychological Association, 1200 17th Street, N.W.,
Washington, DC 20036, 1980.

United Press International Stylebook, compiled and edited by
Bobby Ray Miller; United Press International, 220 E. 42nd
Street, New York, NY 10017, 1980.

U.S. Government Printing Office Style Manual, Superintendent
of Documents, U.S. Government Printing Office, Washington,
DC 20402, current edition.

The Washington Post Deskbook on Style, compiled and edited by
Robert A. Webb; McGraw-Hill Book Company, New York, NY, 1978.

Word Division, Supplement to Government Printing Office Style
Manual, Superintendent of Documents, U.S. Government Printing
Office, Washington, DC 20402, current edition.

Dictionaries

Webster's New Collegiate Dictionary,* Henry Bosley Woolf, editor in chief; G. & C. Merriam Company, Springfield, MA, 1980.
    An abridgment of the Third New International.

Webster's New World Dictionary, David B. Guralnik, editor in
chief; William Collins Publishers, Inc., Cleveland, OH, 1980.
    The standard for The New York Times, Associated Press,
    and United Press International.

---

*Merriam-Webster dictionaries are descriptive--they record the
language as it is used--not prescriptive--there is little guidance
given on preferred forms; for example, you will find "alright"
listed with no indication that many people consider this spelling
wrong.

<u>Webster's Third New International Dictionary</u>, Philip B. Gove, editor in chief; Henry Bosley Woolf, managing editor; G. & C. Merriam Company, Springfield, MA, 1976.
> The standard for GPO and University of Chicago styles.

Books on Grammar, Punctuation, and Spelling

<u>Follett Vest-Pocket 50,000 Words</u>, compiled and edited by Harry Sharp; Follett Publishing Company, Inc., Chicago, IL, 1978.
> This or a similar small book is handy for spelling and word division.

<u>Grammar for Journalists</u>, by E. L. Callihan; Chilton, Radnor, PA, 3rd edition, 1979.
> Textbook and reference for people in the media.

<u>A Grammar of the English Language</u>, by George O. Curme; reprinted by Verbatim, Essex, CT, 1978.
> Two volumes, one on parts of speech and one on syntax, contain thorough descriptions of English grammar and form and trace their historical development up to notable modern writers.

<u>Harbrace College Handbook</u>, by John C. Hodges and Mary E. Whitten; Harcourt Brace Jovanovich, Inc., New York, NY, 1977.
> A standard college-level textbook and reference.

<u>Help Yourself, A Guide to Writing and Rewriting</u>, by Marylu Mattson, Sophia Leshing, and Elaine Levi; Charles E. Merrill, Columbus, OH, current edition.
> A self-study manual, recommended as a refresher course in grammar.

<u>Punctuate It Right</u>, by Harry Shaw; Harper & Row Publishers, Inc., New York, NY, 1963.
> A comprehensive guide to punctuation.

<u>Spell It Right</u>! by Harry Shaw; Barnes & Noble Books, New York, NY, 1977.
> Six ways to improve your spelling.

Specialized Reference Works

<u>A Handbook for Scholars</u>, by Mary-Claire Van Leunen; Alfred A. Knopf, Inc., 1978.
> An authority for the new style of citation that eliminates bibliographic information in footnotes.

<u>Law</u>, by Seymour Bieber, Professional Education Series; National Shorthand Reporters' Association, 2361 South Jefferson Davis Highway, Arlington, VA 22202, 1976.
> An introduction for shorthand reporters; useful for proof-readers to learn the terminology and the concepts.

A Manual for Writers of Term Papers, Theses, and Dissertations, by Kate L. Turabian; The University of Chicago Press, current edition.

>   Especially useful for bibliographic material in the traditional style.

Mathematics Into Type, by Ellen Swanson; American Mathematical Society, P.O. Box 6248, Providence, RI 02904, current edition.

A Systematic Guide to Medical Terminology, by Nathaniel Weiss; National Shorthand Reporters' Association, 2361 South Jefferson Davis Highway, Arlington, VA 22202, current edition.

Typing Guide for Mathematical Expressions, Society for Technical Communication, Washington, DC, 1976.

Books for Further Learning

Bookmaking, by Marshall Lee; R. R. Bowker Company, New York, NY, current edition.

Ink on Paper (2): Handbook of the Graphic Arts, by Edmund C. Arnold; Harper & Row Publishers, Inc., New York, NY, 1972.

Pocket Pal, A Graphic Arts Production Handbook, International Paper Company, New York, NY, current edition.

Primer of Typeface Identification, by A. S. Lawson and Archie Rowan; National Composition Association, 1730 N. Lynn Street, Arlington, VA 22209, 1976.

Printing & Promotion Handbook: How to Plan, Produce, & Use Printing, Advertising & Direct Mail, by Daniel Melcher and Nancy Larrick; McGraw-Hill Book Company, New York, NY, 1966.

Type and Typefaces, by J. Ben Lieberman; Sterling Publishing Company, Inc., 1968; available from The Myriade Press, 7 Stony Run, New Rochelle, NY 10804, 1978.

Books on Usage and Style

The American Heritage Dictionary of the English Language, edited by William Morris; Houghton Mifflin Company, Boston, MA, 1969.

>   Includes comments on usage, prepared with the help of 100 educators, speakers, and writers. Other editions are also acceptable.

American Usage: The Consensus, by Roy H. Copperud; Van Nostrand Reinhold Company, New York, NY, 1979

The Careful Writer: A Modern Guide to English Usage, by Theodore M. Bernstein; Atheneum Publishers, New York, NY, 1965.

<u>A Dictionary of Contemporary American Usage</u>, by Bergen Evans and Cornelia Evans; Random House, Inc., New York, NY, 1957.

<u>The Elements of Style</u>, by William Strunk, Jr., and E. B. White; Macmillan Publishing Company, Inc., New York, NY, 1978.

<u>Harper Dictionary of Contemporary Usage</u>, by William Morris and Mary Morris; Harper & Row Publishers, Inc., New York, NY, 1975.

<u>Modern American Usage: A Guide</u>, by Wilson Follet, Jacques Barzun, and others; Grossett & Dunlap, Inc., New York, NY, 1966.

<u>Words into Type</u>, by Marjorie E. Skillin and Robert M. Gay; Prentice-Hall, Inc., Englewood Cliffs, NJ, 1974.

General Reference Works

Almanac
Atlas
Dictionary of biography
Encyclopedia
Foreign language dictionaries
Street directory
Telephone book
Type specimen books
Who's Who
Zip code directory

Abbreviations Used in Editorial Work*

AA or aa	author's alteration	f.; ff.	and following page (pages)
au	author	FIC**	follow copy, including capitalization
c., ca.	_circa_, about		
CC	carbon copy	FIC & punc.**	follow copy, including capitalization and punctuation
cf.	_confer_, compare		
ch., chs.	chapter; chapters	fig.; figs.	figure; figures
chap.	chapter	fn	footnote
ck.	check	fol.	folio
col., cols.	column, columns	Fol. lit.**	follow literally (no changes acceptable)
CQ	do not change it		
CR	carriage return	fwd.	forward
cxn, cx	correction	FYI	for your information
do.	ditto	graph	paragraph
ds, dsp	double space	hed	headline, heading
ed.	editor; edited by; edition	ib., ibid.	_ibidem_, in the same place
eds.	editors; editions	id.	_idem_, the same
e.g.	_exempli gratia_, for example	i.e.	_id est_, that is
		inf.	_infra_, below
eq.; eqq.	equation; equations	l.; ll.	line; lines
et al.	_et alii_, and others	n.; nn.	note, footnote; notes
et seq.	_et sequentes_, and the following		

---

*Sources: _Chicago Style Manual_, _GPO Style Manual_, _Webster's New Collegiate Dictionary_, _Webster's Third_, and author's preference.

**The U.S. Government Printing Office interprets these instructions as follows: FIC--follow GPO style but keep capitalization as copy shows; FIC & punc.--correct obvious errors, including deviations from GPO style; Fol. lit.--change nothing except type style, type size, and spacing.

NA	not available; not applicable; no answer	q.; qs.	question; questions
N.B.	_nota bene_, take careful note	q.v.	_quod vide_, which see
no.; #; nos.	number; numbers	s.d.	_sine die_, without date
op. cit.	_opere citato_, in the work cited	spec.	special; specifically; specification
p.; pg.; pp.; pgs.	page pages	ss.; ssp.	single space
par.; para; pars.	paragraph; paragraphs	sup.	_supra_, above
		T.	table
PE	printer's error	T of C; TOC	table of contents
pl.; pls.	plate; plates	TK	to come
pt.; pts.	part; parts	viz.	_videlicet_, namely
PU	pick up (type or other previously printed matter to re-use for job in hand)	vol.; vols.	volume volumes

Book Publishers

The following list, designed to be helpful in checking bibliographic citations, is authoritative in spelling, capitalization, use of commas, ampersands, hyphens, plus signs, etc.* If, however, a manuscript is consistent, even though wrong, avoid nitpicking about changes that would be expensive; for example, do not query the consistent use of "and" for "&" in "Harper & Row."

Spacing of initials may deviate from this list (A.S. Barnes, A. S. Barnes), but it should be consistent. "Co." and "Inc." may be spelled out but should be consistent. The ZIP code abbreviations for states are not obligatory; the traditional state abbreviation may be used or the state's name spelled out; again usage should be consistent.

For complete lists of current publishers with correct spellings and punctuation, see the section listing full names in <u>Books in Print</u>, published annually by R. R. Bowker Company, and <u>British Books in Print: The Reference Catalogue of Current Literature</u>, published by J. Whitaker & Sons Ltd. and R. R. Bowker Co.

<u>Publishers</u>

    Abbey Press; St. Meinrad, IN
    Abelard-Schuman Ltd.; New York, NY
    Abingdon Press; Nashville, TN
    Harry N. Abrams, Inc.; New York, NY
    Academic Press, Inc.; New York, NY
    Acropolis Books LTD. (no comma before Ltd.); Washington, DC
    Addison-Wesley Publishing Co., Inc.; Reading, MA
    Aldine Publishing Co., Inc.; Hawthorne, NY
    Allyn & Bacon, Inc.; Boston, MA
    American Photographic Publishing Co., Inc.; New York, NY
    ARCO Publishing Co., Inc.; New York, NY
    Arno Press; New York, NY
    Atheneum Pubs.; New York, NY

    A. S. Barnes & Co., Inc.; San Diego, CA
    Barnes & Noble Books; Totowa, NJ
    Barron's Educational Series, Inc.; Woodbury, NY
    Beacon Press, Inc.; Boston, MA
    Berkley Publishing Corp. (note no <u>e</u> between <u>k</u> and <u>l</u>); New York, NY
    Berkshire Traveller Press (note <u>ll</u>); Stockbridge, MA
    Better Homes & Gardens Books; Des Moines, IA
    Binford & Mort Pubs.; Portland, OR
    Bureau of National Affairs; Washington, DC
    Bobbs-Merrill Co., Inc.; Indianapolis, IN
    R. R. Bowker Co.; New York, NY

---

*Sources: <u>Books in Print, 1980-1981, Volume 4, Directory of Publishers</u>, R. R. Bowker Co., New York, NY, 1980, and publisher's letterhead where it disagreed with <u>Books in Print</u>.

Charles T. Branford Co.; Watertown, MA
George Braziller, Inc.; New York, NY

Chandler & Sharp Pubs., Inc.; Novato, CA
Chilton Book Co.; Radnor, PA
Citadel Press; Secaucus, NJ
William Collins Pubs., Inc.; also
  Collins-World; Cleveland, OH
Columbia Univ. Press; New York, NY
Cornell Maritime Press, Inc.; Centerville, MD
Cornell Univ. Press; Ithaca, NY
Coward, McCann & Geoghegan, Inc. (if necessary, divide
  Geogh-egan); New York, NY
Crane, Russak & Co., Inc.; New York, NY
Thomas Y. Crowell Co.; also T Y Crowell Juvenile Books;
  New York, NY
Crowell-Collier Press (Division of Macmillan); New York, NY
Crown Pubs., Inc.; New York, NY

Da Capo Press, Inc.; New York, NY
Delacorte Press; Delta Books; Dial Press (all are part of Dell
  Publishing Co., Inc.); New York, NY
T. S. Denison & Co., Inc.; Minneapolis, MN
Devin-Adair Co.; Old Greenwich, CT
Dillon/Liederbach, Inc. (note slash); Ojai, CA
Dodd, Mead & Co.; New York, NY
Doubleday & Co., Inc.; Garden City, NY
Dover Pubs., Inc.; New York, NY
Dow Jones Books; Princeton, NJ
Dow Jones-Irwin; Homewood, IL
Drake Publishers (note <u>a</u>); New York, NY
Droke House/Hallux (note <u>o</u>); Anderson, SC
E. P. Dutton; New York, NY

Editorial Experts, Inc.; Alexandria, VA
Wm. B. Eerdmans Publishing Co. (note <u>Wm.</u>, also <u>Ee</u>);
  Grand Rapids, MI
Elsevier-North Holland Pub. Co.; New York, NY
Paul S. Eriksson Pubs. (note <u>ss</u>); Middlebury, VT

Farrar, Straus & Giroux, Inc. (note <u>rr</u> and single <u>s</u>);
  New York, NY
Follett Publishing Co.; Chicago, IL
Funk & Wagnalls Co.; New York, NY

Ginn & Co.; Lexington, MA
David R. Godine, Pub.; Boston, MA
Goodheart-Willcox Co., Inc.; South Holland, IL
Gordon & Breach Science Pubs., Inc.; New York, NY
Gramercy Books, Inc.; New Brunswick, NJ
Stephen Greene Press; Brattleboro, VT
Grosset & Dunlap, Inc.; New York, NY
Grune & Stratton; New York, NY

Hammond, Inc.; Maplewood, NJ
Harcourt, Brace & Co.; New York, NY (books published under this imprint are often cited although the company no longer exists)
Harcourt Brace Jovanovich, Inc. (no punctuation until comma before Inc.); New York, NY
Harper & Row Pubs., Inc.; New York, NY
Hastings House Pubs., Inc.; New York, NY
Hawthorn Books (note no e); New York, NY
D. C. Heath & Co.; Lexington, MA
Hill & Wang, Inc.; New York, NY
Holt, Rinehart & Winston, Inc.; New York, NY
Houghton Mifflin Co. (no comma); Boston, MA
Howell Book House Inc.; New York, NY
Howell North Pubs., Inc.; San Diego, CA

J. B. Lippincott Co.; New York, NY
Little, Brown & Co.; Boston, MA
Littlefield, Adams & Co.; Totowa, NJ
Liveright Publishing Corp.; New York, NY
Lothrop, Lee & Shepard Books; New York, NY

MIT Press; Cambridge, MA
McGraw-Hill Book Co.; New York, NY
David McKay Co., Inc.; New York, NY
Macmillan Publishers Ltd. (no capital m in the middle); London
Macmillan Publishing Co., Inc. (no capital m in the middle); New York, NY
Mason/Charter Publishers, Inc. (note slash); New York, NY
G. & C. Merriam Co.; Springfield, MA
Morehouse-Barlow Co.; New York, NY
Morgan & Morgan, Inc.; Dobbs Ferry, NY
William Morrow & Co.; New York, NY
C. V. Mosby Co.; St. Louis, MO

W. W. Norton & Co., Inc.; New York, NY

J. Philip O'Hara, Inc., Pubs.; New York, NY
Oxmoor House, Inc.; Birmingham, AL

Pflaum/Standard (note slash); Fairfield, NJ
Platt & Munk, Pubs.; New York, NY
Clarkson N. Potter, Inc.; New York, NY
Praeger Pubs.; New York, NY
Prentice-Hall, Inc.; Englewood Cliffs, NJ
Price, Stern, Sloan, Pubs., Inc.; Los Angeles, CA
G. P. Putnam's Sons; New York, NY

Rand McNally & Co.; Chicago, IL
Random House, Inc. (Alfred A. Knopf, Inc.); New York, NY
Fleming H. Revell Co.; Old Tappan, NJ
Rowman & Littlefield, Inc.; Totowa, NJ
Russell & Russell, Pubs.; New York, NY

St. Martin's Press, Inc.; New York, NY
Howard W. Sams & Co., Inc.; Indianapolis, IN
W. B. Saunders Co.; Philadelphia, PA
Schocken Books, Inc.; New York, NY
Science & Behavior Books, Inc.; Palo Alto, CA
Charles Scribner's Sons; New York, NY
E. A. Seemann Publishing, Inc.; Miami, FL
Shambhala Pubs., Inc.; Boulder, CO
Sheed and Ward, Inc.; Mission, KS
Shoe String Press, Inc.; Hamden, CT
Simmons-Boardman; Omaha, NE
Simon & Schuster Publishing Corp., Inc.; New York, NY
Starbuck Inc.; Hartford, CT
Stein & Day; Briarcliff Manor, NY
Lyle Stuart, Inc.; Secaucus, NJ
Summy-Birchard Co.; Princeton, NJ

Charles C Thomas Pub. (no period after C); Springfield, IL
Charles E. Tuttle Co., Inc; Rutland, VT (also correct:
  Rutland, VT and Tokyo, Japan)
Two Continents Publishing Group, Inc.; New York, NY

Frederick Ungar Publishing Co., Inc.; New York, NY

Van Nostrand Reinhold Co. (no comma); New York, NY
Viking/Penguin, Inc. (part of Viking Press, Inc.; New
  York, NY); East Rutherford, NJ

Walker & Co.; New York, NY
Frederick Warne & Co., Inc.; New York, NY
Warner Books, Inc.; New York, NY
Warner Press Pubs.; Anderson, IN
Watson-Guptill Pubs.; New York, NY
Franklin Watts, Inc.; New York, NY
John Weatherhill, Inc.; Salem, MA
Weybright & Talley Inc.; New York, NY
John Wiley & Sons, Inc.; New York, NY
Williams & Wilkins Co.; Baltimore, MD
Wm. H. Wise & Co., Inc.; Union City, NJ
Writer, Inc.; Boston, MA
Writer's Digest Books; Cincinnati, OH

Zondervan Publishing Corp.; Grand Rapids, MI

Table of Equivalents for Verifying Reduction

Proper Fraction	Decimal	Percentage	Number of Times of Reduction
1/20	.05	5%	
1/10	.10	10%	10
1/9	.111	11%	9
1/8	.125	12-1/2%	8
1/7	.143	14-1/4%	7
5/32	.156	15-5/8%	
1/6	.167	16-2/3%	6
3/16	.187	18-3/4%	
1/5	.20	20%	5
7/32	.219	21-7/8%	
2/9	.222	22%	4.5
1/4	.25	25%	4
9/32	.281	28-1/8%	
2/7	.286	28-1/2%	3.5
5/16	.312	31-1/4%	
1/3	.333	33-1/3%	3
3/8	.375	37-1/2%	
2/5	.40	40%	2.5
7/16	.437	43-3/4%	
1/2	.50	50%	2
3/5	.60	60%	
5/8	.625	62-1/2%	
2/3	.667	66-2/3%	1.5
7/10	.70	70%	
5/7	.714	71-2/5%	1.4
3/4	.75	75%	
10/13	.769	76-9/10%	1.3
4/5	.80	80%	1.25
5/6	.833	83-1/3%	1.2
7/8	.875	87-1/2%	
9/10	.90	90%	1.1

Table of Equivalents (Approximate): Inches, Centimeters, Points, and Picas

Inches	Centimeters	Points	Picas*
1/72**	.035	1	1/12
1/36	.07	2	1/6
1/32	.08	2.25	
	.1	3	1/4
1/16		4.5	
	.2	6	
	.25	7	
1/8	.3	9	3/4
5/32		11.25	
1/6	.4	12	1
3/16	.5	13.4	
1/4	.6	18	1-1/2
5/16	.75	22.5	
	.8	24	
3/8	.9	27	
	1.0	28.4	2-1/2
7/16	1.1	31.5	
	1.2	34	
1/2		36	3
	1.3	37	
	1.4	40	
9/16		40.5	
	1.5	42	3-1/2
5/8		45	
	1.6	46	
		48	4
11/16		49.5	
3/4	1.9	54	4-1/2
	2.0		4-3/4
13/16		58.5	
		60	5
7/8		63	
		66	5-1/2
1***	2.5	72	6

---

*Fractions, not decimals, are normally used. With the period, 1.5, for example, represents 1 pica 5 points, not one and one-half picas.

**To be exact, 1 point = 0.01384 inch.

***To be exact, .99648 inch = 6 picas; for all practical purposes, 1 inch is the equivalent to use.

Roman Numerals

Roman numerals are shown below. In Roman numerals, the position of a letter affects its value as follows:

- A repeated letter repeats its value (X is 10, XX is 20)

- A letter placed after one of greater value adds its value (X is 10, XV is 15)

- A letter placed before one of greater value substracts its value (X is 10, IX is 9)

- A bar over a letter multiplies its value by 1,000 (V is 5, $\overline{V}$--handwritten..--is 5,000).

1	I	i	50	L	1,500	MD
2	II	ii	55	LV	2,000	MM
3	III	iii	59	LIX	3,000	MMM
4	IV	iv	60	LX	4,000	MMMM or $\overline{IV}$
5	V	v	69	LXIX	5,000	$\overline{V}$
6	VI	vi	70	LXX	1 million	$\overline{M}$
7	VII	vii	79	LXXIX		Dates
8	VIII	viii	80	LXXX	1600	MDC
9	IX	ix	89	LXXXIX	1700	MDCC
10	X	x	90	XC	1800	MDCCC
11	XI	xi	99	XCIX	1900	MCM or MDCCCC
12	XII	xii	100	C	1910	MCMX
15	XV	xv	150	CL	1920	MCMXX
20	XX	xx	200	CC	1930	MCMXXX
25	XXV	xxv	300	CCC	1940	MCMXL
29	XXIX	xxix	400	CD	1950	MCML
30	XXX	xxx	500	D	1960	MCMLX
35	XXXV	xxxv	600	DC	1970	MCMLXX
39	XXXIX	xxxix	700	DCC	1980	MCMLXXX
40	XL	xl	800	DCCC	1981	MCMLXXXI
45	XLV	xlv	900	CM	1982	MCMLXXXII
49	XLIX	xlix	1,000	M	1983	MCMLXXXIII

A-1.   Roman numerals

How to Proofread Lexitron Copy

(These guidelines, while covering only one brand of word processing machine, illustrate principles generally applicable to other word processing equipment.)

Description of Copy

There are two main operations in producing Lexitron copy--input and printout:

1. Input. A Lexitron operator types on a machine that looks like a typewriter with a TV screen on top of it. The machine records the operator's typing onto a tape cassette or disk. The video screen displays, one page at a time, what is being or what has been typed.

2. Printout. Next to the input machine is the printer, a machine that prints out the contents of a tape.

Each of the two operations uses a different correction method.

Tape Corrections

An operator corrects input errors right on the tape and then makes a new printout of every corrected page. The machine can--

- Erase characters
- Delete and close up characters
- Replace characters
- Insert characters or empty lines
- Delete lines
- Move lines from one part of a page to another or from one page to another.

Printout Corrections

An operator fixes printout errors (after proofreading) by making a new printout with a different--

- Typeface
- Pitch
- Line spacing for a whole page (double space instead of single or vice versa).

The printer has a lever that must be set correctly to prevent printing a degree sign instead of an apostrophe (or vice versa) in certain typefaces.

Proofreading Instructions

Use standard proofreader's marks.

Use a red pencil to mark errors. Any page with an error will be printed out again.

Do not write queries in red. Attach a query slip onto a page so that a page with no errors will not have to be printed out again if the query is not accepted by the project manager.

Mark these errors individually; they will be corrected on the tape:

- Typos, outs, doublets, repeaters

- Wrong word division

- Wrong word spacing

- Watch especially for these errors:

    - only one space after a period or colon
    - one hyphen dropped from an em dash (--)
    - one hyphen dropped from a compound word

- Wrong margins, ragged margins

- Missing empty lines, extra empty lines

- Static (garble, garbage); mark as copy out.

Write a general note for these errors; they will be corrected by setting the printer differently:

- Wrong typeface

- Bad printwheel

- Wrong pitch

- Wrong margins (throughout)

- Wrong line spacing on a whole page (double spacing instead of single and vice versa)

- Degree sign instead of apostrophe

- Wrong paper.

Oversize tables get special treatment:

Use nonphoto blue pencil to mark corrections so typist can make a cut-in correction rather than reprint a whole table.

Make sure there is a "frame page" (page with table number, title, and proper page number) attached to any oversize table.

Make sure an oversize table has a notation in nonphoto blue that says "table ____, reduce for page ____."

Checking corrections requires a special process. Check not only each correction but also the entire line in which a correction has been made and the lines above and below. Watch especially for these errors:

- Only one space after a period or colon

- One hyphen dropped from an em dash (--)

- The hyphen dropped from a compound word

- New errors in word division

- New errors--repeaters or outs--at the end of one line and the start of the next

- Wrong margins, ragged margins

- Widows.

Reproof all changed lines and paragraphs. To find which have been changed, compare line beginnings in the dead copy with those in the live.

If copy has been moved, be sure none has been dropped or repeated on the page or from the end of one page to the start of the next. Be sure moved copy is in the right place. Be sure the place copy has been moved from is merged properly.

Scan each new printout page for garble.

How to Proofread Lexitron Copy
Coded for the Computer

Description

Lexitron copy coded for the computer is sent over telephone wires to a company that does typesetting.

The codes program the computerized typesetting equipment. There is a code for every paragraph or head and for every time a change is made in typeface, type size, or spacing. There are also codes for special symbols, such as superscripts.

Instructions

Be sure the codes in the live copy match those in the dead copy.

Do not mark wrong margins. The computer will set type in the measure the code tells it to. It does not matter if the typed copy is run on, has ragged margins, or has short or long lines as long as every new paragraph (or new line) is coded.

Mark end-of-line word divisions to be typed as single words, or else the hyphens typed at the ends of lines will appear in the middle of a line in the typeset copy.

Be careful not to take out hyphens in compound words, but be sure a compound does not fall at the end of a line, or a space will appear between the hyphen and the following word.

How to Proofread OCR-B Copy
for a Hendrix Typereader

Description

The typereader reads a special typeface (OCR-B) and records the typed characters onto a Lexitron tape.

An operator puts the tape the scanner recorded into the Lexitron, examines the copy page by page as it is displayed on the screen, and makes the corrections you have marked.

Instructions

The scanner reads black and other colors; it cannot read red. Mark scanner copy with a red felt-tipped pen.

The scanner will not record--

- Characters that are crossed out with a black line woɸrd
- A single character followed by the symbol <
- A word followed by <<
- A whole line followed by <<<

Be sure these symbols that tell the scanner not to record are used correctly.

Be sure all characters are sharp so the scanner can read them properly.

Be sure margins are at least one inch on all sides.

Otherwise, mark the same as for Lexitron copy.

Example of Specifications to a Printer

1. Trim Size ___7-2/8 x 10-1/4 inches___

2. Paper: Text ___Offset book, 120 lb., white___ Cover ___Lithocoated, 160 lb.,___
                                                                    white

3. Binding ___Perfect___

4. We will hold proofs:

   a. Galleys ___14 working days per 500 manuscript folios___

   b. Page Proofs ___7 working days per 500 manuscript folios___

5. Number of camera-ready charts, graphs, photographs, etc.:

   ___None___

6. Color of Ink: Text ___Black___   Cover ___Black___

7. Text: Body Type ___Times Roman 10/11 (27Lf 10-11), Clc, FL L & R___
                          ___19 picas wide___

8. Head Schedule:

   Level A. ___Chapter/Part Identifier and Title:___

            ___24 pt Record Gothic Bold (186 Lu 24)___

            ___Clc, FL   Space: 24 pt between identifier and title___
                                    12 pt below title
   Level B. ___Chapter/Part Subhead #1/Appendix Head___

            ___12 pt Spartan Heavy (142 Lf 12-13___

            ___All Caps, FL Space: 24 pt above, 10 pt below___
                                For use with Introduction, Priorities,
            ___F Chapter/Part Subhead #2___   Implementation
   Level C.

            ___10 pt Times Roman Bold (28 Lf 10-11)___

            ___Clc, FL   Space: 10 pt above and below___
                                            (27 Lf 10)
9. Folio: Type ___10 pt Times Roman___ Position ___Bottom, fl with outside___
                                                      edge of outside
                                                      column 1 pica
                                                      below text

                                                   Continued

Figure A-2. Sample printing specifications form

10. Footnotes: Type   8 pt Times Roman on 9 lead (27 Lf 8/9)

                          At bottom of column on page on which the
Position   footnote appears in the text

                        Not to exceed 19 picas wide, flush left
Width   and right

                        Indent first line 1 em; runover is flush left
Indent

Line Rule   Separate footnote from text by a 4-pica hairline
                        rule, with 5 pts of space above and below the rule

11. Page Specifications:

Trim Size   7-7/8 x 10-1/4 inches

Bleed   None

Number of Columns   2

Column Width   19 picas

Gutter Width   1.5 picas

Page Width (from left side of left column to right
side of right column)   39.5 picas

Page Depth (without folio)   53 picas

Page Depth (with folio)   55 picas

Margins (after trim):   Head   5 picas

                              Foot   2.5 picas

                              Inside   4 picas

                            Outside   4 picas

12. Page Make-up Instructions:

    a. Chapter opening pages are always new odd pages. Hang chapter

       chapter title from 11 picas sink. Leave 12 points of space bet.
       bottom of last line of chapter title and first line of text

    b. Top of right column lines up with top of left column.

    c. Indent paragraphs 1 em at first line. No extra space between pars.

Figure A-2. (Continued)

Some Points on GPO Style*

ABBREVIATIONS (See Manual, Rules, pp. 149-156; 166-167; Standard word abbreviations, pp. 156-163; Units of Measure, pp. 163-166; Legal and Latin Phrases, pp. 482-485)
- Acronyms. Use no periods (GPO, HUD).
- Units of measure. Use no periods (Btu, cm).
- U.S. Use abbreviation as adjective before Government or name of Government agency (U.S. Congress), except in formal documents. As noun, spell out United States.
- States. N. Dak., S. Dak., N. Mex., (but N.C. and S.C. for North and South Carolina), Nebr., Oreg., Tex., Wis.; spell out Alaska, Hawaii, Idaho, Iowa, Maine, Ohio, Utah.
- Postal Service State abbreviations. Two-letter forms appear on p. 151.

CAPITALIZATION (See Manual, Rules, pp. 23-32; List of capitalized and lowercased words, pp. 33-60)
- Government words:
  - Generally, cap names of State and Federal bodies and officials given in full (Civil Service Commission, Secretary of Commerce, Virginia Assembly); cap only Federal names in shortened form (the Commission, the Secretary, the assembly).
  - Cap Government for nations (British Government); lowercase government for States, territories, and municipalities, including D.C. (D.C. government).
  - Cap State referring to any of the 50 specifically or in general, e.g., State statutes; lowercase adjectives such as statewide.
  - Cap Federal; lowercase federally.
  - Cap Nation, generally, only as a synonym for the United States.
- References. In text, when no title follows, lowercase references such as amendment 5, appendix C, chapter IV, table 6, treaty of 1919. When title follows, cap (Chapter IV, Further Research).
- After colon or comma. Cap independent (not merely supplementary) clause or phrase (The question is, Shall the bill pass? The answer is: Yes); cap first word in series of introduced items (Voting was as follows: Yea, 22; nay, 19).
- Heads. In head, cap principal words, including infinitives (To Be, To Go), short verbs (Are, Is), and prepositions of four letters or more (With, From), e.g., Price-Cutting War; Forty Homes Are To Be Built; How To File With Exemption From Requirements.

COMPOUNDING (See Manual, Rules, pp. 73-82; List of compounds, pp. 82-130)
- Combining forms, suffixes, and prefixes. Write solid most words with combining forms, suffixes, and prefixes, including those beginning with anti, multi, non, and pre. Hyphenate these exceptions:
  - Duplicated prefixes (re-redirect)
  - Prefixes added to already hyphenated words (pro-mother-in-law)
  - Prefixes added to capped words (mid-April, post-World War I)
  - Prefixed words that could be confused or mispronounced (re-ink, pre-judicial)
  - Words with the prefixes ex, quasi, or self (ex-trader, quasi-academic, self-evident)
  - Words with identical triple consonants (hull-less, bell-like)
  - Words with identical double vowels (anti-inflation) unless formed with the short prefixes co, de, pre, pro, and re (cooperation, deemphasis, preempt, reenter)
- Unit modifiers. Definition of unit modifier (u.m.): adjectival unit of two or more words preceding a noun (This is fire-tested material). Do not confuse with predicate adjective (This material is fire tested).
Do not hyphenate u.m.'s in these cases:
  - When first element is a comparative or superlative (higher income group, best selling design)
  - When first element is an adverb ending in ly (wholly owned subsidiary)

---

*U.S. Government Printing Office Style Manual, 1973.

(continued)

- When elements are normally unhyphenated proper nouns, words in quotes, or foreign phrases (<u>Latin American</u> countries, "<u>blue sky</u>" law, <u>laissez faire</u> attitude)

Hyphenate u.m.'s in these cases:
- When one element is a past or present participle (<u>job-related</u> skill, <u>law-abiding</u> citizen)
- When there are three or more elements (<u>2-year-old</u> child, <u>non-civil-service</u> job), except when first two are adverbs (<u>very well worth</u> reading, <u>not too distant</u> past)
- When first element is a numeral or spelled-out number (<u>8-hour</u> day, <u>two-sided</u> question), except when second element is a possessive noun (<u>1 week's</u> pay)

- <u>Examples of GPO compounds:</u>

antitrust	inservice	nonprofit	shortrun (u.m.)
audiovisual	interrelated	onsite	short-term (u.m.)
checklist	large-scale (u.m.)	part-time (u.m.)	socioeconomic
decisionmaking	long-distance (u.m.)	percent	tie-in (n., u.m.)
first-class (u.m.)	longrun (u.m.)	post card	video tape
follow up (v.)	long-term (u.m.)	preservice	well-being
followup (n., u.m.)	lowercase	reevaluate	work force
in-house	multistory	semiautomatic	workplace

ITALICS AND UNDERSCORES (See Manual, pp. 175-177)

- Italicize or underscore legal cases, except the v. (<u>Smith</u> v. <u>Brown</u>)
- Do not italicize or underscore except in legal usage words of Latin origin (ante, post, infra, supra, id., ibid., et seq).

NUMBER STYLE (See Manual, pp. 179-85)

- <u>Numerals</u>. Use numerals (figures) for numbers with more than one digit--10 and over (except for first word in a sentence), e.g., <u>There are 11 people in the family</u>; <u>The houses numbered 12</u>. Use numerals for units of time, money, and measurement (<u>4 hours</u>, <u>1 dollar</u>, <u>2 miles</u>, <u>9 percent</u>, <u>$1 to $3 million</u>).
- <u>Words</u>. Spell out one-digit numbers--nine and under (except for units of time, money, and measurement), e.g., <u>There are four people in the family</u>; <u>Only eight houses were built</u>, and first word in a sentence (<u>Twelve houses were built</u>).
- <u>Multiple use</u>. In a sentence with two or more related numbers, if any is greater than nine, write all as numerals (There are 16 people in the 3 families; The children were 6, 8, and 10 years old).
- <u>Dates</u>. <u>June 1935</u> (no comma); <u>June 3, 1935</u> (comma); <u>June 3, 1935, was the date</u>.
- <u>Money</u>. <u>$3</u> ($3.00 only in tables); <u>$30</u>; <u>$30,000</u>; <u>$30 million</u> (not $30,000,000).

PLURALS (See Manual, pp. 65-67)

- <u>Data</u>, the plural of <u>datum</u>, always takes plural verbs and pronouns.
- <u>Anglicized plurals</u>: <u>curriculums</u>, <u>memorandums</u>, <u>indexes</u> (but <u>indices</u> in math).

PUNCTUATION (See Manual, pp. 131-132)

- <u>Serial comma</u>. Use comma before "and" or "or" in series (<u>a, b, and c</u>; <u>x, y, or z</u>).
- <u>Plurals and possessives of acronyms and numbers</u>. Use apostrophes (<u>the 1920's</u>; <u>HUD's regulations</u>).
- <u>Punctuation inside closing quotation marks</u>. Put terminal commas and periods inside (<u>"Yes,"</u>). Put other punctuation marks inside only if part of the matter quoted.

SPELLING (See Manual, pp. 61-71) The shorter, simpler spelling is often the choice.

- <u>Examples of GPO spelling:</u>

acknowledgment	combated, -ing	labeled, -ing	rarefy
adviser	dialog	livable	sizable
advisory	diagramed, -ing	marihuana	subpena, -ed
aline (not align)	diagrammatic	marshaled, -ing	totaled, -ing
benefited, -ing	esthetic	moneys (not monies)	toward (not towards)
bused, -es, -ing	gage (not gauge)	programed, -ing, -er	traveled, -ing
canceled, -ing	insure (not ensure)	programmatic	transferred, -ing
catalog	judgment	prolog	vis-a-vis

Some Points on University of Chicago Press Style*

ABBREVIATIONS (See Manual, Rules and lists, pp. 315-36)
- General principles
  - Nontechnical writing. Trend is toward decreased use. Widely accepted principles: (1) Keep out of running text as much as possible (spell out percent, degrees, etc.); reserve for tabular and tight material. (2) Confine such as etc., e.g., and i.e. to parenthetical references. (3) Use scholarly forms (et al., geog.) mainly in other than running text--footnotes, tables, bibliographies, etc.
  - Technical writing. Abbreviations accepted. Trend is toward eliminating periods, as in acronyms (NATO, YMCA) and units of measure (mm, cu in).
- U.S. Except in the most formal writing, abbreviation accepted as adjective in text (U.S. courts); use as noun in tabular and tight material only.
- States. In text spell out when standing alone and preferably when following the name of a city or other geographic term, except in lists, tables, footnotes, etc. Approved abbreviations (p. 321) are same as GPO style.
- Titles. Spell out with surname alone (General Washington); abbreviate with full name (Gen. George Washington).

CAPITALIZATION (See Manual, pp. 147-94)
- Trend is toward lowercase: proper nouns and adjectives up, all else down except to avoid ambiguity. However, rules "can never be final," as they merely provide "a helpful pattern." Important thing is consistency.
- Cap the following when in normal word position as accepted part of proper name, lowercase otherwise.
  - Titles and offices (President Ford, the president; Pope John, the pope; General Pershing, the general). Exceptions to avoid ambiguity (Speaker of the House, General of the Army, Fleet Admiral).
  - Political divisions and place names (Fairfax County, the county of Fairfax; the state of Maryland; Southeast Asia, central Asia; Silver Lake, the lake).
  - Government organizations (Civil Service Commission, the commission; Department of Labor, Labor Department, the department).
- Cap names of political organizations, parties, and movements (but not the words party, movement); lowercase nouns and adjectives designating political or economic systems of thought, unless derived from a proper name (Communist party, communism, Marxism).
- Not usually capped: government, federal, nation, state (U.S. government, federal policy, state statutes).
- References. In text, lowercase references such as figure 3, appendix C, table 6, chapter 4. Use arabic numerals or spell out chapter numbers in text references even when actual numbers are in roman numerals.
- Heads and Titles. In Clc heads and in titles of works mentioned in text, cap first and last words and all others except articles, prepositions, the "to" in infinitives, and coordinate (but not subordinate) conjunctions such as and, but, or, yet, therefore (Forty Homes Are to Be Built; How to File with Exemption from Requirements). In hyphenated compounds, cap second element only if noun, proper adjective, or equal in force to first (Price-cutting War; Nineteenth-Century Poetry).

COMPOUNDING (See Manual, Rules, pp. 130-32, Table, pp. 133-36, and Merriam-Webster dictionaries)
- General principles
  - To follow rules in Manual, distinguish between permanent (found in dictionary) and temporary compounds (coined by author for a specific purpose), between noun and adjective forms, and between adjective forms before and after the noun.

---

*A Manual of Style, University of Chicago Press, 12th edition, 1969.

(continued)

- "There seems to be a preference to spell compounds solid [as one word] as soon as acceptance warrants their being considered permanent compounds, and otherwise to spell them open [as separate words]."
- Temporary adjective forms before a noun are often hyphenated to avoid ambiguity (the best-informed reporters). After a noun, the hyphen is usually not needed (those reporters are the best informed).

- Solid compounds (one word)
  - Prefixed forms listed below are solid, except for homonyms (un-ionized, pre-judicial), capped second element (mid-April), numerals (pre-1914), or multiples (pro-mother-in-law).

anti	infra	pre	semi	ultra
co	non	pro	sub	un
extra	over	pseudo	super	under
intra	post	re	supra	

  - Suffixed forms as listed are solid: ache (headache); book--unless too long or temporary (notebook, reference book, recipe book); fold--as an adjective except with numerals (tenfold, 10-fold); house--as permanent form (boathouse); like-- except with proper name, triple l, or multiples (catlike, Paris-like, bell-like, apple-blossom-like).

- Open compounds (no hyphen)
  - object + gerund, as noun form (problem solving)
  - adverb ending ly + participle or adjective (wholly owned subsidiary, widely known fact)
  - normally unhyphenated proper nouns or foreign phrases (Latin American countries, laissez faire attitude)

- Hyphenated compounds
  - object + present participle, as adjective form preceding noun, and sometimes as permanent compound (problem-solving process; thought-provoking; time-consuming)
  - well-, ill-, better-, best-, little-, lesser-, etc., as adjective forms preceding noun, except when modified (well-known man; very well known man)

- Examples of Chicago compounds

all-inclusive (adj)	half-baked (adj)	quasi corporation (n form)
cost-effective (adj)	how-to-do-it (adj)	quasi-judicial (adj)
cost-effectiveness	in-service (adj)	self-reliant
decision-making (adj before n)	long-term (adj)	short-term (adj)
decision making (n form)	postcard	videotape
follow-up (n, adj)	president-elect	
follow up (v)	(but county clerk elect)	

ITALICS, UNDERLINING (See index of Manual)

- General principles
  - Italics (or underlining) to achieve special effects is used less and less, "especially by mature writers who prefer to obtain their effects structurally."
  - In a study containing many references to books and works of shorter than book length, all titles may be given in italics.

- Italicize (or underline)
  - titles and subtitles of published books and periodicals, but not articles or parts of books
  - foreign language: isolated words or phrases if unfamiliar to reader (He spoke ore rotundo, eloquently); sometimes a full sentence but not two or more (Esse quam videre is North Carolina's motto); sic, but not other scholarly Latin words and abbreviations
  - legal cases, except v. (Smith v. Jones)

- Do not italicize (or underline)
  - titles of published works shorter than book length, parts of larger works, dissertations, lectures, unpublished works (all usually enclosed in quotes)

- foreign language: familiar words or phrases (barrio, menage); scholarly Latin words or abbreviations (ibid., passim) except _sic_; two or more sentences (treat as quotation)

LISTS
- In a vertical list, use period, not parentheses, after letters or numerals enumerating items. Omit punctuation after items unless one is a complete sentence.
    1. item
    2. item
In a list within a paragraph, enclose numerals or lowercase italic letters in parentheses ((1) item, (2) item).
- Ordinarily, use a colon to introduce a list or series (Three areas are critical: France, Italy, and England). Use a colon when a list immediately succeeds the words as follows, the following, or as shown (There are three critical areas, as follows: France, Italy, and England).
- Use a period when a complete sentence intervenes between a complete introductory sentence and a list:
    There are three critical areas, as follows. Note that Belgium is excluded.
    1. France
    2. Italy
    3. England
- Use a comma with expressions such as namely, for instance, or for example, unless at least one gramatically complete clause is in the series (Three areas are critical, namely, France, Italy, and England. Three areas are critical, namely: France, which is the first to be studied; Italy, which is the next in sequence; and England, which is the last but most important).
- Place lists following i.e. or e.g. in parentheses (Three areas (i.e., France, Italy, and England) are critical).
- Use a dash to end an introductory line when items in a list complete a sentence:
    Before the meeting, the custodial staff must--
    1. post direction signs;
    2. unlock conference rooms;
    3. set up extra chairs.

NUMBER STYLE (See Manual, pp. 195-207; for usage not covered use GPO Style Manual)
- General principles
    - Numerals. In nonscientific text, use numerals for exact numbers with three or more digits (100 or over), except for the first word in a sentence. In any text, use numerals for year numbers (44 B.C.), parts of a book (page 2, table 9), fractional quantities (8-1/2 by 11 inches), decimal fractions (2.3 billion), percentages (3 percent), and abbreviations (3 mi) and symbols (4').
    - Words. In nonscientific text, spell out exact numbers of two or fewer digits (ninety-nine and under). In any text, spell out any number beginning a sentence (Four hundred thousand houses were built) and any round number (approximately two hundred).
- Multiple use. When more than one number in a paragraph applies to items in the same category, and the largest contains more than two digits, write all in that category as numerals (Of the eighty-four buildings, nine had 102 stories, seventy had 63 stories, and five had 40 stories.).
- Units of measurement. For measurement of physical quantities such as pressure, acceleration, distance, etc., use numerals in technical or scientific copy (30 volts; 10 degrees, 5 minutes); in any copy, use numerals with symbols and abbreviations (30 v; 10°5'); in nonscientific copy, follow general rule (The temperature rose thirty degrees; the temperature rose 130 degrees).
- Time. Spell out except when emphasizing exact moment (half-past three, 3:37), with A.M. or P.M. (3:30 A.M.), or with military system (0330).

- **Dates.** Preferred form: <u>3 June 1964</u>. Also acceptable: <u>June 3, 1964</u>,... and <u>the third of June, 1964</u>. Spell out, do not cap, generalized references to centuries or decades (<u>the sixties, twentieth century</u>) but use figures for century plus decade (<u>1960s</u>). With numerals, do not use ordinal endings (<u>-st</u>, <u>-d</u>, or <u>-th</u>).
- **Money.** Spell out sums under $100 except for decimal fractions (<u>five dollars</u>, <u>$5.75</u>); use numerals when decimal fractions and whole dollar amounts appear in the same context (<u>The charges were $5.00 for parts and $5.75 for labor</u>). Spell out unit of currency if number spelled out; use symbol if in numerals (<u>ten dollars</u>, <u>$100</u>). Combine figures and words for large sums of money ($2 million, $9.4 billion).
- **Percent and Decimal Fractions.** Use figures (<u>2 percent</u>). Use symbol in scientific and statistical copy (<u>2%</u>).

PLURALS AND POSSESSIVES (Use first plural listed in Merriam-Webster dictionaries, as <u>memorandums</u>, <u>symposia</u>.)
- Omit apostrophe with plurals of acronyms and numbers (<u>1920s</u>, <u>YMCAs</u>); use apostrophe with abbreviations followed by periods (<u>Ph.D.'s</u>) and with cap or lowercase letters (<u>p's and q's</u>, <u>A's to Z's</u>).

PUNCTUATION (See Manual, pp. 103-26)
- **Comma.** Use serial comma (<u>a, b, and c</u>; <u>x, y, or z</u>). Use comma after <u>U.S.</u> in citations of public documents from federal sources (<u>U.S., Department of State, Trade Expansion Act of 1962</u>, etc.).
- **Plurals and possessives of acronyms and numbers.** (See PLURALS, etc., above)
- **Semicolon.** Use before clauses beginning with <u>then</u>, <u>however</u>, <u>thus</u>, <u>hence</u>, <u>indeed</u>, <u>yet</u>, <u>so</u> (<u>Edith says she will start a new job next week; yet she has not submitted her resignation</u>).
- **Punctuation inside quotation marks.** Put terminal period inside double quotes (<u>"Yes."</u>), outside single quotes when used to set off special terms (<u>The gap is narrow between 'yes' and 'maybe'</u>.) Put comma inside closing quotes. Put exclamation point and question mark inside only when part of quoted matter. Put colon and semicolon outside; drop them from inside when they end quoted matter.

SPELLING (See Manual, pp. 127-40, and Merriam-Webster dictionaries)
- Use the first listing in the dictionary. Different from GPO style: align, gauge, dialogue, aesthetic, subpoena, marijuana, programmed, ensure (as well as insure).

Proverbs for Proofreading

<u>Love is nearsighted</u>. When you are the writer, editor, typist, or typesetter proofreading your own work, you will almost surely suffer from myopia. You are too close to see all the errors. Get help.

<u>Familiarity breeds content</u>. When you see the same copy again and again through the different stages of production and revision, you may well miss new errors. Fresh eyes are needed.

<u>If it's as plain as the nose on your face, everybody can see it but you</u>. Where is the reader most likely to notice errors? In a headline; in a title; in the first line, first paragraph, or first page of copy; and in the top lines of a new page. These are precisely the places where editors and proofreaders are most likely to miss errors. Take extra care at every beginning.

<u>Mistakery loves company</u>. Errors often cluster. When you find one, look hard for others nearby.

<u>When you change horses in midstream, you can get wet</u>. It's easy to overlook an error set in type that is different from the text face you are reading. Watch out when type changes to all caps, italics, boldface, small sizes, and large sizes. Watch out when underlines appear in typewritten copy.

<u>Glass houses invite stones</u>. Beware copy that discusses errors. When the subject is typographical quality, the copy must be typographically perfect. When the topic is errors in grammar or spelling, the copy must be error-free. Keep alert for words like <u>typographical</u> or <u>proofreading</u>. Double check and triple check.

<u>The footbone conneckit to the kneebone?</u> Numerical and alphabetical sequences often go awry. Check for omissions and duplications in page numbers, footnote numbers, or notations in outlines and lists. Check any numeration, anything in alphabetical order, and everything sequential (such as the path of arrows in a flowchart).

<u>It takes two to boogie</u>. An opening parenthesis needs a closing parenthesis. Brackets, quotation marks, and sometimes dashes, belong in pairs. Catch the bachelors.

<u>Every yoohoo deserves a yoohoo back</u>. A footnote reference mark or a first reference to a table or an illustration is termed a <u>callout</u>. Be sure a footnote begins on the same page as its callout. Be sure a table or illustration follows its callout as soon as possible.

<u>Numbers can speak louder than words</u>. Misprints in numerals (figures) can be catastrophic. Take extraordinary care with dollar figures and numbers in dates, statistics, tables, or technical text. Read all numerals character by character; for example, read "1979" as "one nine seven nine." Be sure any figures in your handwriting are unmistakable.

<u>Two plus two is twenty-two</u>. The simplest math can go wrong. Do not trust figures giving percentages and fractions or the "total" lines in tables. Watch for misplaced decimal points. Use your calculator.

<u>Sweat the small stuff</u>. A simple transposition turns <u>marital strife</u> into <u>martial strife</u>, <u>board room</u> into <u>broad room</u>. One missing character turns <u>he'll</u> into <u>hell</u>, <u>public</u> into <u>pubic</u>.

Above all, never assume that all is well. As the saying goes, ass-u-me makes an ass out of u and me.

Overview of Proofreading

DEFINITIONS

Proofreading is comparing an earlier version (draft, manuscript, copy, dead copy) with a later version (proof, final copy, live copy), word for word and letter for letter.

Printer's errors (PE's) are deviations from dead copy, specifications, or good printing (or typing) practice. Catching PE's is the proofreader's responsibility; correcting them is the typesetter's or typist's responsibility. Errors in the dead copy are not PE's and will not be corrected without extra charges after they appear in the live copy. The author or editor, not the proofreader, must decide when errors other than PE's must be corrected.

Queries are questions to the author or editor. Queries are often made on errors that have been transferred from the dead to the live copy. Normally only blatant errors--those that would seriously embarrass the author or bewilder the reader--are queried.

Author's alterations (AA's) are instructions to the typesetter to make changes or corrections other than PE's. Proofreaders very seldom have authority to authorize AA's, which are very costly. Instead, proofreaders write queries to the author or editor, who must decide whether or not to have the AA's made.

Single proofing is one-person proofreading and is done well only by professional proofreaders.

Double proofing is two-person, team, or partner proofreading. The copyholder reads aloud from the dead copy to the proofreader, who marks the live copy. Everything is read--spacing, punctuation, caps, changes in typeface, and so on. Equally qualified partners may switch roles. Double proofing is the most accurate method for non-professionals and is the traditional professional method many publishers prefer.

Qualifications for proofreading include the ability to spell; the typographic "eye"; knowledge of printing processes and typography; flexibility to adapt to different requirements, such as different editorial styles (GPO, University of Chicago, for example), different levels of authority for queries and AA's, and different kinds of live copy (camera-ready typing, galleys, page proofs, and so on).

Recommended tools include nonphoto blue and colored pencils (Eagle Verithin Nonphoto blue 761-1/2, Venus Col-Erase red 1277, Venus Col-Erase blue 1276); ruler; leading gauge (ruled in various type sizes), pica pole, and line-up gauge (available from printing and art supply houses).

Recommended references for general proofreading include A Manual of Style (U. of Chicago Press); Vest-Pocket 50,000 Words (Follett); Words Into Type (Prentice Hall); Merriam-Webster dictionary, atlas; almanac. Specific employers may require other style guides or dictionaries.

Standard marks are shown on page 358. Two corresponding marks are made for every error--one in the text to show where a correction goes, one in the margin to show what correction to make. Unlike editor's marks, words or characters are never written in the text. Standard marks are used only for galleys, page proofs, photo-copies, or any kind of duplicate copy. Modification is needed for camera-ready copy, mechanicals, type itself (typeset photographic material) from photocomposition, direct-use typing, or a draft to be typeset for the first time. The modifications may mean that marks are allowed only in the margin, only in the text, or not at all. If no marks are allowed, a list or tissue overlay is used.

Speed should average 5,000 words an hour for a team with good copy. Tables, small type, sans serif type, heavy editing, or handwritten copy reduce speed.

The work day should be seven hours long (not counting lunch or dinner break). Maintaining speed and accuracy takes concentrated effort. A five-minute break is needed every hour. Accuracy drops with longer hours or without frequent breaks.

INTRODUCTION TO PROOFREADER'S MARKS

1. Mark in the text to show where the error is; in the margin, to show what correction to make; for example: poofreading

2. Mark in the margin nearer the error, writing from left to right. Use a slash to separate marks for errors in the same line; for example: Now is te tme for all good pople

3. Use slashes to indicate that the same correction must be made in the same line as many times as there are slashes; for example: Now is the time fr all god peple

4. Insertion. As shown in the previous examples, mark a caret in text and write the insertion in the margin.

5. Closing Up. The close-up sign means "take out all space, close up entirely"; for example: pr͡oofreading

When necessary, use close-up hooks to show whether a character goes before or after a word; for example:

No is the time for all good people
to come to he aid of their country.

6. <u>Deletion</u>. In text, slash or cross through the character(s) to be deleted. In the margin, write the delete sign; for example: Now⁄ is the the time for all good people⁄ *𝒮//*

Use a combination delete-and-close-up sign when the characters on both sides of a deletion should be entirely closed up; for example: *𝒮//* "Proofreading?" "Yes!" she said.

7. <u>Replacement</u>. In text, slash or cross through the wrong character(s) and write the correct character(s) in the margin; for *o/time* example: Now is the ~~moment~~ for all good people

8. <u>Transposition</u>. Mark transposed adjacent words with a double loop in text and (ⓣⓡ) in the margin; for example: Now the is (ⓣⓡ) time. . .

Traditional marking treats transposed adjacent characters the same as words, but GPO style prefers transposed characters marked for replacement: for example:

(ⓣⓡ) Traditional: proofreading

no GPO: proofreading

Non-adjacent characters or words should always be marked for replacement: for example: Now ~~for~~ the time ~~is~~ all good people. . . *is/for*

9. <u>Punctuation Marks and Symbols</u>. Proofreader's marks for punctuation marks and for symbols such as inferior (subscript) and superior (superscript) characters are shown in the list of Standard Proofreading Marks. Note that the comma is marked like an inferior character, the apostrophe and quotation marks like *⌄/ʌ* superior characters: for example: "Proofreaders marks?" "Yes" she said.

Note also that the question mark is marked with the word "set" to distinguish it from a query to the author or editor, and that the exclamation point is treated the same way to avoid ambiguity: for (ⓢⓔⓣ) ? example: "Proofreader's marks" "Yes indeed" she said. (ⓢⓔⓣ)!

10. <u>Spacing Problems</u>. The marks for spacing problems are shown in the list of Standard Proofreading Marks. Leading or lead (pronounced <u>led</u>) is the space between lines in typeset copy. Ems and ens are units of printer's measure.

11. <u>Incorrect Word Division</u>. When words are wrongly divided at the end of a line, the best way to mark them is for deletion and insertion, as shown under Special Marks in the list of Standard Proofreading Marks.

12. <u>Rings</u>. To avoid any possibility of confusion, make a ring around a marginal mark when the mark does not represent the actual characters to be set. An example of this is given above for the word "set."

STANDARD PROOFREADING MARKS

Basic Marks
(delete, insert, replace, transpose)

- delete 1 character
- delete more than 1 character
- delete and close up entirely
- inset from 1 character to 7 words
- insert more than 7 words (out, see copy p.x)
- insert and close up at left, at right
- a   replace 1 character
- than   replace more than 1 character
- transpose (words adjacent) or letters
- or (or) letters

Marks for Punctuation and Symbols

- <   inferior, subscript
- >   superior, superscript
- apostrophe
- :/   colon
- comma
- ! (set)   exclamation point
- =/   hyphen
- period
- ? (set)   question mark
- quotation marks
- ;   semicolon
- (shill)   virgule (slash, shilling)
- (/)   parentheses
- [/]   brackets

Special Marks

- (stet)   ignore marked correction
- to/?   query at author
- (X)//   make same correction as many times as slashes
- (sp)   spell out abbrev, numeral, or symbol
- correct wrong word divis-ion
- correct wrong word div-ision
- do not set ringed explanation in type

Marks for Spacing and Positioning

- eq #   equal 1 space needed
- (run on)   no new line
- (break)   break. Begin new line
- carry over (to run over) next line
- (run back)   carry back to previous line
- new paragraph
- no   no new paragraph
- move right
- move left
- move down
- move up
- (straighten)   align horizontally
- (align)   align vertically
- center horizontally
- center vertically
- close up entirely
- #   insert space
- (less #)   less space

Typographical Marks

- (ital)   italic
- (sc)   small caps
- (caps)   all caps
- (bf)   boldface
- (c+sc)   caps and small caps
- (lc)   lowercase
- S/L/C   single-letter caps
- (Clc)   caps and lowercase (as in a head)
- (Clc)   CAPS AND LOWERCASE
- (x)   defective character
- (wf)   wrong font
- (lig ff)   use ligature (as in off)
- (rule)   use rule

Marks for Typewritten Copy Only

- #   skip a line
- (2CR)   2 carriage returns; skip a line, type on 2nd line
- (3CR)   3 carriage returns; skip 2 lines, type on 3rd line
- (ss)   single space
- 1½#   space and a half
- (ts)   triple space
- (dds)   double double space
- 5   indent 5 spaces, type on 6th
- 5   indent 5 spaces
- 1st   indent to 1st specified indention
- 2nd   indent to 2nd specified indention
- =/   hyphen or en dash; type closed up
- --/   2 hyphens closed up, equivalent to em dash
- (score)   underscore

Marks for Typeset Copy Only

- $\frac{1}{N}$ 1-en dash
- $\frac{1}{M}$ 1-em dash
- 9   inverted letter
- protruding spacing material
- (ld)   in-sert lead
- (ld)   take out lead
- indent 1 em or insert 1-em quad
- indent 2 ems or insert 2-em quad
- indent number of ems shown

General Rules

Mark every error twice--first in the text to show where the error is, next in the margin to show what correction is needed.

Use both left and right margins, according to which is closer to the error.

Slash to separate multiple marginal marks.

INDEX

This index covers both the Proofreading Manual and accompanying workbook. The letter-by-letter rather than word-by-word method has been used for alphabetization. Workbook entries are indicated by a workbook page number (63WB) or an Exercise number (ex. 1WB). Material found in footnotes is indicated with an n following the page number. Answer keys are not separately indexed; however, each exercise contains a cross-reference to the location of its key. The "Questions for Students" sections that appear at the end of the textbook chapters are not indexed.